A Little Book Of Revelations

Dick Bell

ISBN: 1-933899-21-2

Published by:
Holy Fire Publishing
531 Constitution Blvd., Martinsburg, WV 25401
www.ChristianPublish.com

Cover Design: Jay Cookingham

Printed in the United States of America and the United Kingdom

Dedication

To all those wonderful
children and teenagers
with whom we shared the
loveliness of Jesus together
at Upcott, Seaton, Devon.

INDEX

INTRODUCTION

First of all, a convention. In Gen 1:26, God declares that He is plural by saying, "Let us make man in our image..." And the Hebrew word for God there is *Elohim* – a masculine plural noun. The Trinity is embedded in Genesis. But throughout the Bible God mostly calls Himself He. So we also call God "He". Are we speaking of Father, Son or Holy Spirit? It does not matter. It's cumbersome to call God "They" or "Them", although that would be strictly correct. And "You" in English can be either singular or plural. The point is that They are so One that "He" is OK. What we say of One, we say of all Three.

Revelation is a special insight given by the Holy Spirit to enhance and expand Bible themes. Revelation causes us to understand what is not obvious from either a cursory or even a long-distance read of the Bible. God is giving deeper insight to those who want to listen to Him. I believe that every Christian gets Revelations – and it certainly applies to our conversions. Without Revelation at that time we would not and could not become Christians.

I am not a huge reader of Christian literature – or indeed of any literature. I have tried speed reading, but find it hard work, and soon revert to word for word. I do read, of course. But I am not fast enough and I am too busy to be a bookworm. There is a consequence to that. It is that I have no idea at all whether others before me have had similar Revelations to those contained in this book. I just don't know. And, really, it doesn't much matter to me. Therefore you will not find any reference literature at the end of the book. Where I have picked up a trigger from another person, and can remember who they are, I have acknowledged it in the text. And I have repeated that idea briefly in chapter 1 in case people don't read Introductions. My understanding has been reading the Bible and learning at the feet of Jesus.

I experienced an illustration of this earlier in my life. It was at the time when a monthly magazine called "The Third Way" was being published. I enjoyed its contents. But I remember getting steamed up about something I don't now recall and sending in the article to Third Way for possible publication. It was returned. "Where are your references?" "What do others say about it?" I had none, and I had no idea. My song was to tell what God had told me, and was not an intellectual exercise of cut and thrust between myself and other people. I ditched the article and got on with what I was doing. Which is where I am now. The enclosed Revelations are similar.

Some of these Revelations will be new to some of you. They were once all new to me. Some you will not agree with, I'm sure. But taken together they form a secure and positive perspective on heaven – a certainty that comes out of testing over many decades. You will see too that I am a very positive person. I made a decision in my early Christian life never to be negative about anything. It was a very good and life-changing choice.

You will, unfortunately, find a lot of "I's" in this book. That is, I tell what I know. There are two reasons for this. The first is that I do not want to contaminate anyone else with what has come to me, nor tar them with the same brush. The second is that it is very difficult to differentiate in writing between confidence and arrogance. When I say I believe something, it is because the Lord has spoken to me, and I am confidently established in that perspective. It could be interpreted as arrogance – "Who does he think he is to make such controversial observations?" But we have the same trouble with both Jesus and Paul. They were confident in what God had said to them in their roles as Son of God and Apostle. Few would think they were being arrogant in expressing their self-assurance.

Let me give you a brief summary of my life, so that you have the background. I was born in Kenya of non-Christian parents. I am the sandwich between two sisters. I went to secondary school in England at the age of 13 to Rossall, my Dad's old school north of Blackpool on the Fylde coast. I was frozen as you can imagine. My one burning love was (and still is) aeroplanes. I flew in one at the age of 2 and have never wanted to do anything else since. I left school and went to the RAF College at Cranwell – to be both a pilot and an officer. Civil flying was too dull for me! There I was exposed. I thought that I was the best thing the RAF could have done – and they thought I was the worst. I was an overconfident, arrogant little twit. Flying aeroplanes was no problem – being an officer apparently was. I was put on special report and eventually given a one-sided interview with my Squadron Commander, who gave me a fortnight to sort myself out – or they throw me out.

It was the first time I was forced to see myself as others saw me, and it was ugly. I did the only thing that seemed sensible: I got down by my bedside at night (I thought that was an OK way to pray) and prayed, "God, if there is a God, help." A fortnight later I was invited into a Baptist church in Lincoln on the Saturday night by my fellow cadet Tony Cottingham. There, in one and a half hours, I was transformed. The College couldn't make it out. I turned from black to white overnight, and they eventually nearly threw me out for being too "religious", they said. They meant "evangelistic". By a series of miracles I graduated and was flying military aircraft as a Christian for 20 years in the RAF, preferably upside down.

I left at the age of 38 because I wanted to do "coal face Christianity". That is, I wanted a direct confrontation with people that challenged them to live for Jesus, rather than the round about way of being a Christian in a secular job. I joined my girl friend Eileen at a Christian Conference Centre in Seaton, Devon called Upcott, which she and her colleague Jeannie Rookley had begun 6 years earlier. Seven years of "going out" came to an end, and we got married 6 months later. Joanna, our only child, was born two years later. I spent 26 years in that ministry as Bible Teacher, without any formal theological qualifications, to adults but mainly to children and teenagers – whom I love. During that time I started an offset litho printing business, so that I could print the notes for my kids beautifully. It was funded by commercial printing locally and lasted 10 years. I also took part in hovercraft expeditions organised by Mike Cole OBE to Third

World locations: Perú, China, Papua New Guinea and Nicaragua. Then I helped Mike once a year as he built infrastructure (schools, churches, clinics etc) in Nicaragua to try to alleviate its poverty.

When it came to reaching my official retirement age, I asked God what I should do, as I was still bright eyed and bushy tailed. He made it clear that I should go to Nicaragua, and so I became a missionary after the Biblical style of Nehemiah. We fired up a Trust called SIFT (Seed International Fund Trust), and we are set to transform our part of Nicaragua in as few years as possible. Such fun. So – I am as unconventional as they come, and you will recognise that as you read through this book.

I pray that its unconventionality, its inventiveness and its ingenuity will inspire you to be as unconventional as God has already designed you to be, and cause you to step out in faith on God's leading, both in terms of what you do and what you do with your life. There is more of the world for you to change through the grace of God, and, if I read Ephesians 2:10 correctly, God has a unique and inventive mandate for every one who reads this book. Go get it, saints of the Living God!

Chapter 1
REVELATION.

The words "Reveal" and "Revelation" are two of the most important words and concepts for Christians. Until we can grasp the impact, purpose and meaning of "Revelation", we will never travel far in our Christian lives.

We need Revelation. Why? Jesus said (just before He died), and it is eternally true, that "Before long, the world will not see me anymore, but you will see me" (John 14:19). The disciples were mega confused by the statement, but it has been irreversibly and absolutely true from His death onwards. Jesus was the ultimate, perfect and complete visual Revelation and Representation of God. Since then, God has been hidden. The only people who can "see" God are those to whom God chooses to Reveal Himself.

But because man is a spiritual creature, he has written all sorts of novels over the centuries, from his own intellect, to try to bridge that unbridgeable gap. We call those novels "Religions". Every one is a figment of man's imagination, but every one contains sufficient elements of truth to make them sound reasonable to other people who also have no Revelation. They include all the mainline Religions, the billions of personal philosophies, and modern religions like Humanism and Evolution. So what is the ultimate Truth? Jesus said, "I am the Truth" (John 14:6). Christianity is therefore not a Religion: it's a Relationship. And that Relationship is eternally hidden from all people until Jesus chooses to Reveal Himself to them individually. It is clearly written in scripture (e.g. John 8:43, 47). But we have difficulty with this concept. So let's start with the problem.

The major problem we have is intellectualism.

God made our intellects beautiful. Without a mind the human does not function. We are thinking beings. So important do we think knowledge is that we spend all our lives gaining it. We are curious creatures, and God has made us such. The more we study, the more we realise how much more there is to study. Universities now run courses on many more subjects than they did 30 years ago. In the micro they are discovering vast areas of knowledge that they previously knew nothing about. Details, for example, of the structure of the human cell, the genome, and parts of the body fill the PhD opportunities with more and more things to analyse and discover. So it is with nano-technology. So it is with the psyche and the study of human behaviour. So it is with animals, birds, marine creatures and vegetation. There are vast tracts of information that man knows he does not know. The more he tries to find out and study, the more he realises there is to find out and study.

This is not only true of the micro. It is true also of the macro. The study of planet Earth is not enough for some. The solar system has its own fascinations, and we know lots about it, but never enough. Space probes (costing billions of whatever currency) are being burned into space to uncover the mysteries of even our own sun and planets – much less beyond into the universe. With a billion stars in our own galaxy and 100 billion galaxies (a guess), there's still more for man to discover. It seems to me that man will never come to the end of finding things to study, and each generation on the earth will increase our knowledge and understanding of this amazing, beautiful, vast and intriguing world and universe in which we live. There will always be more for every new generation to get their teeth into and to find a life's fulfilment that will satisfy their intellectual curiosity.

Knowledge itself comes out of knowledge. We base our research on other people's discoveries. And if we go backwards through the logic of that statement, the knowledge that begun it all was still there, although hidden, and it is immense. The beginning was knowledge and intelligence, not Nothing – as many logical and intelligent people keep trying to convince us.

We arrive at the fact that the universe is one cohesive, ordered, intelligent whole, full of laws that governed it and bound it together from the beginning, and long before man ever dreamed of defining any of those laws. No research of man has been able to uncover disorderliness in the universe. If the laws had not been there from the beginning – gravity, motion, chemistry etc, what would have happened to the cosmos?

The structure of a cell, for instance, is incredibly complicated, amazingly put together, and actually works. Cells have worked from the beginning. There is no evidence of a partial cell. We have rogue cells, but never disorderly or incomplete ones. It is an example of "irreducible complexity", a phrase coined by Michael Behe, a micro-biologist. And the logic is that in every area of human intellectual discovery, the details must have been designed and put together by an Immense Intellect. Think this way: not even 15 billion years of evolution is enough to produce the immensity, complexity, variety and completeness of a universe that actually functions. It works.

As I see it, man does not create. He manipulates with material he has already been given. But to create – to form matter, to make life, who can do that? Man only discovers. What he discovers is already there, and has been since the beginning. We call it creation. Any thinking person (and we all are in our small or large way) cannot escape the possibility – no, the probability – of an enormous Intellect behind Life. The Name He has given us of Himself is God, so that is what we call Him. If not even man in all his brilliance can make Life (vegetable, animal, human, micro, macro or any), what chance has Chance got for Life to pop up spontaneously from Nothing? That introduces God, who must be bigger, more intelligent, more beautiful and more intriguing than any man could ever intellectualise. Knowledge is based on knowledge, which in the beginning directs us to a fount of all knowledge and a law-giver. His name is God.

The reason why He hides Himself so effectively is because He wants us to walk by faith and not by sight (2 Cor 5:7). The reason for *that* is that faith is creative, sight is not. He is *so* obvious that

He is amazed by any person who cannot perceive Him there. Wasn't Jesus surprised so often by a lack of faith among His own disciples? It's so obvious. How come you keep missing it?

One certain reason is our own intellect. As I said, it's a big problem. We think so much that we think we've thought of everything. And we haven't. But we are so proud of our "thinkability" that we are entranced by it. Can anything live beyond my own understanding and knowledge? Well, yes. Practically everything! The older one gets, the more we know we don't know, and a little intellectual humility opens a door to more knowledge. To Revelation in fact.

Let's go to our Bibles. 1 Cor 1 summarises it perfectly.

> "As the scriptures say, "I will destroy human wisdom and discard their most brilliant ideas." So where does this leave the philosophers, the scholars, and the world's brilliant debaters? God has made them all look foolish and has shown their wisdom to be useless nonsense. Since God in His wisdom saw to it that the world would never find Him through human wisdom, he has used our foolish preaching to save all who believe." (New Living Translation).

It seems as if Paul had as much problem with intellectualism in his day as we have in ours. There it is made abundantly clear that knowledge, wisdom and intelligence can never, repeat never, get us close to God, or give us a knowledge of God. He has cut off that avenue to knowing Him – or anything of His heaven. How slowly and reluctantly we mind-centred people learn that lesson. And what is true of initial introduction is true all the way down through our lives.

So why do I consider that important? Because if God made all things, a knowledge of God will introduce us to all sorts of intriguing things we never thought of before. Knowing God is a key to much more knowledge of all kinds.

From a new understanding of God flows a new understanding of all things. That's what God does to us and for us. Luther and Calvin opened up a "thinkers'" approach to the Bible, which gave people access to Revelation which opened up their minds to a million new possibilities in every sphere of life. It was very good. Divinely initiated. So what did mankind do as a result of all this new found knowledge? We captured it, worshipped it and made it our god. We became intellectuals. We lost the new Life God had given and became mind-centred beings. We educated – and based our education on the Greek philosophers (the word "philosophy" is Greek, and means "lovers of wisdom") and the battle went straight back to 1 Cor 1 some 15 centuries after it was written.

In the non-Christian world everything became secular, logical, mind-centred and man-centred. "Satan", said Jesus "savours the things which are of *man*." Satan relishes man-centredness. It keeps men away from God. That's got to be the major reason why so many clever people think God is a myth. Do they know they have been duped?

In the Christian world, intellectualism mirrored the secular world, and became the norm for Christian ministry. Calvin wrote his *Institutes*, which were Doctrinal in the extreme, intellectually put together. "Doctrine" became the norm and the guiding rule of Christianity. Read the Puritans and you will see what I mean. And think of this: every Christian denomination (that is, every Christian division that leads to disunity and separation), separated on a *doctrinal* basis. Some people have divided on anger, criticism, control or jealousy, but they have soon turned to Doctrine to justify their pride, lack of submission and separation. Doctrine is still the great barrier that divides Catholic from Protestant today. How can this possibly be of God? Did Jesus not say that all men would know that we are His disciples by our *love* for each other? And the Bible adds that "Love covers over a multitude of sins". The greatest of which is division, and the second of which is mind-centred intellectualism masquerading as Christianity.

Intellectualism and mind-centredness is of man, not of God. Therefore it is sin (see chapter 7). So, if I am saying that mind-centredness and mind-centred Christianity is sin (which I am), what alternative can I suggest?

Revelation.

It's what the Bible teaches. It is God's *only* way of getting to know Him and to keeping on knowing Him. All else is cul-de-sac; dead end; useless waste of time; death.

So what is Revelation? Put simply, it is God telling us what He wants us to know. The word itself in Greek is *apokalupsis*, which is used to describe the drawing aside or opening of a curtain. It is only God who can open the curtain – we have no ability to do so. And it is God who shows us (Reveals to us) what lies behind that curtain.

Throughout this book I have used the word "Revelation" to indicate God's direct and spoken communication to us. There are other words that can be used (like *Rhēma* in the next chapter), but I have tried to stick to this one Biblical word so that I do not confuse you.

We don't "work it out". We receive it. And it therefore comes to us in an illogical order, in illogical ways and at illogical times.

I have long taught that God is both illogical and irrational. That is not because He is *sub*-logical. It is because he is *super*-logical. He is Spiritual. The realm of the Spirit is so much higher and greater than our realm that, in comparison, we are pathetic, ignorant, sub-logical little dunces. All of us. For instance, is Jesus not at present "upholding the universe by His word of power"? (Heb 1:3). So how do our puny efforts compare with that? The trouble is that we compare ourselves with one another, and think ourselves so marvellous; the Bible calls that "foolish" (2 Cor 10:12). "My thoughts are completely different from yours," says the Lord. "And My ways are far beyond anything you could imagine. For just as the heavens are higher than the earth, so are My ways higher than your ways and My thoughts higher than your thoughts." (Isaiah 55:8-9).

Knowledge of God comes *only* and *always* by Revelation. God is the initiator. His revealed information is always needed, always appropriate and always timely.

Let me give you an example from my own stupidity. For many years I thought and taught that, if I had been God, I would have scrapped creation and started again after Adam and Eve had sinned in the Garden of Eden. Think what a lot of tragedy would have been saved if He had. But many years later, *many* years later, He just popped into my head this statement, "I couldn't. The first one was perfect." That answer was itself perfect. How could He or anyone improve on a perfect creation? Therefore the tragedy of Eden meant that another solution had to be found. And, indeed, the redemption through Jesus was also perfect. As well as necessary if God was going to achieve His planned destiny for the earth and for mankind.

All the rest of the chapters of this book are Revelations – as indeed is this one. That is, God popped these intriguing new thoughts into my head at some time in the past. Some of them came through channels, and, where I can acknowledge those channels, I have.

In order that we don't go astray in some fancy area of our own, God has given us the Bible to check every Revelation against. No Revelation given to us directly can ever go against the most universal and greatest deposit of Revelation – the Bible. This is the safeguard. But God can give us understanding and insight about the truth already revealed, as well as direct guidance on specific issues of life. All of the Revelations that I open up in this book are based on scripture. If I were to make any comment about the Christian church as I have found it throughout my life, it would be to say that we have not read or recognised the small print, nor analysed *how* the Christian life really works. That's why I am writing what I am writing.

So, how does Revelation work? Very simply. A new thought that I have not meditated on or that has not come out from my own mental calculations "pops" into my mind without warning. As a result of that thought, I then know because I know.

God's Revelations come complete. Nothing needs adding to them and they are a "soul" thing as well as a mind thing. They come as a package to the whole being. Now I *know*. There can be no possibility that I have thought this out myself. That would be impossible. God has *given* it to me as a package. I have developed this theme – of how Revelation comes - in the chapter "Hearing the Voice of God".

Let's look at a few scriptures first to establish the principle. Then we can look at how and when it comes (the italics are mine).

> Dan 10:1,2. "In the third year of Cyrus king of Persia, a *revelation* was given to Daniel (who was called Belteshazzar). Its message was true and it concerned a great war. The understanding of the message came to him in a vision."
>
> Amos 3:7. "Surely the Sovereign LORD does nothing without *revealing* his plan to his servants the prophets."
>
> Matt 16:17. "Jesus replied, "Blessed are you, Simon son of Jonah, for this was not *revealed* to you by man, but by my Father in heaven."
>
> Luke 2:26. "It had been *revealed* to him [Simeon] by the Holy Spirit that he would not die before he had seen the Lord's Christ."
>
> Luke 10:21. "At that time Jesus, full of joy through the Holy Spirit, said, "I praise you, Father, Lord of heaven and earth, because you have *hidden* these things from the wise and learned, and *revealed* them to little children. Yes, Father, for this was your good pleasure.""
>
> John 6:44. "No one can come to me unless the Father who sent me draws him." That's 100% of people!

Rom 1:17. "For in the gospel a righteousness from God is *revealed*, a righteousness that is by faith from first to last, just as it is written: "The righteous will live by faith.""

Rom 16:25. "Now to him who is able to establish you by my gospel and the proclamation of Jesus Christ, according to the *revelation* of the mystery hidden for long ages past, ..."

Gal 1:12. "I did not receive it from any man, nor was I taught it; rather, I received it by *revelation* from Jesus Christ."

Gal 2:2. "I went in response to a *revelation* and set before them the gospel that I preach among the Gentiles. But I did this privately to those who seemed to be leaders, for fear that I was running or had run my race in vain."

Eph 1:17. "I keep asking that the God of our Lord Jesus Christ, the glorious Father, may give you the Spirit of wisdom and *revelation*, so that you may know him better."

Eph 3:3. "that is, the mystery made known to me by *revelation*, as I have already written briefly."

So how does Revelation come? Through what channels? Let me try to put them in order of the best and most frequent.

- Directly by the Holy Spirit.
- The Bible.
- Sermons.
- Worship.
- Songs.
- Nature.

When God speaks through the Holy Spirit, He speaks directly into our minds – or souls or hearts. In this chapter I just want to give you the principle: other chapters expand on exactly *how* God speaks and *how* we hear and understand Him speaking. This issue is so important that I needed to devote another whole chapter to it.

Let us look at the Bible.

The Bible is a spiritual book. It is pure Revelation from beginning to end. Men, inspired by the Holy Spirit, wrote as they were led by God. Over the centuries, the Holy Spirit separated wheat from chaff, and the 66 books we now have are the ones that we can guarantee as Inspired (God-breathed – 2 Tim 3:16).

It is through its pages that God breathes His Revelations. I have expanded the delights and difficulties of that in a more detailed way under the chapter 5 The Bible.

So why has He given us intelligence? Not to find Him, but to be found by Him. When *He* fills our minds with understanding, it is a life-changing experience, is eternal, and gives us a wisdom that neither our years nor our intelligence deserve. There is no question about it – Revelation is a life-transforming occurrence. Look at the Apostle Paul. He was chief among his contemporaries, mega intelligent. But from Gal 1 we read that he had to unlearn *all* his University knowledge, become a little child again, and be re-taught from God by the Holy Spirit.

> "Dear brothers and sisters, I solemnly assure you that the Good News of salvation which I preach is not based on human reasoning or logic. For my message came by direct Revelation from Jesus Christ himself. No one else taught me." (Gal 1:11, 12).

It was so revolutionary that it took the Christian Church 300 years to ratify what Paul wrote and acknowledge that it was from God. Even Peter said that Paul wrote some things that were hard to understand (2 Peter 3:15). Paul's letters are not logical treatises – the calculations of a trained mind. They are higgledy-piggledy.

But they are Life and Truth. And satisfying to the reader who wants God to speak to him.

The same pattern is true of sermons, Christian songs and worship. God gives Revelation to open hearts, not thinking minds.

We have to change. Western culture is mind-centred. Christians have to reject that altogether. We have to become Spirit-centred. We have, in another idiom, to stop being Greek and start being Jewish. Without compromise. That's where Life is. And then our lives become useful and a blessing wherever we go. "The wind (or Spirit – same Greek word) blows where it wants to. You cannot tell where it is coming from or where it is going. So it is with everyone who is born of the Spirit." (John 3:8).

Please, Lord, give us the "Spirit of Revelation".

SUMMARY

It is impossible for mankind to know God. The *only* way is for God to initiate it by Revealing Himself to them.

Chapter 2
LOGOS AND RHĒMA

You may not be familiar with Greek. Neither am I in any seriousness. But I commend even a cursory interest in it. Once you get to recognise its strange alphabet (ἀ = alpha, β = beta, γ = gamma etc), an interlinear New Testament can be a great help in evaluating Bible passages. Which leads me to today's Revelation. This one is pure Bible evaluation, and has been most helpful in bringing me Revelation and thereby understanding.

The two Greek words *Logos* and *Rhēma* mean Word (I will use the capital for clarity). But they mean and imply very different uses of Word. Let's start with *Logos*.

The word *Logos* is used 329 times in the New Testament. It is the general word for Word, and represents a written word, thought word, idea, spoken word, studied word, and covers all the uses of the word Word. Further below I have given you a few samples.

In English the words Logic and Logical come from *Logos*, and the dual words Bio-logy, anthropo-logy, geo-logy and many more also do. This latter use is very interesting. It arises from the Greek civilisation in its heyday when knowledge and study were all the rage. In those days they found that knowledge was so vast that it needed to be sectioned off, such that people could study particular areas of knowledge on their own, uncluttered by other disciplines. Those who wanted to study vegetable life, "bios", would gather together under one umbrella. Soon that discipline divided down and became known, for example as "*The* Word on vegetable life", and they coined the word "Bios logos" – Biology. So with "geo" – land, "anthropos" – man and so on. So *Logos* was used in the Greek university equivalents as THE WORD on _ _ _ whatever. So *Logos* is a big and multi-faceted word.

Let's see some of its uses in the New Testament:

Matt 8:16. "When evening came, many who were demon-possessed were brought to him, and he drove out the spirits with a word and healed all the sick."
Matt 12:37. "For by your words you will be acquitted, and by your words you will be condemned."
Matt 24:35. "Heaven and earth will pass away, but my words will never pass away."
Mark 7:13. "Thus you nullify the word of God by your tradition that you have handed down."
Mark 8:38. "If anyone is ashamed of me and my words in this adulterous and sinful generation, the Son of Man will be ashamed of him when he comes in his Father's glory with the holy angels."
Mark 16:20. "Then the disciples went out and preached everywhere, and the Lord worked with them and confirmed his word by the signs that accompanied it."
Luke 4:22. "All spoke well of him and were amazed at the gracious words that came from his lips. "Isn't this Joseph's son?" they asked."
Luke 7:7. "That is why I did not even consider myself worthy to come to you. But say the word, and my servant will be healed."
Luke 24:19. """About Jesus of Nazareth," they replied. "He was a prophet, powerful in word and deed before God and all the people."
John 1:14. "The Word became flesh and made his dwelling among us. We have seen his glory, the glory of the One and Only, who came from the Father, full of grace and truth."
John 17:17. "Sanctify them by the truth; your word is truth."
Heb 4:12. "For the word of God is living and active. Sharper than any double-edged sword, it penetrates even to dividing soul and spirit.."

Do you see the variety that *logos* contains – every different kind of Word?

But the best and most significant use of this word *logos* is by John in 1:1-14. "In the beginning was the Word (*Logos*). And the *Logos* was with God, and the *Logos* was God. And the *Logos* was made flesh and lived among us, full of grace and truth". I owe a debt to David Pawson for his superb analysis of this passage, which I heard many years ago on a tape. There was a certain Greek philosopher called Heraclitus (540-480BC) who, particularly, defined the use of *Logos* in the specialist way I have already written about to describe individual disciplines. For instance "The Final Word on Bios" is to be found in the discipline of Biology. John, knowing this background and inspired by the Holy Spirit, wrote of Jesus. He is THE ULTIMATE WORD on the Whole Universe – all things were made by Him. He is the Ultimate Revelation of God – The *LOGOS* that experiences and describes God to the fullest extent, the "express image of God" (Col 1:15). By using *Logos*, Word, John is saying that Jesus is the full and final expression of all God was, is, and will be. There is nothing that Jesus *said* or *did* that will ever be contradicted in the universe, or superseded. He was the initial expression of God. He will be the final expression of God; He is THE WORD. And that WORD covers all the variety contained in the Word *Logos*.

It also means that God's Words and God's actions are one and the same thing. What He *says* is what *happens*. He spoke the Creation into existence, through Jesus, and it happened. In addition Jesus "holds all things together" (Col 1:17). Please note it is in the Present Tense. That is, God does and is still doing it through Jesus.

Consequently, all actions in the created Cosmos were performed by Jesus, are performed by Jesus and will be performed by Jesus. Because Jesus was the Creator Agent, He is responsible to God for the things He made. That's why Jesus had to be the Redeemer - He had to take responsibility for allowing sin into the world. His Father abandoned Him on the cross - He alone had to be accountable for dealing with sin. And that's why Jesus will personally come again and put an end to wickedness on the earth because He is responsible for putting it right. 1 Cor 15:24-25 says "Then the end will come, when he (Jesus) hands over the kingdom to God the Father after he has destroyed all dominion, authority and power. For he must reign until he has put all his enemies under his feet. "

> "In the beginning was the *Logos*. And the *Logos* was with God, and the *Logos* was God. And the *Logos* became flesh and lived among us, full of grace and truth."

As an aside, it tells me that every person will be held accountable for every action they have initiated. If God holds His Son responsible for the things He did then He will certainly hold us responsible for the things we do. Whatever a man sows, that will he also reap. (Gal 6:7-9).

I need to ask the question: "What is the connection between *logos* as we would understand the Bible to be and *Logos* as we know Jesus to be?" Many people make them the same. They say Jesus is the Word of God, and the Bible is the Word of God; therefore they are the same. This would be error. Jesus is *far more* than the Bible. You will find Jesus throughout the Bible, as He said (John 5:39). But you will find Him in a million other places as well.

So we see that *Logos* is a multi-facetted word, has many applications, and bears fruitful study of the places it appears in the New Testament.

So now what is the difference between *Logos* and *Rhēma*? *Logos* is the general word for Word. *Rhēma* is absolutely exclusive; it means only one thing; that thing is A Spoken Word. It is always and only a spoken Word, nothing more and nothing less. We can see the exclusivity of it if we consider the English word derived from it – rumour. That also is exclusively a spoken word.

A study of *Rhēma* in the New Testament gives us vital clues to living the Christian Life, tying up especially with the word Revelation from the chapter I have already written. In addition, a study of *Rhēma* could easily knock one or two of our favourite doctrines on the head. So let's look at a few of the 69 instances, one at a time, and please allow me to give Revelation where the Lord has given it to me. He will also give you Revelation as you ponder the implications with Jesus.

> Matt 4:4. "*Jesus answered, 'It is written: 'Man does not live on bread alone, but on every word (rhēma) that comes from the mouth of God.''*"
> Man must live on the *spoken* word of God, not on anything else.

Matt 12:36. "*But I tell you that men will have to give account on the Day of Judgment for every careless word (rhēma) they have spoken.*"
Luke 1:38. "*I am the Lord's servant," Mary answered. "May it be to me as you have said (rhēma)." Then the angel left her.*"
Luke 3:2. "*during the high priesthood of Annas and Caiaphas, the word (rhēma) of God came to John son of Zechariah in the desert.*"
God *spoke* words to Mary in her home and John the Baptist in the desert.

> John 3:34. "*for the one whom God has sent speaks the words (rhēma) of God, for God gives the Spirit without limit.*"
> Jesus' only method of communication is the *spoken* Word, not the written Word. Jesus uses the written Word as an opportunity through which He can communicate His spoken Words. It is Jesus' *spoken* Word that contains Life. The written Word is lifeless until Jesus *speaks* into it and through it.

John 5:47. "*But since you do not believe what he (Moses) wrote, how are you going to believe what I say? (My rhēma)*"
I have given this key in my chapter on Genesis. If we do not believe the Genesis (and other writings by Moses), how can we

possibly hear those vital words that Jesus speaks to us, using the Divine communication system that God has ordained?

> John 6:63. *"The Spirit gives life; the flesh counts for nothing. The words (rhēma) I have spoken to you are spirit and they are life."*
> The words Jesus *speaks* are always Life. If I understand these scriptures correctly, this is the only way that Life can come to us. Jesus *speaks* it into our spirits and souls.

John 6:68. *"Simon Peter answered him, 'Lord, to whom shall we go? You have the words (rhēma) of eternal life.'"*
John 8:47. *"He who belongs to God hears what God says (God's rhēma). The reason you do not hear is that you do not belong to God.'"*
We need to take encouragement from this. If we belong to God, we ***really do*** hear God speaking to us. The question is whether we recognise Him speaking or not.

> John 12:47. *"As for the person who hears my words (rhēma) but does not keep them, I do not judge him. For I did not come to judge the world, but to save it."*
> John 12:48. *"There is a judge for the one who rejects me and does not accept my words (rhēma); that very word (rhēma) which I spoke will condemn him at the last day."*
> These are illuminating verses. They are saying that judgement does *not* come to those who fail to act on Jesus' promptings (even though every prompting generates salvation). Judgement comes to those who hear the promptings and reject Jesus and/or reject their author as being Jesus. They got the Revelation but missed the Relationship! Man is blessed beyond his wildest dreams if he has a relationship with Jesus, but judged beyond his deepest fears if he doesn't. And the dividing line is *how* we acknowledge Jesus' *rhēma* Revelations. But

it also tells me that non-Christians hear God speaking *rhēma* words to them.

John 15:7. "*If you remain in me and my words (rhēma) remain in you, ask whatever you wish, and it will be given you.*"
We are to position ourselves permanently in Jesus. But we also need to position Jesus' *spoken* words in our hearts (note not His written words in the Bible). If we do, that promise is astonishing in its potential. Learning Bible verses has value, but it is limited. When *Jesus* speaks a Bible verse into our lives, it remains there eternally, never to be forgotten. According to John 14:26, the Holy Spirit will remind us of everything *Jesus speaks* to us.

John 17:8. "*For I gave them the words (rhēma) you gave me and they accepted them. They knew with certainty that I came from you, and they believed that you sent me.*"
Jesus expects *us* to live by His spoken words. He knew why. That's the very way *He* lived and therefore managed to live a perfect life on earth, He recommends that we follow His example.

Rom 10:8. "*But what does it say? "The word (rhēma) is near you; it is in your mouth and in your heart," that is, the word (rhēma) of faith we are proclaiming:*"
Rom 10:17. "*Consequently, faith comes from hearing the message, and the message is heard through the word (rhēma) of Christ.*"
These two verses tell us something very important. They tell us that the kind of faith that God honours is first given to us by the *spoken* word of God. He talks to us (it's a living thing), and with His *rhēma* comes the faith to live by it and to do God's will. Moreover, preachers need to be preaching God's *rhēma* rather than anything else (see John 17:8 above).

Rom 10:18. "*But I ask: Did they not hear? Of course they did: "Their voice has gone out into all the earth, their words (rhēma) to the ends of the world."*"

God's *rhēma* can actually be heard throughout the earth. Isn't that good news? There is nowhere we cannot find Him, and nowhere He cannot find people.

Eph 5:26. "*to make her holy, cleansing her by the washing with water through the word (rhēma),*"
This is also very interesting. It is talking about the Church. She is cleansed by the *spoken* word of God. That word also keeps her (us) clean.

Eph 6:17. "*Take the helmet of salvation and the sword of the Spirit, which is the word (rhēma) of God.*"
The sword of the Holy Spirit is the *spoken rhēma* of God, not the written *logos* of the Bible. The Bible tells us truth that we can understand and even live our lives on. But understanding is of man, not of God. However, when the Holy Spirit brings God's *Rhēma* to us through that same Bible passage, then it becomes Life to us, becomes fused into our souls and transforms us in every way. There are many Christians who think Life is in the Bible. It is not. Life is only in Jesus. Many people just do not recognise that they have actually been spoken to, and place their trust in the wrong place – their Bibles. It may seem bizarre that we can learn a verse and forget it, but when the Holy Spirit teaches us that verse, we can remember it for ever because He will be our memory. That means that when God speaks to us, that very word has power to do all sorts of things. It cuts through barriers, it demolishes strongholds (2 Cor 10), it opens closed doors, it provides sustenance of every kind, and it defeats all enemies.

Heb 1:3. *"The Son is the radiance of God's glory and the exact representation of his being, sustaining all things by his powerful word (rhēma)."*
Jesus' present job (among a million others) is to keep this cosmos consistently together, from the micro to the macro, by His *rhēma* word. He is *speaking* it into being continuously. How awesome is that?

Heb 6:5. *"who have tasted the goodness of the word (rhēma) of God and the powers of the coming age,"*
This is a very hard passage to handle. It tells about the possibility of falling away from God. So, have we tasted the goodness of the *rhēma* of God? Hang in there if you have, and don't fall away.

Heb 11:3. *"By faith we understand that the universe was formed at God's command (rhēma), so that what is seen was not made out of what was visible."*
1 Peter 1:25. *"but the word (rhēma) of the Lord stands forever." And this is the word (rhēma) that was preached to you."*
We often talk (and I have written) about the indestructibility of the written word of God, the Bible. This is true of the Bible. But it is the *rhēma* word of God that stands for ever. The point is this: God's *Rhēma* Word is far more extensive than His written (*Logos*) word. It is the *Rhēma* word that tells me how to live my daily life. The Bible *Logos* only gives me the principles. And that *rhēma* word is what we should be hearing and preaching. So when God speaks to you and calls you to do something, it is that *rhēma* word on which you must rely. You can check if it's valid and that you heard it right. How? It will *never* contradict either the principles or the themes of the Bible. If it doesn't, then you are onto a winner.

Rev 17:17. *"For God has put it into their hearts to accomplish his purpose by agreeing to give the beast their power to rule, until God's words (rhēma) are fulfilled."*

> Not even satan in all his power, accompanied by wicked and powerful men, can defeat the *rhēma* words of God. What God says will happen.

So how do we reconcile *logos* (the written word) and *rhēma* (the spoken word)? First we need to see that Life is not in the written word: it is in the spoken word only (John 6:63). Second, we need to see that the whole of the Bible was originally given as a *rhēma* word of God. "Men spoke from God as they were carried along by the Holy Spirit." (2 Peter 1). The authors, whether historians, poets, prophets or apostles, all heard God speak first, and then they wrote down what He told them to write. Those writings that were not God-breathed (2 Tim 3:16) were eventually discarded as not being "inspired", and the final canon of scripture was confirmed in the Council of Carthage in 397AD. Thus we have the *logos* of the Bible.

But I have to say now that the *logos* of God as we describe the Bible to be is, in itself, lifeless. Dead. It came from a *rhēma*, but lost its life as man wrote it down and it became part of this earth. It has no life *in itself.* God has hidden Himself inside the Bible. It is only Jesus through the Holy Spirit who can bring it to Life. He does this individually as a person reads it.

So what brings it life? Only the *rhēma* of God. It is the *rhēma* that brings life – the flesh counts for nothing. So reading the *logos* with one's mind cannot bring life – as no doubt all of us have found throughout our Christian lives. The *logos* needs to be transformed back into *rhēma* by the Holy Spirit as we read. Reading with our spirits rather than our minds brings life. When we do that, we will find that every single verse in scripture can be an avenue for God to speak anything He wants through it, applying it in the most versatile way. What many Christians fail to recognise is that they *need* the Holy Spirit to bring light and understanding through their Bibles. Nothing else will. The *rhēma* of God and Revelation are one and the same thing. They are Life because they come from a *living* God.

So we have a sequence of *rhēma, logos, rhēma. Rhēma* to the authors, *logos* from the authors, and *rhēma* to us as we read. That is how the Bible becomes an eternal book, bringing Life to any person in any century in the history of the earth.

So, will the *Rhēma* of God ever conflict with the *Logos* of God? *Never!* But the *Rhēma* Word of God is *far more* than the *Logos*. The *Logos* points us to Jesus (John 5:39), but it is only Jesus who can tell us what to do and how to live in our daily walk on earth. Therefore living a consistent and faithful Christian life is governed entirely on our recognising those *Rhēma* words that come to us daily. They are tricky to identify. Why does God make it so difficult? Because He wants us to walk by faith and not by rote. This is so important that I have expanded it in the next few chapters, and it constitutes the major theme of this book.

Now I don't know how much your view-point of the Christian life has been changed by these scriptures. But mine certainly was as I studied them in time past. All the solid things that we have previously relied on to give us hope and expectation in our Christian lives (our Bibles, our fellowships and churches, our companionship with other Christians, our Pastors, Vicars, Priests, Ministers and Leaders, our worship, the preaching, the counselling etc) do not in any way compare with the thing that seems to be most elusive to modern Christians: - the *rhēma* words of God. Indeed, if we put our trust in any of those things mentioned, our Christianity will certainly die or become lifeless. Yet these Bible verses suggest that if we have those *rhēma* words, hear them and obey them, we actually have the real goodies that Jesus came to give us. Without them, we actually have nothing – or maybe we just have mist.

May the *Logos* of God open up to you the most precious conduit and artery you can ever secure to obtain your full redemption – His *rhēma* words.

SUMMARY

Rhēma is the *spoken* word of God. It alone has Life, power and creativity. God created and governs the universe through His Now, *spoken* word. The Rhēma of God and Revelation are the same thing.

Chapter 3
HEARING THE VOICE OF GOD.

Ridiculous title, that. How can anyone possibly hear God's voice? Very few have literally done so. So let's discount for ever a literal hearing through ears, shall we? It is very rare and if it happens we need to be careful we are not mistaken.

I'm really talking about communication. God says He speaks to us. So if He doesn't speak in a voice we can hear, how does He speak? That's what I want to unravel. In case you don't think it's important, pause awhile and rethink. If we don't actually know *how* God speaks to us, how are we going to do His will?

In reality, it is amazing how few Christians there are who can find a clear and unambiguous answer to how God speaks to them. Even geriatric Christians who have been on the road decades seem mainly to have missed it. *Did* they ever know His will? How can anyone be so vague about something so important?

God uses many channels through which He communicates when He speaks to us. The Bible is, however, the least contaminated and the most used. The best way to look at the Bible is that it is a *channel* for Revelation from God. If we listen to God through it, He will speak to us through it. If we want intellectual information, we can also get that, but will not hear God speaking. God also uses sermons, Christian songs, visions, prophecies, conversations, confrontations, other Christians, nature, circumstances and loads of other things as a means of bringing Revelation. He uses what and whom He chooses.

But here I need to add one *very* important matter: Every Revelation we have ought to be confirmed somehow. We always need a double check. Satan is the arch counterfeiter and "appears as an angel of light". (2 Cor 11:14). If he can dupe us and get us off God's track, he will. That's his job, and he's pretty good at it. So, somehow, we must get confirmation that what God has said to us is right. This *particularly* applies to prophecies and visions. Get them confirmed. "Every matter must be established by the testimony of two or three witnesses." (2 Cor 13:1). The best confirmation is your Bible. Then there is the confirmation of fellow Christians. If even one person among your group of Christian companions has a doubt or caution, go back to God again in prayer. Don't move until all have peace over the decision (Phil 4:6-7). Making independent decisions is full of danger and stinks of satan. Beware!

In that list of suggested channels through which God speaks to us, they come in a descending order of certainty. The Bible is the most certain; circumstances the least certain. But all need time and waiting on God for His double check in our hearts.

So – how *does* God speak to us? Let me give you the key first, and I will then unravel it bit by bit. He communicates into our soul and spirit.

That might leave you just as confused. The difficulty is that it's not really a simple thing until you get the hang of it. The more you can identify the *method* of communication inside your soul /spirit, the easier it becomes to identify it again later.

So let's start with the spirit. All humans are spirit beings, although we are not particularly aware of it and would have a lot of trouble identifying which part of us inside is spirit and which is soul. Do not worry. God is also Spirit (John 4:24) and in 6:63 Jesus says: "The things I speak to you are Spirit and they are life". Now this system of communication I am about to share with you I got from my friend Andrew Palmer. He said that God is Spirit, is plural and they are One. In order to run this universe, they are continually discussing with each other what should be done. So there's a lot of communication going on continually. In fact, the communication system they have must be the most sophisticated, efficient and perfect system in the universe. How do they communicate with one another? They just do. Each knows the thoughts and desires of the others instantaneously, and the Trinity collectively runs the universe that way. (Rom 8:26, 27 – "And he who searches the hearts knows the mind of the Spirit, because the Spirit intercedes for the saints in accordance with the will of God").

Enter man into the agenda. Firstly manhood in the form of Jesus; He has taken mankind into Heaven for ever. Secondly, intercessory prayer. We read that Jesus "ever lives to make intercession for us" (Heb 7:25), and the Holy Spirit is also interceding for us (Rom 8:26). So we (every human on earth, but especially Christians) figure hugely in God's agenda, and that is how and why, in terms of God's thought life and prayer life, we become a part of the Divine communication system.

Even so, *how* do we get Revelation? We just do. It "pops" into our system and we know, because we know, because we know. It is a "whole life" thing. It's not just information but certainty and faith as well. Without being able to separate soul from spirit, both inside parts of us are aware together that we have been spoken to and we have no questions. (Someone said that before we become Christians, we were all questions with no answers. After we become Christians, we have no questions). That's Revelation. That's God speaking. That is Spirit to spirit communication. That's the way the Trinity does it, and, as we get sucked into the Trinity, we join in their communication system.

Let me give you a couple of examples from my own life about big occurrences.

The first was when I was in the RAF. I was a Flight Commander in a Lightning F3 Squadron (29 Sqn). At that time the whole of the Lightning force was losing one aircraft a month to technical and servicing difficulties. One of our Squadron pilots, Captain Bill Povilus (USAF on exchange) experienced a fire in one engine at night, low level, out in the North Sea. It was pitch black. He used his ejector seat to bale out of the aircraft, and in the total darkness, managed to do everything perfectly. He got into his dinghy, inflated it, got out his SARBE rescue beacon and was rescued intact. All by feel. Awesome. As I considered his adventure, a mini fear grew inside me that I would probably not be able to copy his example and get away with my life. I pondered over it for a bit and then dismissed it. Some months later, when it was long forgotten, I was doing some Bible research for a talk I had been asked to give in a local Church, when I happened upon Is. 52:12 in RSV. There it says; "For you shall not go out in haste, and you shall not go out in flight; for the Lord will go before you, and the God of Israel will be your rearguard." I instantly joined God's communication system and the Lord spoke to me directly, clearly and unmistakably – "You will never need to bale out of an aircraft," That is, "You will not go out in flight." It was such a bizarre application of scripture that I did not immediately believe it. "A text out of context is a pretext" is a saying I attribute to David Watson, and I felt it applied here. But as I mused over it over the succeeding months, God confirmed it within me in a multitude of different little ways. It was not until 6 months later that I dared share it with other Christians. And, later, when I was a Test Pilot on Lightnings, I had a few engineering disasters myself, had to call on that promise a number of times, and was able to save both the aircraft and my life. That word had become life and action to me. Knife-edged, but successful. That's what God does for us.

The second occasion of clear Revelation I want to share with you is how I went full-time into serving God in Nicaragua. I had been going out to Nicaragua once a year for some 5 years with Mike Cole and the Peace and Hope Trust. We built schools, clinics, Churches and stuff. In 2000 we went out in January, and round about the 15th we were accosted by not a few families who asked us for 30 Cordobas to register their kids at school. That's about £1.50, and less than $2 US. Desperate parents and despairing children came around in their Sunday best and silently looked up at me with their huge brown pleading eyes. I've always been a sucker for kids, and their unspoken pleas were irresistible. I emptied my pockets of both dollars and Cordobas, as did the rest of the Team. I knew nothing of the Nicaraguan Education system, but later learned that it cost that to register each child in school at the start of each year, and then the same per month if they want a reasonable school. I dismissed the incident and got on with my work. In May that same year I was back in the UK and had been asking God what I should do with my life after I retired, which would be soon. Every one of those incidents were disconnected and I was walking down town musing that it was extraordinary that in this modern 21st Century, there were still people who could not afford £1.50 a month to educate their children. How did they eat? Right outside the Post Office, God said to me, "You can do something about that." Indeed I could, I immediately thought, no one in the UK would miss £1.50 a month, or even £3.00, so that the families could buy exercise books, school clothes etc. I stood still for about 2 minutes working out how we could do this, and then suddenly woke up to realise that God had called me to do something radical and new in Nicaragua. That was the beginning of SIFT; God had told me to start a work out there. It was crystal clear. Revelation. It happens every now and then, when God has clear directions to give us. Spirit to spirit communication.

Every Christian will have similar spasmodic incidents in their lives that they can call on with confidence. But that is not how He guides us daily. So let me introduce you to your soul. The soul is the "Inner working Me" and consists, most would agree, of our minds, our wills, and our emotions. Let's deal with these 3 backwards.

The *Emotions* are fickle, nice, but utterly unreliable in terms of getting guidance. They are often governed by time of day, time of month, sunshine or cloud, before meals or after, whether I'm in love or not, and all sorts of other irrational and irrelevant inputs. None of us can rely on emotions for guidance – ever.

The *Will* is ours and never touched by God. My will is my own, and makes me accountable for every word and deed I do in this body. That's why God doesn't touch it.

The *Mind* – ah, there's a place God can infiltrate, so let's look at it in depth.

The human mind is a remarkable bit of organic "computery". All sorts of thoughts race through it moment by moment. Please be assured that satan also has access to your mind, and can put thoughts in there just as easily as you can or God can.

Temptation starts in the mind – "First the look; then the thought; then the fascination; then the fall." (From a Moral Rearmament Booklet). But so can God. So can I. The difficulty is knowing where this moment's thought has come from.

There are a number of inputs and sources of thoughts in the mind, and I have catalogued them thus:

- Me - by calculation. I am thinking something through.
- Me – by memory. I recall inputs from time past.
- Outside sources – what other people say and have said, books, circumstances; past; present; etc.
- God. – He puts thoughts directly into my mind.
- Satan – He starts temptations in the mind and argues with me in there.

Let's eliminate satan first. He is a demanding spirit. When he puts temptation into our minds, he cuts off practically every other input. It's *that thing* only that it is the total focus of our thoughts. At first it doesn't seem like temptation; and it is nearly always highly desirable. Like Eve, in Eden, when "she saw that it was good for food and pleasing to the eye, and also desirable for gaining wisdom, she took..." Now satan is not allowed to *make* us sin – and God has placed the same restriction on Himself in terms of goodness; He will not *make* us do good. Satan is allowed to tempt, and God will also put in His inputs at the same time. But we choose. We are responsible spiritual creatures. That's the will. We select which way to go, the right or the wrong, and for that selection we are eternally accountable. All that battle takes place in our minds. Check it out. If you weren't aware of it before, you'll have another opportunity to analyse it before the end of today! Check out satan's arguments and his tactics. Check out your decision and how you made it. And do it right after the temptation is over – whether you have sinned or not. (If you sinned, confess it immediately. But still analyse it while it's fresh in your mind). I suspect, but don't know, that satan cannot hear or read what God puts into your mind. It's as if he is deaf when God speaks or walks away at times, and is just not available. But I'm not convinced about the total validity of that one.

Let's deal with calculation next. We will all be aware of personal thinking. It starts in our own minds. It ruminates around our own minds. It concludes in our own minds. We will all be so aware of it that I need spend little time on it.

Outside Inputs? These mainly come from memory. We recall the past – circumstances, situations, words, information – just like I have done in writing this book. Sometimes the external input is current – what someone is saying to me right now, or a situation that is confronting me right now. How I react or respond is governed by how I am at that moment, how much of Jesus I have within me (to respond in His way), and what I think. External inputs come in from outside, but dealing with them comes up from inside.

So, how about God's inputs?

Firstly, let's look at Jesus. He claimed that every word He spoke and every action He did was first prompted by God (John 14:10). And that must have been so from the very beginning of His life, because at His baptism, and before He had done anything miraculous, God said, "This is My Beloved Son with whom I am well pleased." So, eating, sleeping, working, worshipping, going to the toilet, looking after Mary and Joseph and His brothers and sisters, in the home and in the workshop, down town, with people, and then being head of the household after Joseph died – all was in response to His Father's inputs. Jesus never "reacted to the circumstances", as we so often do. He always got God's mind on it first. God can and wants to direct us in every minute of every day in everything we do. If He did it for Jesus, He does it for us. That means communication is current and continuous. Jesus, I guess, did it perfectly and better than us because He was able to identify when His Father was speaking and when man or satan were speaking, and always chose God's way (e.g. Matt 16:22-23). But this one thing I am certain about: Jesus never cheated. It's no good any of us saying, "Well – He was the Son of

God and therefore had an advantage over us." No, He laid aside His glory and became fully man just like we are. And if we are re-born from above, we have the same inputs and opportunities as He had. If Jesus could please God in every moment of an ordinary life, so can we. At least, the promises are all fully there, if only we would access them! (And see chapter 8 on Righteousness).

God never cheats.

All right then. If God can and does speak to us at any and every point of our working day, how do we identify Him speaking?

So, it is in the mind. It comes in the form of *thoughts*. The great disadvantage of "thoughts" is that their sources are not identifiable. If you spoke to me I could establish who you were by the cadence, pitch and accent of your voice. Every voice in the world is different – another of God's miracles and our individual uniqueness. But not thoughts. They are soundless, emotionless and unidentifiable; they are almost as inanimate as things. So, how do we distinguish God's thoughts in our heads? I have 7 keys for you:-

- They "pop" into our minds without any pre-warning and without any pre-calculation. That is, they don't come up from inside, they come in from outside.
- They are always good. They prompt us to do good, kind, nice things – things that God in His excellence would do. That will distinguish them from satan's inputs. "Perform random acts of kindness to strangers" is a start. Remember James 1:17: "Every good and perfect gift is from above, coming down from the Father of heavenly lights..."? *Every* good and perfect gift. Not just some.
- They never, repeat never disagree with the Bible.
- They are always gentle and undemanding. (Matt 11:28).
- They are almost always something we never thought of before.

- They always tie up with Peace in the heart. (Phil 4: 6, 7).
- They always leave us with choice, and include a way out if they are in response to a difficulty we are in. (1 Cor 10:13).

OK so far? Sure, but *how* do we "hear" them?

They are simply thoughts that pop into our minds. Tell me, have you ever argued or discussed an issue with yourself in your mind? Of course you have! And the answering thought - the thought you were speaking to – was that *really* you? Methinks not. It was God. Very simple. Very ordinary. Sounds just like me. But always putting a view-point that is right, righteous and helpful. But we thought that was ourselves! Or our conscience. Indeed we did. But next time you do it – it will happen within the next 24 hours – sit back and analyse both the content and the style, and analyse the viewpoint it is suggesting. You'll get the point pretty quickly. What "felt" like you talking to yourself (although, of course, you felt nothing), what "sounded" like you (although, of course you heard nothing), was in fact the Lord answering you instantaneously as you "discussed" the issue together. He is so immediate and so "ordinary" that we miss it being Him, consider our discussion as having been between me and me, and dismiss the incident as being of little value. But God has actually been guiding me by thoughts in my mind. And if we don't recognise that it was Him speaking, we attach no faith to it, and even if we do what He suggests, thinking it was me, and a good idea, it will fail because "without *faith* it is impossible to please God." (Heb 11:6). But the moment we cotton on that it is God speaking, our whole attitude changes, we listen more carefully, "believe" that it is He who is speaking, and all sorts of wonderful things can come out of our faith and obedience.

So why does He hide Himself like that? If He made Himself more obvious, there would be less room for faith. The more room there is for faith, the bigger the ensuing miracle or divine input. Get it?

Or again, did you ever wonder how Jesus read other people's minds? Analyse every passage in the Gospels where it says "He knew what they were thinking." Every single occasion was an accusation against Him. He read the accusation before they managed to express it – He knew what they were *thinking*. Now, satan is the "accuser of the brethren", so all accusation comes directly from him. Moreover, it is always based on half-truth. It's never the whole story. (Read any daily newspaper and you'll see what I mean about accusation being based on half-truth or part-truth). Later He then goes on to say that everything He did we can do also (John 14:12. "I tell you the truth, anyone who has faith in me will do what I have been doing. He will do even greater things than these, because I go to the Father."). So we can read accusation in other people's minds, just like He did. What actually happens is this: satan's accusation communicates with *us* as well as the person to whom it comes at the same moment – spirit to spirit. The accusation thought that is going on in their minds also comes directly into our minds, and we know it before they actually express it. If we are quick enough, we can identify the half-truth, tell them what they are thinking, bring them the whole story and kill the accusation. Just like Jesus did. Check it out for yourself.

Let me try to make it as simple as I can for you. If you can ever say, "It occurs to me that ...", you have almost certainly heard the communication of God in your mind. Analyse it. Where does a new thought that you think come from? If you examine the occurrence dispassionately, you will realise very clearly that you did not initiate it – it did not arise from your own calculations. It just came in. It was suddenly there. It is so ordinary, so normal and so common that you have always assumed that you thought it. But did you? *You* didn't think it – *it* suddenly appeared in your mind. That's different. Analyse your own internal experience.

But why does He talk my language, so that I can barely distinguish between me thinking and Him thinking in me?

Here I picked up a key from Judson Cornwell on a tape he made at one of Don Double's missions. The Lord had led him in preparation to look up the Hebrew of Gen 6, talking of Noah. The Hebrew word for Noah was *Nun-het.* As Judson read down the passage, he came across verse 8, "Noah found grace in the eyes of the Lord", and to his astonishment the Hebrew for "grace" there was *Het-nun.* Grace was the mirror image of Noah.

What was the Lord telling him through this scripture? That Noah found in God a perfect mirror image of himself, and God called that *Grace.* What Noah discovered was that in God he had found a perfect – yes, perfect complement to his own character. I went on thinking about that. So I liken it to a ball. On our own we are half a ball. We roll around for a while and then go clunk – onto the flat bit. Then we need someone to come around, prise us up, and off we go again. But Jesus is the exact other half to each one of us. He complements us perfectly, and completes us perfectly. Stuck together we become a complete ball and never fall flat. (By the way, he is the only One who can do this – no other human being or animal can complement any of us perfectly like He does). To me He is wonderful. He thinks the way I do, uses the same expressions, understands my personality traits, knows fully the whole of my background, and lives life inside me in my style. He is my perfect companion and is "acquainted with all my ways." He is my perfect mirror image. Suzanne cleverly pointed out that I was therefore making God in man's image – which was a shrewd observation. But no. He is *your* perfect complement too. And 6 billion others on this planet today. He is all things to all men. He is the eternal diamond with the infinite number of facets, each one of which perfectly fits some human being that has ever lived on earth. That's how He can relate to each of us so perfectly, and give us all a unique ministry. He humbles Himself to come down to our level exactly.

So? Well, when He talks to me in my mind He sounds exactly like me. He addresses me in my language, my style, bearing in mind and reminding me of my whole background and experience, using people and situations that are familiar to us both. That's why His inputs into my mind sound like I am talking to myself. And that's why it's difficult to separate Him from me inside. And *that's* why it's so difficult to exercise faith that it really is Jesus talking to us and guiding us every moment of every day. But now that I have given you the key, you will more easily be able to tell which voice inside belongs to God.

If Jesus is not saying anything to you, don't you say anything either. He had nothing to say to Herod, and little to say to Pilate and the Chief Priest. Don't drag up good advice from inside – that's man. Wait for inputs to come in from above. Then you will find that the Lord has the key to every situation you find yourself in.

I have coined the expression "Hold all things lightly." Why? Because we get it wrong so often. So don't let your imagination or dreams grip strongly onto anything, because if they fail your disappointment and depression could be awful and you could lose your faith. Many have for that very reason. The *only* thing on earth that we must hold strongly is Jesus. And living with Him is unpredictable; He is "not a tame Lion."

He also has the key to every other person's innermost heart – things you have no natural way of knowing. In a counselling situation, He gives you that key that unlocks the logjam that is inside them. Sometimes that's called a "Word of Knowledge". And it's easy to come by if you know how – once you have been able to identify the "voices" inside your own head.

Eileen and I are house-sitting for a friend. We call it holiday. Last night the Holy Spirit said to me: "Pray for this house." Immediately I did – for its security, protection, permanence, peace and the blessing of the Lord in Jesus' Name. The natural question to ask was: "Why?" But if God chooses not to tell me that, then I have no need to know. He who can see to the end of time knows exactly why that needs to be prayed, and I need to trust Him for that. We are family, the Trinity and me. Together we work goodness and grace into mankind through prayer, and God's priorities for this moment are His affair, not mine. The Holy Spirit knows God's mind, prompts me (or you) to pray, and it is accomplished for ever – so long as we do pray. Protection is now fixed eternally for this house. Do you see the simplicity of it?

Don't be nosey or stupid and ask questions you've no reason or right to know.

There may be those among you who disagree with this chapter; God does not guide you this way. Is Dick unique and abnormal in the way God speaks to him all the time? What you cannot surely deny is the Biblical truth of the previous two and the next two chapters (Faith and The Bible) – that God runs His universe and us through revelation, His Spoken Word. So if His Spoken Word comes to you in another way, make haste to find out exactly *how* that Word comes to you. For if you don't know that, how are you going to know how to think right, and therefore how to do right? Or you might end up like some teenagers who, when asked when God spoke to them last, replied, "Well, three years ago ... " or "Five months ago ... " which was the last time they knew for certain that He had spoken to them. Does God say *nothing* in the gaps in between? Paul says "We walk by faith and not by sight." Faith in what? That would be Jesus. So, how? I've worked it out in me. Have you in you?

When once you have distinguished the voice of God inside your mind, you are on the highway to having an effective Christian ministry, built on faith, and to living a fruitful Christian life. Try it; you will see how very simply and how wonderfully it works. Doesn't it say in the Poetry Books somewhere (one version): "God has made man plain and simple, but we have made ourselves very complicated."?

Following that, "Those who get the prompting, do the job." It is not enough to recognise that God has spoken to you. Go and *do* it.

SUMMARY

God directs Christians by His Rhēma word into our souls (minds) all the time. We need to identify them and receive them by faith.

Chapter 4
FAITH

Faith is a strange thing. God asks us to trust Him whom we cannot see, cannot hear, cannot touch or feel, and over issues that are illogical in terms of timing, necessity and common sense. Yet we *have* to. "Without faith it impossible to please God" (Heb 11:6), and "Whatever is not of faith is sin" (Rom 14:23). That last verse is very harsh, but it is unambiguous. What's more, it describes perfectly some 80% of the average Christian's daily life. What is not of *faith* is *sin*. Very nasty.

Clearly, Faith does not come naturally. By nature we all live from a position whereby we consult our own minds first and other people second in most of our activities and living. Not God. For the vast majority of people, never. For many Christians, seldom. For a few very special servants, a little bit more often than seldom. The Biblical perspective of "we walk by faith and not by sight" (2 Cor 5:7) is reversed for some 80+% of Christian people in 80+% of their daily lives.

Is God therefore asking the impossible of us? Absolutely. Certainly. Indubitably. So how can *any* of us ever please God? We can't. Humankind as a concept from God was brilliant. Humankind as we've all turned out is an absolute disaster. We are all total failures. Few of you readers will agree with me on that statement – you will all have a mini reservation somewhere that thinks: "Surely I have *some* good in me?" I'm afraid not, if we are to take Scripture as it is written: "The scripture declares that the whole world is a prisoner of sin..." (Gal 3:22). Not even a teensy-weensy bit? Nope. Not even a teensy-weensy bit.

And it applies 100% to Faith as it does to sin. We are all 100% sin by nature: and 100% all have No Faith by nature: 100% of us cannot please God. So has God therefore asked of us something that is impossible to fulfil? Yes; exactly. So isn't that a teensy-weensy bit unfair? Well, no. Why not? Because *God* has produced a different and un-natural solution that is 100% fair to all people of all ages, all cultures, all over the world. Take His solution, and all please Him. Reject or ignore His solution, and all displease Him. Even I can understand that principle – it's simple.

So what is the solution? Here it is: He *gives* us Faith; the only kind of Faith that pleases Him: Jesus is "the author ...of our faith" (Heb 12:2). It's very simple. God makes it simple just for people like me. And maybe you too.

How does He do that? Revelation. Very simply, He tells us what to do. And with that telling comes the Faith to believe that it is possible. In my chapter on Revelation (which I hope you have read before this one), I explained that Revelation is a "whole person" experience. It ministers to the whole soul as well as the mind and the spirit. Sometimes the body too, in the form of a happy or nice feeling.

Do you see the beauty of this system? When God wants to do something stupendous and/or life-changing, He hunts the earth to find someone who can carry it through and finds *YOU*! Then He tells you exactly and simply what He wants to do, and/or what He wants *you* to do. With it comes the Faith to believe it and receive it. So you leap up, punch the air with your fist and shout "Yes!" (or whatever your style is). You believe because God has given you not only the *what* to do but the *how* to do it (by Faith). You pray about it, confirm it, and believe it. Then, after a suitable length of time predetermined by the Lord, whatever it was happens.

Soon we will look at Biblical references for this, because it's all in there. But first let's see the counterfeit.

The counterfeit is *very* subtle. And every one of us Christians has been caught by it many times. Simply it is this: you see a *verse in Scripture* that seems to apply to your situation, accept it, and then you come into "faith" on it out from your own resources. We think: "This is the word of God. Therefore, because God is consistent and faithful, He will answer my longings through prayer and down the line of Scripture. Therefore I will get what I asked for." We try. And we don't get what we asked for. It doesn't work. I have known many many Christians who have fallen away from God simply because, in their need they have prayed "according to the Scripture", and the heavens have been like brass and the ground beneath them like iron. God has failed. If He didn't help me in my hour of need, then presumably He has abandoned me and I'm on my own again. So we walk away from Him, and all is downhill from then on.

So what happened? Our "faith" was from man and not from God. He didn't initiate it, we did. We didn't ask His approval, we told Him what we wanted, and tried to blackmail Him by using Scripture. It's called Presumption. We "presume" God is our servant to do as we ask Him – and can quote loads of Scriptures that would back up that style. For instance: "Ask, and it shall be given you ..." (Matt 7:7). And it does not work.

Let me give you two very common examples of our use of this counterfeit: Healing and Prosperity.

Healing is the most common example. The Scriptures are quite clear that God heals. Jesus healed *everyone* who came asking. There are plenty of examples in the Gospels and Acts of the disciples doing the same. So – of course God heals. "By His stripes we have been healed" (Is 53). Therefore it's obvious that Granny Jones, suffering from cancer and in pain, is going to get healed. Oh yes? Who said? Try it, and you'll find, as thousands of Christians have found, that Granny Jones (GJ) does not get healed and dies. So what went wrong? No one asked God's opinion in an unbiased and unprejudiced way. *We* want GJ to be healed. We *all* want GJ to be healed. So, it's obvious, God must too. Not necessarily so. Faith is given by the spoken word of God through Revelation. We must first ask: "Lord, how do *You* want us to pray?" Then we must wait for His Revelation, after which we can only pray along that line, because we now know His will. He is, after all, Sovereign over the whole universe.

There is a story about Harry Greenwood. A group were in the Caribbean somewhere and Harry was the speaker. The guests were enjoying a swim in the beautiful tropical waters. One of them got into trouble, and others had to drag her out senseless onto the beach. No one knew what to do. Someone suggested calling Harry, who came along. He prayed. But he did not pray for the lady's healing or survival; he prayed that she should find the Lord in her coma, and become a Christian. (Harry had never met the lady before). Someone asked if he shouldn't pray for her healing? He replied that he had no freedom from God to do so. He only had freedom to pray for her salvation, so that was what he did. And off he went. Eventually some medics came along, took the lady to hospital where, after some days, she recovered. And when she woke up, she was a Christian. She had met the Lord while she was "out". Get the point?

The Bible is *laden* with verses we can "presume". But the word of God is dead until *God* gives it life. All else is presumption. There is *nothing* automatic about the Christian life, nor about the Bible. It is all ebb and flow by a continual relationship with God through the Holy Spirit. God is *living.* He's *alive.* What works is *Life.* Not assumptions or presumptions.

It is the same with Prosperity. There are those who say that there is no prosperity teaching in the Bible. They would be wrong. There is plenty. There is also plenty of teaching on Poverty, and I have written a separate chapter on that. Both Poverty and Prosperity are Biblical. But neither can be presumed. Others (and I) have fallen into this trap often. For example, I am in debt, and I know God doesn't like to see me in debt. So I presume that, if I follow the rules, He will prosper me. (The rules, by the way, are neatly summarised in Psalm 1). But not so. I pray. I stay in debt. God does not bail me out.

How Christians would all love to win the Lottery to be able to give substantially to others in need, and, of course, we wouldn't tell another Christian that we had entered it, or where we got our money from. Surely it's gambling? A game of chance? Hmmm. Can anyone find for me a Scripture that specifically forbids gambling? Didn't Old Testament people find the will of God through casting lots? That's gambling – chance. Please don't get me wrong – I am not thereby approving either of gambling or the lottery. But I am saying that God is Sovereign over all, and we need to ask Him first. After all, there are some Christians to whom God has given the ministry of making money. Their task is to provide for those in Christian work who do not have any. Not for selfish purposes, but for the Kingdom of God. There are two principles laid down in 2 Cor 8 & 9. Firstly, those who have now give now to those who don't, so that the roles can be reversed later. The illustration is the manna in the desert.

And the second principle is "He who supplies seed to the sower and bread for food will also supply and increase your store of seed and will enlarge the harvest of your righteousness." (2 Cor 9:10). God gives increase so that it can be fairly divided between eating and sowing. If we use it all for eating (selfishly), and have a whale of a party, there's nothing left to sow for next year, and we starve then. If we give it all away and sow into the Kingdom, we starve today. Actually, *all* of us have to heed this principle, not just rich people. But how much goes into which area? That's where we ask the Lord, and He brings guidance, assurance and prosperity in both areas of use. The principle is laid down in Scripture. The practice and application of that principle is lived out daily in our lives, in collaboration with the God of Life. He alone knows the best use of our money, and we come into Faith according to His Revelation, *not* according to Scripture. Wow! That's challenging, and should chop a few of our neat Christian prejudices and assumptions to pieces.

In SIFT we have this all the time. We have the need (and the need is not necessarily the call); we talk to the Lord; and we move according to what the Lord says. There are many times when we go out to Nicaragua with less money than we need to meet the occasion and the promises. So both those out there and we here have to wait for the Lord's perfect timing. It teaches us patience and a greater and greater reliance on the Lord's perfect knowledge of all things.

So both Healing and Prosperity come through Revelation, not through Scripture. Of course Revelation can come through

Scripture. But without *Revelation* we have no divine Faith, and nothing works, Scripture or no Scripture.

So what Scriptures are laid down for Faith after the pattern I am suggesting? Let's look at a few.

> Jesus answered, "It is written: "Man does not live on bread alone, but on every (spoken) word that comes from the mouth of God."" (Matt 4:4). (See the chapter on *Logos* and *Rhema* for an analysis of the Greek word "Word").
>
> "Consequently, faith comes from hearing the message, and the message is heard through the (spoken) word of Christ." (Rom 10:17).
>
> Did you get that one? *Faith* comes from *hearing* the message, and that comes from the *spoken word* of Christ? Got it?
>
> "I tell you the truth, whoever hears my word and believes him who sent me has eternal life and will not be condemned; he has crossed over from death to life." (John 5:24).
>
> "Do not work for food that spoils, but for food that endures to eternal life, which *the Son of Man* will give you. On him God the Father has placed his seal of approval." (John 6:27).
>
> "For it is by grace you have been saved, through faith— and this not from yourselves, it is the gift of God— not by works, so that no one can boast." (Eph 2:8-9).
>
> "Let us fix our eyes on Jesus, the *author* and perfecter *of our faith*," (Heb 12:2).

> "This is the confidence we have in approaching God: that if we ask anything according to his will, he hears us. And if we know that he hears us—whatever we ask—we know that we have what we asked of him." (1 John 5:14,15).

So what is the Principle behind Faith as we find it in the Bible? The Principle is that Jesus has accomplished *every* thing that is needed for:

- Our salvation.
- Our survival.
- Our work.
- His work on earth through us Christians.
- The future in terms of what's going to happen to earth and its people.
- The new Heavens and the New Earth.

Nothing can be taken away from it – it fulfilled the whole will of God. Nothing can be added to it – it is complete with or without us. God has chosen to do it with us, but not using our contributions. Only our obediences.

It's quite galling really. We have talents and contribute excellently to running this world and making it tick over well. Isn't God interested in our talents, and our using them for His Kingdom and glory? Nope. Not at all. Never. Let me explain. Let me let you into another secret: using our talents and energies for God and His Kingdom is sin. Stinking, self-centred, nasty, horrible sin. I'll explain why in a jiffy, but first to say that I have heard that perspective recommended from the pulpit more times than I can count. It sounds so holy; so reasonable; so Biblical; so spiritual – "Don't use your talents for yourself, use them for God." But it is not any of those things. Why not? Ask who is deciding and controlling the *use* of the talents? Me or God? Answer: Me. ***I*** am choosing to do stuff for the Kingdom. Because I am in charge of the choosing, it is just as much sin as choosing to work for myself, the firm, the government or my own ends. God is not mocked. Sin is defined as "me doing my own thing". No matter how philanthropic that "thing" is, it's still *me* doing it. That's why it's sin. Me choosing to burn out for God leaves God cold and unimpressed, and I ruin my life and waste my years never doing God's will. Do you see the wickedness in it? Only a total surrender to *His* will, so that He makes all the offers of choice is good enough for the Kingdom. I am to be God's servant and slave, and no one else's. Not even my own. Especially not my own. All visions are to be God's visions, not mine. Running under God's direction requires Faith of the Divine kind, and a permanent, daily, total surrender to whatever God wants. And if He is not asking anything of you right now, take a holiday. Like the disciples going across the lake after John the Baptist's beheading, holidays in Jesus don't last very long. But do not, above all do not do your own thing. 80% of Christians are for 80% of their time.

If you are on a sailing boat and the wind dies, don't get out the oars and row. Take a rest. "The wind blows wherever it pleases. You hear its sound, but you cannot tell where it comes from or where it is going. So it is with everyone born of the Spirit." (John 3:8). Trim your sails to catch the wind. Rowing is not any alternative to sailing – if you get the metaphor.

Let me make as simple as I can what Faith is not and what Faith is. Faith is *not*: just faith ("I've got faith"). Faith is *not*: faith in faith ("I believe in faith"). Faith is *not*: believing in Jesus (that is restricted to the day we became Christians). So what is Faith? Faith *is*: hearing what God is saying, believing that it is He who is saying it, and doing what He asks. Is that simple enough? (It has taken me years to work that out. You have the benefit of my decades of trials and errors).

It's amazing that God achieves anything in this world; if He only has Christians who have insight into His will, how slowly does the Kingdom of God advance? "Surely the Sovereign LORD does nothing without revealing his plan to his servants the prophets." (Amos 3:7). So where are they, those prophets? Their inputs could stop an awful lot of wasted effort.

Let me move onto "sanctified common sense". I had it given to me (often) when I was a young Christian. Maybe I needed it then. But it caused me to think and pray about it. Common sense is so essential to living in this world. It keeps our feet on the ground and stops us being silly or so sanctified and holy that we are no earthly use. God is a practical God. One of the most "spiritual" things He did was to make an earth. So most of the spiritual things He asks us to do are practical, earthy and often full of common sense. But we must distinguish between what is of God and what is of man. A secular non-Christian person *needs* common sense. A Christian doesn't. And there's hardly a thing called "sanctified common sense". So what is there? Only the leading and prompting of the Lord as we walk daily with Him on earth. For some who do not recognise God's voice or cannot distinguish it from other voices that crowd their minds, "sanctified common sense" may, possibly, be a useful tag. I guess it means being earthly and practical and doing good with it at the same time? But to live like that means I am either not communicating with God or I haven't yet worked out which voice coming into my mind is His. Therefore it is not of Faith. Therefore, by definition of Rom 14:23, it is sin. Please can we remove the concept from the Christian vocabulary, and show people "the more excellent way"? If God is not leading us all the time, then He has failed. But God does not fail; therefore the fault lies within us – we just don't know when He is speaking. And, certainly, therefore, we don't take heed.

What's more, very often God's suggestions are definitely *not* common sense!

So how does God's kind of Faith work in the secular world in which most of us earn our bread? Have you ever noticed how many Christians divide secular from spiritual? They (maybe) pray at the beginning of a day, ask God to rubber-stamp all their decisions, and turn off God as they close their front doors? There they remain for the rest of the day, doing a secular thing in a secular way using secular expertise that they have accrued by a secular use of their brains in a secular college or university. (All universities spawn and multiply secular – and atheistic - information. Is the best way for a Christian to train their minds to contaminate them with man-made and man-devised information? Does it advance God's Kingdom in us and for us, or man's? Just asking, that's all). Do we not know that ALL knowledge of EVERY area of science, humanities, society, history etc etc lies in Jesus? Want to know mathematics? Learn at Jesus' feet. Sir Isaac Newton did. Physics? Chemistry? Geology? Biology? Human society? Tell me what things in all areas of knowledge that man thinks he knows so much about that Jesus does not know more? There actually is no such thing as "secular". That's a concept made by men who want to leave God out of everything. It stinks, really. Don't you think so? People who walk without God may well advance the causes they favour, but those causes will veer towards man, satan and evil. It's inevitable. If you leave God out, how can His goodness be advanced? It can't. They will receive no blessing from God or advance goodness, wisdom or grace on earth. Sad really. Everything that is not of Faith is still sin. Always will be. (Chapter 7 on Sin is helpful here).

The best way we can see this is our own conversion and new birth. How come we changed from having nothing to do with God to being open to Him, and then surrendering to Him? Easy really. It was He who started to talk to us inside. We discussed it with ourselves (or so we thought), and gradually came to realise that what Christians were talking about had sense. Who gave us that realisation? Jesus did. And with it He brought the Faith to believe it and receive it. His spoken words inside us galvanised our faith. Did we realise it? Not at all. But have we come to realise now, in retrospect, that that was exactly the way it occurred?

Guess why God wants us to pray for non-Christians? That's easy too. Our praying releases Him to talk to those people inside. They may be able to avoid us on their outside, but they cannot avoid King Jesus on their insides. So why doesn't God do it on

His own without us? That's also easy. We are family, God and us, and the family work together as One.

Alongside God's kind of Faith lies Faithfulness. Or "stickability" if you prefer it. When God tells you what to do, and you start to pray it through, just watch to see how long it takes for it to happen. Sometimes – instantaneously. Sometimes – even quicker than that and you realise that you are walking into well prepared ground. But not very often. Mostly – longer than you expect or want. So Faith and patience join together. And Faithfulness unites them both. We hang in there in accordance with the Revelation God has given until we see it fulfilled in front of our eyes.

I recall a story of Colin Urquhart's that I picked up from a tape of his. It was at the time when they had asked God for the money to buy Roffey Place for their work. It was going to cost $1,000,000. Colin was in Australia ministering as the deadline approached. He rang Caroline every evening to give her a run down on his day, and asked if the money had come in. Daily, no. At the very last minute, the day before the deadline, Caroline told him that the money had arrived. When Colin had replaced the phone, he said to the Lord, "Why did you do that?" God replied, "That was when you wanted it, wasn't it?" The gap between asking and receiving is either a gap of anxiety or a gap of Faith. Faithfulness ensures it's the latter.

So Faith is imparted. That's the only kind of Faith that works. God gives us the task, and supplies the Faith to believe it is He who has spoken, and we mobilise the Faith by action into fulfilment. We stick like glue to God's spoken words, and see them through to the end. That's called Faithfulness; it's much the same as Faith, only stretched. That's the Christian life for you!

So why, in this chapter, have I not written anything about the marvels of Faith? What about some teaching on Hebrews 11? Nope. *Everything* is possible *to him who believes.* I really didn't think I needed to. If once you have got hold of how to get real Faith, and avoided the counterfeits, you will find out for yourself just how brilliant Jesus is, and start to do real, eternal, effective exploits in His name. God wants *you* to write the next chapter in the eternal Book of Faith. This is your generation. This is your hour. This is your life and your *only* opportunity. Go for risky, illogical, impossible, but divinely inspired works of Faith! And see what enormous fun you can have in your life!

SUMMARY

The only faith that works is that given and generated by God's Rhēma words.

Chapter 5
THE BIBLE.

God has placed five solid things into this world that point us to Himself. He is spiritual and so huge that He cannot be seen or detected using any of our senses. But we have these five to show that He is alive and well on planet earth as well as in the Cosmos. They are: Jesus, The Creation, Israel, The Christian Church and the Bible. Let's briefly go through these one at a time.

Jesus was an historical man. There is more historical evidence for His existence than there is for the existence of Julius Caesar (according to the Alpha Course). *Christians* know that He once lived because they know Him today. But outside the Christian Church Jesus is relegated to a swear word or to history, where, like others who existed back along, He is discarded as ancient, old fashioned and irrelevant in today's modern society. So what if He did live on earth? So what if He did claim to be the Son of God? What's that got to do with me? Satan is continually working to throw the life of Jesus in the mind of today's society into the waste bin.

The **Creation** as written in the Bible is also discarded and considered to be a myth. Romans 1 tells us that man cannot escape the hidden knowledge of God because it is revealed through the Creation. "For since the creation of the world God's invisible qualities – his eternal power and divine nature – have been clearly seen, being understood from what has been made, so that men are without excuse." I notice that no one has yet made anything that wiggles that approximates to life as we observe it. I have written elsewhere that intelligent men think and believe that Nothing created Life when intelligent men cannot even do it. What folly! But still the Great Lie of Evolution has successfully eroded Creation as good hard evidence for the existence of the Creator God.

Israel were and still are God's chosen people. By and large, the Jews are disliked by practically everyone on earth, and are a particular sore in the side of Arabic nations. It is illogical that they should be, so there must be a spiritual reason for it. Demonic in fact. But the survival of Israel is one of the most astounding features of this planet. Despite their abandonment of God with whom they have made umpteen covenants, God has kept His side of the bargain by protecting them and granting them success. As a nation their success in all matters of art and commerce is grossly disproportionate to their numbers, and they are streets ahead of the rest of the world in terms of talent. Moreover, they should have disappeared into other cultures long before now, for they have been removed from their promised land many times. Indeed, these last decades have seen the direct fulfilment of prophecy; 1948 saw the restoration of Israel back into their own land in fulfilment of Ezekiel 37:11-22 and other Old Testament prophecies. 1967 saw the fulfilment of Luke 21:24 when they recovered Jerusalem for themselves. Indeed, Israel's precarious existence today is a testimony to the faithfulness as well as the existence of God. Their survival is a miracle, and they should have been absorbed into the nations thousands of years ago. Yet here they are still. And still they get up people's noses, and are no longer regarded as "chosen". But they still are.

The **Christian Church** is an historical fact emerging out of the life of Jesus. There has been no break in the continuity between His life and today, and the witness to His existence has been carried through the centuries by faithful followers of The Way. But it has been hard for every generation to gain converts, except when God has sent revival. In the valleys between the fervent peaks the Christian Church has been persecuted, marginalised, discarded, considered to be irrelevant, and confined in the minds of outsiders to poor old ladies who need it for a bit of comfort in the evening of their lives. Besides, "By schisms rent asunder and heresies distressed" her witness has been tarnished. In addition, there are other main line religions who also claim to have an historical background, and people now consider them to have just as valid a claim as Christ does. If only they really examined those claims for themselves instead of believing what someone else has casually fed into them. Most people's belief system is a conglomeration of the view points of all their friends, and which they adjust inside their minds so that it is comfortable to live with and not too disturbing to their hedonistic or self-centred life style.

Satan has managed to erode those solid evidences of God's existence so that they no longer have the bite they once had. But he has had difficulty with the fifth – the **Bible**. Jesus said that while the earth exists, not one tiny speck will disappear from the law until everything is accomplished. Many generations and many cultures have tried to burn or destroy the Bible, but it has divine protection. Burn one and two more spring into being in its place. The Bible now remains the major safe and secure indicator of the existence of God. But it does need to be read. Thus satan has a campaign to stop people reading anything today, and to get all our knowledge and opinions from the Tele. We are being fed daft stuff – the opinions of men – and entertained. We prefer that to anything sensible or solid on which to secure our lives.

I tell you another way in which satan is succeeding to destroy the Bible. It is through translations. There are now over 100 versions in English, and most have been written to help us understand in a better way what God wants us to know. But that door has opened sloppy and purposeless translations that make a mockery of its integrity and that deliberately leave out challenging passages. Even the genuine ones can have an adverse effect on us Christians. Once upon a time we were able to learn and quote Bible verses, thus knowing what it said, but now with so many versions, we do not even know for certain exactly what it does say any more. Used wisely, differing version have something genuine and helpful to say to us. But for the new convert the proliferation is huge and very confusing. To modern man the KJV is ancient (and its language really is), so it becomes confined to old people again. A new convert introduced to the KJV has to fight his way through Shakespearian English to read it, and has to retranslate it in his mind to make it relevant to his today world.

So satan has done and is doing a very good job in marginalising God.

Let me now give you some clues on the Bible.

It is God's purpose-built deposit of Truth. He has managed (miraculously) to get all the authors to write down things that will be common for every Christian to know, and to discard all the writings that do not have that inspiration or purpose. For example, what happened to the third letter to the Corinthians, or Paul's letter to Laodicea?

Let me give you an illustration of what the Bible is. God clearly speaks to those who love Him every waking moment of their days (if they did but listen). I am not only talking about what He is saying today, but what He has said throughout the ages of earth. If you think of it, that's an awful lot of communication. That communication I picture to be like one very long sheet of metal stretching back to the beginning of time. Into that sheet holes have been cut and it now looks like chicken wire. The holes represent the communications of God to individual people that were relevant *only* to those people to whom they were given, but are irrelevant to everybody else on earth. So He cut them out and "lost" them. What is left is a framework of truth (and looks like chicken wire) which God has made relevant to *every* person in *every* age in the history of earth. Thus the *principles* of eternal truth are permanently there and will never be erased.

Into that framework God is then able to refill the gaps for everybody in every Now situation. This leaves lots of opportunity for God to talk to every individual on earth and direct them in the unique way He wants them to go through their Bibles. Thus, for each and every Today for each and every person, the chicken wire becomes a solid sheet again. By way of illustration let's take Ps 51 – David's confession of his sin with Bathsheba. "Wash away all my iniquity and cleanse me from my sin." This Psalm does not mention his adultery, lying and murder. So God removed the details from which David penned this Psalm. So for us today whatever sin we feel guilty about is echoed in the principles written, and the Holy Spirit pin-points for me what I need to confess to God today – my thoughtlessness, meanness, stubbornness or whatever.

Then He steered His people to put it all together in 66 books and in one volume. That makes the Bible unique. And it makes it very precious and essential for every person on earth, regardless of their age, language, tribe, culture or nation. The Bible is the foundation, the rock, the base for the knowledge of God for ever. As a framework of eternal truth, it neither needs to be added to or subtracted from. *Everything* in its pages is relevant to today's human being, regardless of who they are or when Today is.

What is really miraculous about the Bible is that every verse is a window to heaven. God can say anything He wants to anyone through any passage, thus filling up those gaps in the chicken wire. The Bible is merely information to those who read with human eyes. But it is the gateway to heaven for those who read it with spiritual eyes. God has so adjusted it that it alone is the only fully uncontaminated opening to seeing Him and finding Him. Other Christian writings also act as gateways to finding the Lord, but the Bible is the least contaminated. And will always remain so. The Trinity is One. The Bible is One with Them. We can look at the Bible rather like being the framework of the Trinity, where the Trinity is fully all things. Or, if you like, the Bible is like a leafless tree in the winter showing all its branches and twigs. God is not just the tree fully leafed and flowered, but like the whole forest. Every sentence in the Bible is available to the Holy Spirit to reveal knowledge, understanding, guidance or correction from anywhere in it. The Bible is used by God as a trigger to initiate something relevant He wants us to know or do appropriate to our modern situation. God is in charge of that, not us. What we are asked to do is to read it. Then He will speak. He gives as He gives, and withholds as He withholds. But everything that God does is perfectly tuned and perfectly timed. He is *Good.*

"You diligently search the scriptures because you think that by them you possess eternal life." (John 5:39). Meaning? Your thinking is wrong – the scriptures don't give you eternal life. If you are studying your bible to find eternal life in them, or to gain knowledge, *stop wasting your time.* You have been deceived. Then Jesus clears up the deception: "These are the scriptures that testify about me, yet you refuse to come to me to have life." Meaning? Only in *Jesus* is there life. It you search for Jesus *through* your scriptures, you will find life. But Jesus Himself says that many of us don't. We try to find life in a thousand other places, and refuse to come to the one and only place it can be found – in Jesus. This applies to born again Christians. We get tired of Jesus, particularly in the desert times. So we experiment with "other things" to see if they can be a satisfying substitute to Him. Even in our Bibles.

Now I have to say something that sounds unbiblical. I really believe that God adds to the Bible. I am aware of the verse in Rev 22 that says that if anyone adds to the words of that prophecy they will collect all the curses in it etc. And Christians get all hot under their collars when I talk like this. But surely the Lord really does add to scripture? I mean, where does it tell us in scripture about how to work computers, modern technology, cars, aircraft and so on? Nowhere. So if the Lord is going to lead us in this modern age, He is going to have to communicate with us on issues that are relevant to our daily lives, but definitely missing from scripture. The point is this: the Bible gives us the *principles* on which the Lord works, and leaves the Holy Spirit to fill in the gaps. So, Matt 4:4, "Man shall not live on bread alone, but on every (*rhēma,* spoken) word that comes out of the mouth of God" is the principle. So when the Lord tells me not to pass a vehicle on the road because there's another one coming round the corner which I can't see, technically He is adding to scripture. (But, note, never taking away from it - because God never contradicts His Word in the Bible).

Another illustration I use is that the Bible is like the root of an oak tree (or any other). The root is definitely oak, and will grow no other tree but an oak, because the entire oak DNA resides in the root as much as in the leaves or the acorns. The trunk and the branches and the leaves will always and only be oak. So it is with scripture. The Bible is the root, and it contains all the DNA of the Kingdom of Heaven incorporated in it. *We* are growing the branches and the leaves – that is, adding to the root with the same DNA that the root contains. The Kingdom is founded on the root, but developed and growing on the guiding words of God through His Holy Spirit. Every branch is different, but still Kingdom. My life is founded on Jesus, rooted in the Bible, and I develop and illustrate all the Bible themes as I live my three score years and ten. I am adding to scripture in the sense that I am a unique and different 21st century demonstration of all the Bible says. Isn't it just so clever that God should do that through every person who ever lives on earth?

The Bible is not God's whole Truth. Jesus is God's whole Truth, but the Bible is the best *Written* route to finding Him. The Holy Spirit is also the Spirit of Truth, and is the best *Living* route to finding Him. The Bible is not complete. Only Jesus is complete, and He completes every incompletion - both written, universal and human. The truth is that God has made *Jesus* to be the only and perfect way of knowing Him. That exclusivity is worked into everything in the universe – including the Bible. You cannot find God in the Bible: you can only find God through Jesus, and He is best revealed *through* your Bible.

Certain Christians use the Bible as a kind of promise box – almost like reading one's stars in the back of silly magazines. Guidance does not come out from Scripture by reading and thinking, but *only* by Revelation. The Bible is a *channel*, a downpipe to the water of God's personal relationship and His Revelations. Some people study the downpipe. They spend hours looking with a magnifying glass at the structure, the content, the Hebrew, the Greek, and the doctrines of the Bible. Many of those who do so miss the water – or even know it exists. But why study the downpipe when it is only the water that brings life (John 4)? If we do not use the downpipe to find the water, what value is it to study the downpipe for its own sake (see John 5:38-39 above)?

Dr Luke wrote more of the New Testament than anyone else. Isn't it surprising that God caused a Gentile (non-Jew) to do that? Indeed, if it wasn't for Acts, we would have little handle on things like baptism, the baptism and filling of the Holy Spirit, local church organisation and governance etc. What Paul wrote was fellowship letters to his converts and friends, and deals very little with their entrance into Christ. Acts does that. But the whole thing was inspired by God - God-breathed. The New Testament is the richest, fullest, deepest and most complete analysis of the heart of God for his people, and 100% appropriate throughout this epoch of Grace. Most of the Old Testament grants us illustrations of man's dealings with man and God, and God's dealings with man, so that we can gain wisdom for our own lives before making silly behaviour mistakes unnecessarily.

Contemporaries of Jesus had half a Bible – the Old Testament. So did the first few generations after Him – the Canon of Scripture only being ratified in 397 AD at the Council of Carthage. One presumes that the Holy Spirit was the Guide and Director in those early days before the Council met. But since that memorable date we have had a foundation from which faith and knowledge of God could spring. Paul got good Revelation when he penned "...You are fellow citizens with God's people, built on the foundation of the apostles and prophets, with Christ Jesus Himself as the Chief Cornerstone." (Eph 2:19, 20). That foundation is still with us in the form of letters the Apostles wrote to early Christians. Since there have been no extractions or additions to the Canon of Scripture, only translations, we can presume that Jesus' words of Matt 5:18 apply to the Bible we now have. Time has established its Divine authorship. It remains the unremoveable foundation of faith, and the most secure and unalterable channel through which we can meet with Jesus.

A thought occurred to me that has been expressed by a number of sharp teenagers over the years. It is this: how come the New Testament was written in Greek? Surely Jesus and his disciples spoke Aramaic? And why do we make such a fuss over various Greek words when many of the same nuances are not found in Aramaic and many of the distinctions disappear in the original spoken idiom?

The comment is a good and fair one. But it leaves God and culture out of the equation. In the decades after the death and resurrection of Jesus, Christianity spread very fast throughout the Roman Empire. Because there was peace in the Roman Empire, and travel was easy in the brilliant communication system set up by those Conquerors, the gospel travelled with tradesmen and merchants throughout the lands. It even reached Britain by 40 AD, 10 years after Jesus' death. Moreover, Christians carrying the gospel realised very quickly that its message was relevant for every tribe and nation under heaven. Therefore to keep it boundaried inside Aramaic soon became a nonsense. Prior to the Romans conquering the Mediterranean, the Greek General Alexander the Great had trodden and vanquished much of the same territory. With the Greek Empire came both culture and language. The Greeks had been a long way ahead of all other cultures (except possibly the Chinese) in thinking and philosophy. This excellence they bequeathed to their defeated foes. So when the Roman armies tramped over the same lands, bringing them under their political domination, Greek was already the common spoken language of every territory. Of course, tribal and indigenous languages still existed and were still used (of which Aramaic was one). But if anyone wanted to communicate outside a nation, they all used Greek. It was the common language of the common man throughout the Roman Empire. Most importantly Jesus' disciples - at least those who wrote the New Testament - realised that the Gospel was life for the common man, so they wrote in Greek. All the New Testament documents were written in colloquial, common Greek - the Greek of the streets. Only the introductions to Luke and Acts and the Book of James were written in Upper Class sophisticated Greek. Greece brought language and culture; Rome brought stability, peace and communication. That's why the gospel spread so fast.

That's the cultural reason why the New Testament is in Greek. But God had another purpose too. Greek is a rich language, many words carrying shades of meaning that cannot easily be expressed by literal translations. (Hence, in English, the Amplified Bible). This richness gives much flexibility to all other languages as people translate from the Greek.

Now, every one of us as Christians has experienced many occasions when, as we read our Bible, it tasted like dried weetabix: it was dull, uninteresting, hard work, boring, and, indeed, dead. Of course. There are Professors of Theology in Universities using the Bible as their text book, and to whom it is also dead – lifeless. It's just a text book. How can this be? The reason is that the only way we can get Life and/or know God from our Bibles is by *Revelation from the Holy Spirit,* not by learning or calculation. See Luke 10:21. And if I or anyone does not have a heart connection with God at the point of reading, no Revelation comes, no inspiration occurs and the Bible at that point is dead. "It is the *Spirit* that gives Life. Human effort accomplishes nothing. And the very words that I have spoken to you are Spirit and Life," said Jesus. (John 6:63).

All of us will also be aware that, on other occasions, as we read our Bibles, Life jumps out at us in unpredictable ways and with unpredictable messages. We feel warm, completed, intrigued, challenged and made whole. That is Revelation. God has spoken into our souls and spirits. To read the Bible with the *mind* leads to information not inspiration. We get the facts, but we miss the Life. It's amazing how intelligent people miss the Life. But then, God has ordained that no one will know Him by intelligence. Truly, the Bible is an amazing book. It is both hidden and open, dead and alive. Only Revelation gives it Life, and that is the personal decision of Almighty God in a moment of time.

The motive behind many new translations is so that we can *understand* what the Bible says. If that is so, it is error. No one can understand the Bible unless God opens it by Revelation. No amount of easy translations can give us what God has reserved exclusively for His Holy Spirit. However, if we find Life through

Revelation in any new translation, then that is the inspiration which we need. If *God* uses your modern translation, then it is Life for you. Be glad and rejoice, and continue to drink from it as long as it retains its Life. I recall Dr Martyn Lloyd Jones saying that if a verse is in one translation, it's good enough for him. That is a very healthy way of looking at our Bibles and translations.

I want to introduce you to another difficulty that God has placed in the Bible. He has so arranged it that no one can be absolutely certain that the Bible he is reading is the real one. How is that so? We do not have any of the originals. All we have of the original Hebrew Old Testament and Greek New Testament are copies and fragments of copies – none of the originals exist any more. On top of that, we read translations. Greek is a very rich language and all sorts of shades of meaning can exist in the one word. It says one thing in one translation and something different in another. So no one reads an original. Thus the element of certainty has been removed from every Bible read today.

I believe the Lord has done that deliberately. He does not want us to be *certain* from a human, logical stand point. We must never be *sure* that what we believe comes from our knowledge, and is therefore provable. It has to come by faith alone. It has to come out from our knowledge and walk with *Jesus*, and not from anywhere else. Remember, *Jesus* is God's answer to all things. Not the Church, not the Bible, but Jesus. The Holy Spirit tells about Jesus with unvarnished truth. But it is Jesus alone whom God has insisted is the only Way for every man to reach heaven. It is very clever of God to erase *certainty* from our Bibles and make sure that the only access we have to understanding it is by faith and Revelation alone. Isn't He just brilliant?

Let me say one last thing about the Bible. Because all of it was a *Rhēma* Revelation directly from God ("For prophecy never had its origin in the will of man, but men spoke from God as they were carried along by the Holy Spirit." (2 Peter 1:21)), then everything it says was and is eternally true. The history it contains in unvarnished truth – that is *exactly* the way it happened. Moreover, the precepts and advice for living are not just good ideas. They are not part of a debate on "How can man live his life?" They are unchanging, unalterable truths as solid as granite, as inflexible as a rock, as permanent as the cosmos itself. The prohibitions in, say, the 10 commandments are irreversible – stealing, lying, coveting, committing adultery for example will always be wrong no matter what we call them or however we might try to disguise them. The principles and precepts are not just good counsel; they are eternal truths as permanent as gravity and light. So when it says that we will reap whatever we sow, that is irreversibly inevitable, whether good or bad. So it becomes very sensible to read our Bibles and to adjust our lives according to what it says, because we will never ever get away with behaviour or thinking that conflicts with it.

Let me summarise. The Bible is God's word and will never be destroyed. It is not a substitute for Jesus, and never will be. We must not worship the Bible – we must worship Jesus. It is the major avenue for Revelation. Relationship issues with Jesus contained within its pages are hidden from every eye except those with faith. To some people it is a book of reference. To others it is a dust carrier. But to those whose lives are hidden with Christ in God, it is a window through which wonder, knowledge, understanding and life comes that Kings and Rulers would give their eye teeth to possess.

SUMMARY

The whole Bible was inspired by God's Rhēma words to the authors. God is hidden inside the written words, and can only be found individually when He reveals Himself by speaking Life through the Spirit.

Chapter 6
GRACE.

I have written in my chapter on the Four Epochs (later) that we are now living in the age of Grace. What a privilege. There are many people more worthy than I who have written at length about Grace, and I commend every one to your readership. I think Philip Yancey's book "What's so Amazing about Grace?" was the catalyst that sparked off most Christian's renewed interest in it, and must stand as the major classic of our generation. Grace is so vast an issue that I don't think we will ever get to the bottom of it or come to the end of it.

But I too received Revelation on it, and I doubt I can do justice by this little attempt to tell you what I discovered.

But some background first.

Beyond doubt, Grace has been, perhaps, the biggest difficulty I have had in all my delving into the heart of God. I, like the rest of us, *needed* Revelation.

First of all, the simple stuff. I found all sorts of definitions of Grace. For example: Love in action; God's Riches At Christ's Expense; God's heart of love etc. These told me what Grace did or does, not what Grace is or was. So they didn't satisfy my curiosity.

Over a two-year period I was involved with a Strict Baptist (Calvinistic) church. They were lovely people, and still are. Previously I had had an RAF friend who was also a Calvinist. I was glad to belong to this group of Christians, and they served to open my mind to a biblical perspective that had previously been hidden from me. That's what Revelation is all about, and we learn as we grow.

The major doctrine that holds Calvinism together is Grace. I was happy to acknowledge that. But their teaching on Grace didn't really help me to understand what Grace is. Instinctively I realised (or wanted to realise) that Grace is a beautiful, sweet, attractive, lovely thing. Calvinism seemed to make it a harsh, polarised, exclusive thing. I ploughed through the debate on Calvinism and Armenianism, but it still didn't help me. Grace stumped me. What was Grace? God's exclusive choices? Hardly. For 40 or so years I did not know and it bugged me. Philip Yancey's book was beautiful, but still I missed it. I still had the difficulty of discovering what Grace *IS* as opposed What Grace *DOES*.

The door was opened to me by Revelation through Mark Pavey. He was only quoting someone else, and refused to take credit for it. But I give him credit for being the messenger. We were at Upcott. Mark was talking to teenagers, and I was sitting uncomfortably on the windowsill. His quote: "Grace is the power of God released to man to enable him to be everything God wants him to be and to do everything God wants him to do." God hit me with joy and understanding.

It still didn't tell me what Grace is but it opened the door. Let's look at those two one by one.

It enables man "to be everything God wants him to be." So God has a picture of who I am and who I should be. He has me already completed in every way in perfection and power. So whatever barriers and difficulties got or get in God's way that hinder that happening, Grace has enabled God to remove them. *Nothing* is impossible to remove. Not my stupidity, nor my limitations, nor my sin, nor my sins, nor my stubbornness, nor my unwillingness (provided it's not terminal), nor my untimely life or death; there are no barriers that God's grace is unable to dismantle. It cost him manhood. It cost him the cross. It cost God everything to accomplish this extraordinary thing - making Dick Bell into a saint that will help God rule over his new heaven and earth in power and great glory alongside his brothers and sisters. *Everything* that God has planned to make me and give me has been and will be released to me by Grace. It's God's Grace that enables this astonishing miracle to happen. I have the full power of God at my disposal to accomplish the impossible. It's turning the wooden Pinocchio into a real boy. And God's inexorable plan is continually to pump power and enabling ability into my heart and soul to transform me into someone just like Jesus - full of kindness, gentleness, wisdom, forgiveness, beauty, and Grace. Those who know me also know that that work is still incomplete. But be of good cheer - one day everyone will like me because the Grace of God cannot fail, and that which God has planned will be accomplished and I shall be perfectly likeable! What is true of me will be true of all Christians.

The Bible often commends that we grow in Grace. So my view point of other people has also changed as I soak up God's Grace to me. No longer do I see people as rivals; I see them as friends - companions on life's journey. That's Grace. No longer am I jealous or envious of others; that's Grace. No longer do I see people (even non-Christians) as sinners going to hell; I see them as friends who can reveal to me another aspect of God's immense variety; that's Grace. No longer do I see congregations as sitting ducks ready for me to persuade into a deeper relationship with Jesus; I see them as fellow saints on the same road as me, helpers in my life, and needing all the encouragement I can give them; that's Grace. No longer do I get resentful of others who get the better of me (a particular vulnerability of mine); I see them as needing as much prayer as I need; that's Grace. In all aspects and in every fundamental attitude with which I was born, and in every prejudice that I have accrued in life, I see the Grace of God transforming me into someone alien to all my assumptions and dreams. What I've always wanted to be God has bypassed and is making me what He wants (prefers) me to be. And to be truthful, I like His vision better than any of my own. I am and have been astonished at the unnatural and unusual reactions to situations I have inside that contrast so markedly with the normal reactions I have had for ages. Grace is changing me. It's amazing. It's the power of God released freely to enable me to be everything God wants me to be.

It's also the power of God released "to enable me to *do* everything God wants me to *do*." What I do on earth is a test run for heaven. By that I'm not saying that if I perform well down here, I'll get a Managing Director's job in heaven. God forbid! To sit at Jesus right and left hand in heaven is for those for whom God has prepared them, and is not governed by "Brownie Points" on earth. Neither is our "job" in heaven governed by our job on earth; that is, preacher on earth will not be a preacher in heaven. Heaven could never be quite so childish. The work we have on earth is for this time alone. Everything changes across the great divide of death. But, Grace enables us to accomplish the things God asks us to do on earth. Ephesians 2:10 says that God has got a unique and different work for every Christian on this earth. It is that work that Grace enables us to do well.

How does it work? Grace is the power of God to enable that work to "succeed". Please don't get diverted by the word "success". What God thinks is successful and what man thinks is successful are two very different concepts. Let's not go down man's route. God releases the Holy Spirit, equipped with the full knowledge of what God intends to achieve when He asks us to do "x" or "y", to make "x" or "y" accomplish what God desired, providing we are obedient. For example, Jesus told Martha to roll away the stone. When Martha obeyed, Jesus brought Lazarus back from death (John 11). Martha did what she was told; Jesus did the miracle; Martha gets the credit; Jesus gets enmity from the Pharisees. That's Grace. That's what happens to us. Jesus told me to do something simple and easy to help poor Nicaraguan children get an education. The result? *Hundreds* of children are helped, an orphanage supported, a large medical work is established, families are emerging from poverty and the gospel is gaining a hearing and a following. So what did we do as a Trust? Very little. What did God do? Huge bits - equivalent to raising someone from the dead. That's Grace. He says: we do: and "great Grace is upon us all."

There are 1000 hindrances to a work like ours in Nicaragua ever succeeding or even getting going. But, by the Grace of God it has flourished and multiplied at an exponential rate. Grace has surmounted or circumvented all the reasons why our work in Nicaragua shouldn't succeed and grow. There is the mindset of the UK population to overcome; there is the mindset of local Nicaraguan people to overcome; there is the bureaucracy and intransigence of Nicaraguan officials to overcome; and there is the mindset of the Evangelical Church in England to overcome. Part of a poem from my scrapbooks: -

Somebody said that it couldn't be done,
But he with a chuckle replied,
That maybe it couldn't, but he would be one
That wouldn't say so till he'd tried.
So he butted right in with the trace of a grin
On his face; if he worried he hid it.
He started to sing as he tackled the thing
That couldn't be done, and he did it.

Somebody scoffed, "Oh you'll never do that,
At least no one ever has done it."
And he took off his coat, and he took off his hat
And the first thing they knew he'd begun it.
With the lift of his chin and a bit of a grin
Without any doubting or quiddit,
He started to sing as he tackled the thing
That couldn't be done, and he did it.

God's Grace accompanies all those who do something at the prompting of Jesus that no one has ever done before. Those without faith and those without a call can only see difficulties. Those with faith and with a call can only see possibilities. I have a quote from George Bernard Shaw stuck on the front of my computer. It says: - "You see things as they are and ask "Why?" But I dream things that never were, and asked "Why not?"" (Copy that into your own scrapbook).

As I continued to meditate on the Revelation God gave me, I got more and more insight.

First, I leapt the Calvinistic barrier of "harsh, calculating and exclusive grace." I saw Grace as something so vast, so extensive, so beautiful, so flexible that it was impossible to describe. Just how many lives does the Grace of God cover on this earth? In *principle*, the cross of Jesus has redeemed every human being that has ever lived on earth; the *promise* only comes to those in Jesus Christ. Does Grace, for example, still bring into heaven those who once had a relationship with Jesus but haven't now spoken with Him for years? What about all those who have never heard - how does Grace deal with them? Or those, like Saul of Tarsus, who feel with enormous zeal that they are doing God's will by persecuting and killing Christians? How much does honesty and integrity play a role in how Grace handles someone we would call a non-Christian?

I remember a story I heard in a sermon when I was young. A rich man wanted a new chauffeur. He asked each candidate the same question: "You are driving along a narrow cliff road. How close do you think you can drive to the edge?" One said a foot. Others said inches. But one driver said, "I don't know sir. All I know is that I would stay as far away from the edge as I can." He got the job. The preacher then asked: "How close can you get to sin and not do it? Stay as far away from it as you can." So, for those "non-Christians" who do avoid sin in their lives, how does Grace reward them?

Once upon a time, I was very black and white on this issue, and the Bible bids me to remain so. But Grace has taught me that there is not one person on earth who is unredeemable. Every human being is a unique gift from God, has an enormous contribution to make to this earth, and could one day be part of the Great Dance and Song of heaven. Grace has taught me to love everyone I meet, to care for them, to serve them, to honour them and to long that they may be my friends for ever. In this I believe that Grace has revealed God's heart to me; that's the way

He feels about everybody too. And He is longing that everyone would open their hearts to enjoy His Grace like I do.

Secondly, I have discovered how beautiful and endearing God's Grace is. It's a gorgeous thing, sweet, attractive, lovely, forgiving, promoting, encouraging, inclusive, and open to all. Amazing Grace. Its capacity to forgive is legendary. Its magnanimity (big-heartedness) is beyond expectation and never ends. So gentle; so quiet; so peaceful; so joyful; so full of patience; so consistent - Grace is astonishing. Words tumble out of me and then stop because I have run out of words, not because Grace has stopped or has stopped getting better.

The understanding I have reached is to say that Grace is the fundamental and foundational attitude of God's character. God is Love. Certainly. God is Light, Life, and Spirit. Certainly. God is a million beautiful and good things and does a million beautiful and good things as a consequence. But I feel that Grace is the root one. It is the beginning of Him who had no beginning. It is the first of all the good things, and is the base from which all other good things proceed. I know I can't really say that for God is much bigger than roots, bases or processes. But of all God's excellences, I am saying that Grace is the greatest. He is the complete God, as I have written later. But Grace begins Him all, and Grace completes Him all. Grace is the beginning, middle and end of all God is and does. Greater, indeed, than Love. Grace is the source of love, not the other way round. (At the end of 1 Cor 13, it says, "And now these three remain: faith, hope and love. But the greatest of these is love." That is, the greatest of *these three* is love). I believe that when He revealed Grace to mankind, He bared Himself. He stripped himself of all outer coverings and showed us His heart - who He *really* is. Now we *know* what God is like - He is full of Grace. No wonder I had such difficulty finding what it is; no wonder it took me such a long time searching until I found. And still I know that however long I search I will never come to the end of the beauties of Grace. It is Infinite - where all good things never end.

So is this just a gut feeling, or is there more substantial evidence? The latter. What was it Jesus came to reveal? What aspect of God did He bring? "The law came through Moses, but Grace and Truth came through Jesus Christ." (John 1). Jesus was not just God's son. Not just God's best. Not just God's champion of whom He was mighty proud. Not just God's solution to all things wicked. Jesus revealed the very heart of the Father - full of Grace and Truth. That has to be the greatest gift God can reveal to us, and the greatest Revelation that He can give us. Once we have captured the real concept of Grace (or the concept of real Grace), nothing else captures us in quite the same way, nothing else satisfies us to quite the same degree, and nothing else encourages us to quite the same extent. Yet I do not want to deceive you: Grace is not a thing; Grace is a He, a Him. God is Grace.

Have you noticed what the predominant preaching themes of the early Church were? Grace and the Resurrection of Jesus. The consequence? Many people were captured by it and "great Grace was upon them all." Paul starts every one of his letters, and finishes most of them with "Grace ... be with you." Oh that we could recover the enormity of it once again! Oh the beauty of it! Oh the all-enveloping and all-embracing loveliness of it! Grace that is greater than all our sin. Have you noticed in early Romans what Paul writes? Adam and sin; Man and sin; none righteous, no, not one; all guilty and all condemned. But *how much more*, again and again, *how much more* did Grace neutralise and erase it all! In every direction, for all people for all of time and beyond, Grace has been more than conqueror over every inadequacy. Amazing Grace. Amazing God. Amazing redemption. Amazing Jesus.

Paul wrote often about "Mysteries." He explained what he meant. A Mystery is a truth that has been hidden in past ages but was now revealed through God's apostles and prophets. The Church was one mystery and I am certain that we have yet to come to the bottom of that one. But Grace is another. We can find Grace in the Old Testament, and Noah was given a bundle. But God held it back for a specific time and a specific occasion.

That time was the birth of a Galilean carpenter, and the occasion His life on Earth. Jesus revealed God's Grace. God left His best Revelation to His best Son.

And now we live in the age of Grace. There is judgement and assessment of accountability - of course. But it is delayed until the end of time. His wrath and justice will be revealed one day (soon?), but meanwhile we are granted the luxury of sunbathing in the sunshine of today's epoch - the age of Grace. Come and get it, you who are thirsty. You who hunger for a purpose, Grace is freely available. You who yearn for significance, Grace is freely lavished on those who ask and seek. We can love life, love earth, love people, love being, love doing, love laughing, and love all things - all because God's Grace has been lavished upon us without measure.

"Oh the love that drew salvation's plan;
Oh the Grace that brought it down to man;
Oh the mighty Gulf that God did span
At Calvary.

Mercy there was great and Grace was free,
Pardon there was multiplied to me;
There my burdened soul found liberty -
At Calvary." (Newell & Towner)

"'Tis Grace has brought me safe thus far,
And Grace will lead me home." (John Newton)

SUMMARY

Grace is the attribute of God that caused Him to rescue mankind. It is the root attribute in God, brought to earth by Jesus. Salvation is by Grace alone through Faith alone. Grace is a very beautiful thing.

Chapter 7
SIN

It's a really nasty word, this word Sin. Anyone with any kind of Christian background knows it well. It's a happy hunting ground for preachers who have little empathy with people, and all of us will have experienced fierce denunciations of it from time to time from a pulpit or two.

Sin is a generic word that incorporates all kinds of wickedness and evil. So why do we not call it "evil" instead of "Sin"? I guess because Sin is always considered to be a deliberate act of evil perpetrated by a human being. The devil doesn't sin – at least I don't think the Bible says so. He's just plain 100% evil. But none of this is the purpose of this Revelation, so I had better get on with it.

I want to try to make the point that there is a vast difference between Sin and sins. Sins are what we do; Sin is what we are. We do sinful things because they come out of sinful beings. If I was not Sin, I wouldn't sin. I am not Sin because I do sinful things: I do sinful things because I am sin (if you get my drift). I do not think it is profitable to pursue the fact of sins. But I think it is profitable to pursue the fact of Sin.

So, I will start with what I see Sin as being. What is it? Sin in a human being describes his state. It is what I am – or was before I was redeemed. It is what I was born as. It was as much part of my nature as humanity is part of my nature, and as much as male is part of my nature. I was born male, human and Sin – or sinful, if you prefer it. That is, full of Sin. Not full of sins – but full of Sin. My spirit, soul and body, individually and collectively were Sin. "In Sin did my mother conceive me." (Ps. 51:5). That does not mean that the sexual act is or was wicked. It simply means that Sin was as much a full part of my parents' nature as mine. Cats beget cats. Dogs beget dogs. Humans beget humans. Sinful humans beget sinful humans. I inherited Sin from my parents, who inherited it from theirs all the way back to Noah and Adam. There has not been one human being in the whole history of mankind who has been conceived outside the sin-line from Adam. Whoops! Wrong again. Jesus alone. That's why the virgin conception is so important. He was not conceived in sin – His Father was God. Therefore He did not inherit the Sin of His ancestors through Mary. He was without Sin. Then, by choice, without sins.

As a matter of passing interest, those who do not believe in the literal nature of Genesis are going to struggle with this. Without a literal Adam and Noah, the line of Sin would have been broken, and we would have found some human beings conceived outside the Adamic blood and sin line. But I think the New Testament makes it clear (Rom 4:12-21) (and human experience would confirm it) that every human being has inherited both Adam's Sin as well as his humanity.

This brings me to where and how it began. It is of little value my reproducing Genesis 3 for you here when you should be perfectly capable of reading it yourself. You should know it backwards anyway – it is a foundational chapter to the whole of the Bible and explains perfectly and simply the whole history of Sin in mankind.

Both Adam and Eve knew 100% that to eat the fruit of the Tree of the Knowledge of Good and Evil would cause them to die. But even that wasn't the first point. The first point was a relational one between man and God. By eating they would break the harmonious relationship. We are not sure whether either Adam or Eve knew what "die" meant, and we, perfect in retrospect, knew it meant spiritual as well as physical death. Eve was tempted. Adam was not. 1 Tim 2:13-14 makes that quite clear. Because Adam was the founder of the human race, he had to choose between God and Eve. He was neither deceived nor blinded, and he had not found a companion quite like Eve – not among any of the animals and not even God Himself. He chose Eve instead of God. He ate the forbidden fruit. He suddenly knew good and evil. And interestingly, Eve did not know good and evil until *Adam* had eaten. He was responsible for all mankind, including his wife. Death of every kind started in them both. Adam was culpable and could have chosen otherwise, because God later said to him, "Because you have listened to the voice of your wife . . ." (Gen 3:17), so clearly he needn't have. That's when Sin started in him. Adam introduced Sin and death to earth and the whole cosmos. To earth certainly because from then on the land started to produce thorns and thistles, and pain came in as did enmity. Work from then on became one of toil and sweat. It was very important that this choice was made before Adam and Eve had children. God made sure that Adam's choice - whichever it was - between evil or God would govern all his descendants down to you and me.

God knows what was, what is, what will be, and also what might have been. Let me give you an illustration. In 1 Sam 23:9-13, David was in Keilah, and King Saul was pursuing him. David asked the Lord if the men of Keilah would hand him over to Saul. The Lord said "They will." So David left Keilah. That which God knew would happen never did – He knows what might have been. And the fact that we were chosen in Christ from *before* the foundation of the earth (Eph 1:4) means that we would still have existed, still be Christians, but the method of both birth and new-birth would have been very different had Adam chosen another path in the garden of Eden. But here and now we are under the situation of the sin of both Adam and Eve, and we are where we find ourselves.

Now Adam's choice was singular, and led to all or nothing. All perfect or nothing perfect. He, the representative human, chose for us all. We got the latter.

Consequently, death occurred in the whole human being – spirit, soul, body.

In our *Spirits* we were cut off from all divine inputs. We did not stop being spirit creatures, but our spirit was now aligned to satan and his great rebellion. In heaven there are good angels and bad angels (commonly called demons). There are no in-betweens. In man, our spirits are similarly fully aligned with God or fully aligned with satan. No in-betweens. That's the nature of spirit life. And our spirits were all born aligned to satan and the cosmic rebellion. We were born in Sin. More of which later.

In our *Bodies* the mark of death is obvious. From the moment we are born, death is inevitable. We live in sinful bodies. These will never be redeemed here on earth. They are limited, are part of the world, carriers of the flesh, and permanently available for the devil to use for temptation. No one can be complete on this earth in this age with a sinful body. It is the source of all temptations (via satan of course), and will either have to die and be resurrected at the 2nd Coming of Jesus or transformed at His Coming. Please don't try to be perfect – you will be *permanently* restricted by a sinful body. Waste of time.

The *Soul*? The Inner Working Me? My mind, my will and my emotions? That is also conceived and born in Sin. My thinking, my desires and my decisions are all totally aligned with the world, flesh and devil, and all my choices are self-directed, self-decided and self-determining. From birth – or rather, from conception. I am saying that nothing I am by birth is on God's side. I am born in Sin. I am sin. There is no good in me by nature, and I *cannot* please God (Rom 8:8).

But what about the good things I have done? I'm afraid they are not good enough. Why? Because the only human being that pleases God is Jesus, more of whom later. So the only things that please God are the things that Jesus prompts in me, and I in faith do them. So if none of my best words, deeds, thoughts that I did came from Jesus, then none of them please God. That's the fact. The trouble is that we compare ourselves with our fellow humans, rather than with God. I am much better than *him, and* her. Also, don't we teach our children that X behaviour is wrong and Y is right, and we then expect them to choose Y? Certainly. God deliberately put Law in place and put us under Law by giving us a conscience so that we would not go berserk by only and always doing our own selfish thing. Otherwise we would be totally anarchical like the people in Noah's day. So we are now under Law, and therefore do much better than they did. That still does not stop us being sinful in essence and failing dismally to please God. Before we get a divine input, we are *totally incapable* of pleasing God. We are Sin. We do not please God. We cannot. That is our inheritance.

The Apostle Paul goes out of his way both to state this and confirm it. In Rom 3:10-18 he pulls out eight quotes from the Old Testament telling his readers that "There is no-one righteous, not even one." He goes on to explain how the sin of Adam has contaminated all, because he is the representative man. He then compares the first Adam with the second Adam, Jesus, who, as Representative New Man, opened the door of redemption. But Paul concludes that "the wages of sin is death." (Rom 6:20). Note sin (singular), not sins (plural). Death, both physical and spiritual is a result of our state or condition, not so much of our actions.

So now let me define Sin. Sin is independence of God. It is man being totally independent and having reference only to himself, and not to God. In fact, independence is also the root of satan's evil, and we find that in Is 14:12-17. So, in fact, when man acts independently, he is in truth acting in reference to satan, did he but know it. Because Adam and Eve submitted to satan in the garden, all spiritual reference lined up with satan rather than God. It has been like that for all mankind since that momentous day.

Is. 53:6 says, "We all, like sheep, have gone astray. Each of us has turned to his own way and the Lord has laid on him (Jesus) the iniquity of us all."

So let us turn our attention to Jesus, the Author and Finisher of our faith. Now I am about to share with you something that could possibly be mega-controversial, and that I have not come across any other Christian so far stating. So I will try to be as careful as I can and as Biblical as I can. If you don't want controversy, skip the next few paragraphs. I will not destroy your faith – but I might well challenge your theology. So here goes.

I have already established from Is 53:6 above that Iniquity = Independence, and Independence = Iniquity. Now let's read 2

Cor 5:21: "God made Him (Jesus) who had no sin to be sin for us, so that in Him we might become the righteousness of God." Note sin (singular), not sins (plural). So, God made Jesus to BE sin. When did He do that? Everyone would agree that it was on the Cross. But when? How? I believe this may be the answer.

In John 10:18, Jesus said "No one takes it (my life) from me, but I lay it down of my own accord. I have authority to lay it down and authority to take it up again. This command I received from my Father." Ah! An independent action – "of my own accord." By *God's* definition, an act of iniquity. But not, you will note, an act of rebellion against God (like satan, demons and man), but an actual Commandment from God. God *told* Him that He could choose to lay down His own life and gave Him the right to choose when; God gave Him permission. More, He gave Him a command. This one act of Independence from Jesus was necessary "to fulfil all righteousness". (Laying down our lives like that is something, by the way, that mankind has no natural power to do). The choice of when was entirely His – an independent act at a moment of His own independent choice. So then, on His way to the Cross, man was not able to kill Jesus – "no man takes my life from me", despite the scourging, pain and torture etc. On the Cross, we know precisely what happened – God withdrew from Jesus. "My God, My God, why have you forsaken me?" For the first and last time in the History of the Trinity, it was separated. The Father abandoned His Son (although God was in Christ reconciling the world to Himself) (and I have no idea whether the Holy Spirit did as well along with God). So Jesus was now *forced* to make an independent decision. Just like Jesus was silent before Herod and had nothing to say to him, God was now silent before Jesus, and had nothing more to say to Him. Theoretically the Universe should have disintegrated; how could it stay together if the Trinity was separated? But it didn't because it was all in God's plan of redemption. In that abandonment, Jesus exercised His God-given right and "gave up His Spirit." Every single account in the Gospels of Jesus' death tells us that it was a deliberate act of His.

He *gave up* His spirit. An independent act – right down the line of the authority and command He had been given by His Father.

Can one member of the Trinity act independently of the other two? That's the conflict. I believe so in this one instance, because that one member had taken on humanity, and as Representative New Man, had to identify fully with mankind, fulfil an act of independence, and, with it, carry all the sin of the creatures He represented. His choice and death were fully acceptable to God because it was necessary – Jesus was perfect and without personal sin. Note Sin, as well as sins. Jesus died for man's sin – the root cause of sins. It was exactly then that God made Jesus to *BE* sin, and the consequence of sin is death. So, Jesus became sin, and straight away died. By choice (bless Him). And by divine necessity. Both.

Consequently the root *state* of sin in mankind has now been died for. The price has been fully paid. This now releases God to offer to all mankind the possibility of reconciliation between man and God. Before the cross it was not possible, and reconciliation was only temporary through the death of bulls, sheep and goats (which paid for *sins*, not for Sin). Now the price has been paid "once and for all" and the offer remains permanently open. What was really happening on the cross was hidden from satan, who thought he had won a tremendous victory: 1 Cor 2:8 "None of the rulers of this age understood it, for if they had, they would not have crucified the Lord of glory."

What Christian people object to in this is that they think I say "Jesus sinned." I didn't and don't. I say He acted *independently*, and, as a consequence, He *became* sin by an act of God. In God's eyes it was the same, but not the same. I trust you see the difference? Moreover, Jesus' independent act coincided with His death – the act *was* His death. Therefore there was no time for Jesus to have continued in a life of Sin on the earth. Isn't God so brilliantly clever?

I cannot express to you the enormity of the death of Jesus. I use the word "hoover", but in case it's a metaphor with which you are unfamiliar (it's a vacuum cleaner), I should use the phrase "sucked up". In that one act of "being made sin" for us, Jesus sucked up all the sin of all mankind from the dawn of time to its sunset. (Sins (plural) were also dealt with). But it's not as if He collected every evil deed in that moment of time and it all descended upon Him. I would think it was more like He "hoovered" up the principle and nature of sin. Because of Adam's decision, mankind was locked into sin eternally – like satan and the demons (demons have no redemption). But how could God unlock the eternal separation in man caused by that sin? There I have to call on a greater than I. CS Lewis in the Narnia book "The Lion, the Witch and the Wardrobe" spoke about a greater magic from before the dawn of time that the Witch knew nothing about. If someone innocent died on behalf of someone guilty, "death started working backwards." That is resurrection. A Brilliant description. Jesus' death broke the eternal chain of separation dividing man from God. Jesus was perfect man, and therefore His voluntary death on behalf of mankind confirmed Him as Representative Man Mark 2 (Adam being Mark 1). That's why His life-style of "By Grace alone through Faith alone" is the only successful one to copy. That's how He managed to live a perfect human life – and so that's how we can do it.

I cannot emphasise strongly enough the perfect and complete erasing of Sin by Jesus on the cross. Sin (the self-centred root from which all wickedness flows) has gone. Christians are no longer self-centred - we are Christ-centred (but see the next paragraph). And that's why law is no longer relevant to Christians. The purpose of Law was to make us feel guilty for our sin. Sin has gone, so Law is redundant as a lifestyle director. Man Mark 1 always needs Law to curb his wickedness through guilt. Man Mark 1 thinks that righteousness comes through the Law, which is why they are adding more and more to it daily. Man Mark 2 only needs and has the Holy Spirit as His life-style director. For them the Law is perfectly fulfilled in their new behaviour pattern (Romans 8:4), and is even exceeded (Matthew 5:20)! Listening to and obeying the Holy Spirit more than fulfils the Law. And with ease. (See the next chapter on Righteousness for a fuller view of this issue).

Some may object – that is too cut and dried. Which would be true. There is a feathering in of Grace throughout our lives, and a feathering out of self-centredness. But for the Christian, sin has been redefined – it now registers as disobedience to Jesus' inputs rather than the breaking of Law. A Christian no longer deals with Law and Judgement – he deals directly with Jesus, His redemption, His forgiveness and His Grace. Jesus will always back up what is written in the Bible. The Holy Spirit confronts us with the scriptures, rather than with secular society.

Let's face it, no one but Jesus has come anywhere near a perfect life–style on earth, so there's no one else to follow that's any good. Other religions? All their founders were men like us. Their philosophies? Limited. Their life-style? Laws and legalism. Christianity? Not a religion – a relationship. Not law – grace. It's the only good and effective one there is on earth.

But I'm getting ahead of myself.

So how does the redemption of Jesus work in our lives? Remember we are spirit, soul and body – each part of which has eternal sin locked into its existence. The Bible talks of 3 stages of salvation (a better more modern word might be "rescue"). They are: I *was* saved, I *am being* saved and I *will be* saved. Past, present and future. These 3 Biblical verb tenses apply to the 3 parts of the human make-up. That is - I *was* saved in my spirit; I *am being* saved in my soul; I *will be* saved in my body. Let's see these 3 separately.

Firstly, *Spirit.* I am a spirit being. From what we can gather from angels and demons, heaven has either one or the other. As I have said, there are no grey angels/demons. It's not possible for any spirit to be partly on God's side of light and partly on satan's side of dark. So any spirit in heaven must be fully light or fully dark. As I have said, we humans are all born fully dark – satan's chicks. The act of yielding to the "drawing" of Jesus (John 5:44), surrendering to His sovereignty, and accepting Him as Lord over our lives has the effect of enabling the Holy Spirit to enter our spirits, unlock the eternal separation padlock, and transform our spirits from darkness to light. That's the process of transformation. It's called in John 3 "being born from above." What the process is exactly I don't know, and the human experience that accompanies it is unique to every Christian, perfectly adjusted to their personality and character. That's when we become Christians – when we came into a personal relationship with Jesus (or the Trinity, whichever you please), when our eyes are opened to heavenly things (the reverse of Adam and Eve in Eden), and our spirits come alive. Whatever processing speed we went through – slow, sudden or in-between – the nature of the new birth was instantaneous. It was then that "I *was* saved." In my *spirit.*

What about the *Soul*? Of course, the soul was heavily involved in that process. Why? Because God will always leave every final decision of our lives to our own will. I am a fully spiritual person in my own right, and God has made us all that. Therefore I make every decision that affects me as a person. My *mind* must be convinced, my *heart* is made hungry for God, my *conscience* longs for freedom from guilt, and my *will* decides to side with Jesus. I come to Jesus willingly, or not at all. (Just like Jesus went to the cross willingly for me). So my soul is 100% involved in the decision of where my spirit aches to go.

I will return to the soul later, but I will now deal with the *Body*.

The bodies we were born with are of the earth –"dust you are and to dust you will return." (Gen 3:19). They are eternally locked into the earth, are eternally locked into Sin, and eternally locked into death. They will never change – except to get older and deteriorate. They are therefore locked into satan's kingdom (he is the prince of the power of the air, the god of this world).

These bodies will never be redeemed. Therefore we are stuck with a limited, earthly, sensual, fleshly body all the days of this life. They will always drag us back and down. They are the channel through which satan tempts us. We can (and must) discipline our bodies – that is our personal responsibility and for which we are accountable. We must control what we eat, what we drink, our indulgences and our physical fitness. Lack of self-control leads to self-indulgences, which amounts to abuse and/or murder of our own bodies. Old age doesn't help. When we've grown in wisdom so that we can rule the world (!), our bodies fall into decay. Eyes, ears, hair all atrophy as do the muscles, until they give up altogether and we die. Sometimes old age is the hardest phase of life to endure with grace. Paul calls it "this body of death".

The body comes under the scripture of "I will be saved." We live with and in this body until death. But the Grace of God and scripture promises us all a resurrection body. None of us will precede another. We all get a resurrection body at the same time – when Jesus personally appears in the clouds at His Second Coming. All Christians already dead will get a new body instantly created for them, which will rise from the earth and be joined with them in the sky. Those of us who are alive on this earth at the 2nd Coming will have these bodies instantly changed into resurrection ones and we will be caught up to meet Jesus in the sky. (1 Thess 4:13-18, 1 Cor 15:42-57).

What will our resurrection body be like? Just like that of Jesus – and you can read about it at the latter end of all 4 gospels and in Acts 1. He is "the first-fruits of those who have fallen asleep."(1 Cor 15:20) We will have a body "like His glorious body" (Phil 3:21). One thing I know is that our resurrection bodies will not contain blood. They will not be air-breathing internal combustion engines, and will not therefore have need of blood.

Let's now return to the soul. The soul, after we become Christians, is "piggy in the middle." The "inner working Me" is now having to decide continually between the spirit within (into which God speaks) and the body (into which satan speaks). Every moment in life has both inputs, and the soul, through the will, is having to decide between God (by faith) and satan (by sight). ("We walk by faith and not by sight." 2 Cor 5:7). Every decision we make for Jesus changes our souls into the likeness of Christ – and it happens bit by bit one at a time. Throughout our life on earth, therefore, our souls "are *being* saved." We are "*being* changed from one degree of glory to another, as by the Spirit of the Lord" (2 Cor 3:18). It is important to note that our souls will never be perfect while they are still attached to this body. Romans 6 rightly says, "Dead men don't sin" (my translation). By implication, live men still do (see my chapter on Our Besetting Vulnerability).

I think the New Testament encourages us never to sin, and says that ample provision has been made for us not to. But God knows that all of us are weak, and He also knows that we get better as we grow more experienced as Christians. There are Christians who disagree with me, and feel we can live perfect lives. Certainly, I have known days when I have not disobeyed the Lord and not sinned. But then, I have known many days when I have. Therefore I disagree with them. And God is gracious.

The trouble is that the sin that we have inherited is so deeply embedded within us that it takes a life-time to get to the bottom of it all. Actually we never do. Praise God that the separation of our bodies from our soul/spirit at death enables the grace of God to do a miraculous work of finishing the redemption that started when we became Christians. But how does this "being saved" work? It's all to do with the transformation of the soul. The more I take God's leading, the more I see His hand of goodness and blessing become effective in my life. Consequently, I will trust Him more. There will be a number of times when He asks me to give up "that thing." Those are real crunch times. There are certain things that we have retained from our childhood that we want to keep and not let Jesus take control of. Habits are a good example. But Jesus is both persistent and terrific. He is able to take the addiction to That Thing and turn it into profit in our lives. It stops being in control of us, and we take control over it. It's terrific when that happens – we feel a huge burden has lifted off our shoulders. There are some things He reveals that we never knew we had. Just accept that He knows best. He knows the depths of sin within our souls far better than we know ourselves. (I have more on this in the chapters on Intimacy and My Besetting Vulnerability).

Do you know what a custard Christian is? One who gets upset over trifles.

There are also some things that we feel certain we cannot either control or get rid of. No amount of repentance will help. In these instances we just have to hand the whole issue over to Jesus and ask Him to deal with it as He knows best. And sometimes we have no idea whatever what He does. There is no conscious knowledge of any process going on inside us. It's just that we know we had "it", and then we know "it" has gone. Often what God has done in us emerges when someone attacks us in some way, and we marvel at our new gracious reactions.

So, I have dealt with the depth of Sin that we all have had (and been) from the beginning. I have dealt with the way Jesus has dealt with that sin. I have looked at the process of redemption in our spirits, souls and bodies. All I have left is to suggest that, if you have not started this process already, start it as soon as you can; it's the only freedom in the universe. If you have started it, don't, please, ever give up. There is no guarantee for those who give up part way, for "Because of the increase of wickedness, the love of most will grow cold, but he who stands firm ***to the end*** will be saved." (Matt 24:12-13). But for those who continue to the end – sin is for ever vanquished and a glorious future awaits you. Guaranteed.

SUMMARY

The whole of mankind is totally sinful, inherited from Adam. That is, cut off from God eternally, and locked into satan. Sin was broken in principle for all mankind when God made Jesus to be sin for us. Appropriation is individually by God's initiative through Revelation and received by faith.

Chapter 8
RIGHTEOUSNESS

Tricky subject, Righteousness. Why? Because it is unobtainable. If I was writing this in Heaven, it would not be a subject of any consideration – all will be righteous, therefore there would be no debate. But here I am still on earth (and longing for Heaven), so Righteousness has always been and will continue to be an issue of conflict, debate, problem and mystery until the end of time. All discussions go round and round and are seldom resolved satisfactorily. My discussion also goes round and round. Ready?

There are those who don't care to be Righteous. I will hardly discuss them. They used to have a conscience but presumably have squashed it and now have a "seared conscience" as the KJV so quaintly puts it. I leave them to the Holy Spirit to deal with in love.

For all others, Righteousness is a struggle of conscience. CS Lewis' book "Mere Christianity" is a brilliant argument for the divine nature of conscience, and I point you in its direction for your further consideration.

Enter Law.

(By "Law" here I am not merely referring to the five books of Moses. I am referring to all rules and regulations from every source that apply in our lives).

Righteousness (as mankind normally defines it) cannot exist on earth without the presence of Law. Law brings in bench-mark standards by which we can assess our moral position – how righteous we are or how evil we are. Where there is no Law, there is neither Righteousness nor evil. Or, as Paul wrote, "Where there is no Law, there is no knowledge of sin". (Rom 3:20, 4:15, 7:7). So Law is an integral part of our Righteousness. *Good and evil* become nonsense if there is no Law. *Conscience* is inoperative if there is no Law. *Divine Judgment* does not work if people have no perception on whether their behaviour is good or evil (Rom 5:13).

We have a brilliant illustration of this occurring in Biblical history. All those who lived before the flood had no Law. There had been only one Law. That was the one given to Adam; and he broke it in Eden before anyone else was born. So, the rest of the population ended up doing exactly what they pleased, had no conscience about it, and were so evil that God grieved that He had made man and destroyed all but eight. But He couldn't punish any of them because they didn't know they had been doing wrong. That's why Jesus went and preached to them in the three days between His crucifixion and resurrection (1 Peter 3:18b-20). For them (only) He gave a second bite at the cherry – a second chance. But as soon as Noah's Ark landed on Mt Ararat and all were ready to leave, God started to issue rules and regulations to mankind through Noah (Gen 9:4-9). Since then the whole of mankind has been subject to Law – and also a limited life-span so we won't get up to as much sin and mischief as our ancestors. What those antediluvians were into was Licence – more of which later.

So what does Law do? It differentiates right from wrong, good from evil. It sets standards for behaviour. It releases guilt to work through conscience. It gives God's Judgment evidence to bite on – whether good for reward or bad for punishment. Through guilt it restrains evil (Gal 3:24). It reveals evil (Rom 3:20). It is perfect (Rom 7:12).

And it is the hardest taskmaster that any person can bow down to.

Unfortunately, we all have to bow. We are born utterly self-centred, and very early in life our parents bring us "under law" to curb and redirect that self-centredness. God's way for the non-Christian is to be under Law, and we all start off as non-Christians. From the cradle to the grave we are confronted with an impossible standard, an undeviating taskmaster, and an unrelenting judge. Every person in this world is born "under Law" and it is what keeps wickedness at bay – along with the Holy Spirit's prompting through conscience. Unfortunately Law is not a person. It therefore has no flexibility. It cannot forgive. For all of us less-than-perfect people, it is therefore a tyrant. Unrelenting, critical, silently condemning – we are all as guilty as hell before its fearsome gaze. How man longs to be free from its shackles! When people talk about "freedom" they mean freedom from the restraints and restrictions of Law. This would instantly take them back to the Anarchy of those in Noah's day. And look what happened to them!

Gal 3 tells us that Law is our schoolmaster – literally *paidagōgos,* a whipping slave – to drive us to Christ.

So what has He, Jesus, got to do with it?

Jesus is the only person in the world who can set us free by God's definition of freedom. Slavery to Christ sets us free from Law.

There are three ways of living a life on earth (beautifully summarised in Gal 5:16-18):

What Authority	**Definition**	**Termed**	**Description**
Self – or flesh.	Doing "my own thing".	Licence	Anarchy
Law	Doing the "in" thing or the "done" thing. "Should, ought, must."	Legalism	Bondage
Holy Spirit	Doing "Jesus" thing.	Liberty	Freedom

According to Gal 5:16-18, all mankind has only these three Authorities to live "under", and we all may choose which of them we wish to be subject to. There are no others. By birth we are "under self". We are brought very quickly "under law" by our parents. To live "under the Holy Spirit" is to be set free from both the flesh and from the Law.

Let me deal briefly with Licence, and there is more about it in chapter 10 The Four Epochs. Licence is Me Doing My Own Thing. That would be regardless of laws, regardless of anyone and anything else. It is extreme self-centredness – I, I, I, Me, Me, Me. It is satan's whole life-style, so we know where we have got it from. Biblically, it is beautifully described in Isaiah 53:6.

Striding Edge is a ridge in the Lake District in England. It joins two mountains, and there is a path running right along the top of the ridge. Walking the Christian life in Liberty is like walking Striding Edge: it's a fine balance. One side is the abyss of Licence. The other side is the abyss of Legalism. We all topple over either side frequently, but God wants us to keep on the path of Liberty, the Holy Spirit continually easing us back into the narrow centre of God's way and will for us. Licence governs our indulgences. Legalism governs our concept of Righteousness.

So what has Jesus got to offer that it better than Law?

1. He sets us free from the Law. He has abolished rules and regulations and the demand of them (Eph 2:15 "...by abolishing in his flesh the law with its commandments and regulations"). In Jesus we are no longer "under the Law", but "under Grace". Neither are we under Licence – to do our own thing. We are under Jesus, to do His thing. God calls that Liberty.

2. He sets us free from the *demands* of the Law. No longer do we have rules to direct us and keep us on a straight path. We are not *under* Law.

3. So what guides us? Take away the rule-book and what do we have left? The Holy Spirit! The release of God Himself into every believer's heart in the form of the Holy

Spirit is one of the most remarkable consequences of the Cross. What does He do? He tells us moment by moment what we can do or mustn't do. That's why "Revelation" is so vitally important. How come God can live with sinful people?

a. Jesus, through His Cross, has forgiven every Christian every sin, past, present and future. He took them all and carried them away "as far as the East is from the West" (Ps 103). I am therefore no longer a sinner in God's sight – only and always forgiven. (Of course, we need to access this daily through repentance and faith).

b. We have Jesus living within us. The Trinity always sticks together, so that is all of God inside us.

c. We are Righteous in God's sight. (I will expand this later).

d. He sets us free from the consequences of failing to obey the Law. We are guiltless. There is no condemnation to everyone who is in Christ. (Rom. 8:1). Ever.

e. There is no hell for Christians. From 100% guilty under Law and destined for punishment in hell, Jesus has given us 100% forgiveness and reward to all in Him. Judgement for Christians is a prize-giving (see the chapter on Humility).

So; choose your Master – Self, Law or Jesus.

Let me delve into Law for a moment more. Just like we all have and see our own individual rainbow, so we all have our own set of Laws. What our parents gave us, what our schools set before us, what society demands of us, what our bosses require of us, each of us has a set of rules that differ from everyone else's. What makes you feel guilty doesn't necessarily make me feel guilty. Those who read their Bibles add a perfect set of moral rules to all the rest. "The Law" is therefore mainly individual, and what is right for one may be wrong for another, and vice-versa. We all relate to the rules we know. Paul expands this individual nature of Law in Rom 2.

So when we "Break the Law", we are breaking *the rules we know*. God knows all our individual rules too, because He is God and He has been living with us from the beginning. As a non-Christian then, guilt is always personally felt and individually applied.

The second observation I have is that I am not talking here about physical laws – Mathematical, Chemical, Physical, etc. No one disputes those laws of God. Everyone who lives on earth lives under those laws without question or debate. If we didn't we'd never have got to the moon. It's the *Moral* Law of God that gets up people's noses. Moral Law is what I am talking about here.

Now I have observed that many Christian people have a problem with Law. Even though Jesus has set them free from all Law and the consequences of failing it, even though He has given us an alternative way of living that works perfectly, they still insist on living "under Law." What's more, they teach others also that Law is still to be read, studied, learned and obeyed. Somehow they feel that teaching others that the Law is cancelled is unsafe, and they have no idea how Law or Liberty might still fit into their lives. They know the very letter of the Law and they try to live by it. The Christians who do this are normally intelligent and self-controlled people, and it is happy hunting ground for many preachers – especially the "Hell Fire and Damnation" bunch. While agreeing with the freedom that Christ gives, they still operate a "Righteousness according to the Law" lifestyle. Law, and adherence to it, is the more important facet of their mindset and lifestyle. We call them Legalists.

The logic to them is obvious (I know - I used to be one of them): If God has set the standards of the Law, then the Holy Spirit is not going to demand any less of us if we rely on His leading. So why don't we teach and live Legal Standards to help the Holy Spirit do His job? But those who think that way have it so wrong. The Holy Spirit doesn't demand less: He demands different. *God's* priorities for our behaviour and how we are going to achieve a Righteous life are absolutely different from *man's* priorities. And what those legalists leave out and are ignorant of is the enormous alternative universe of Grace. So let's look at Righteousness.

But now a righteousness *from God*, apart from law, has been revealed, to which the Law and the Prophets testify. (Rom 3:21).

"For in the gospel a righteousness from God is revealed, a righteousness that is by faith from first to last, just as it is written: "The righteous will live by faith."" (Rom 1:17).

Righteousness according to God's new way of Grace has nothing whatever to do with Laws, and nothing whatever to do with standards. For the Christian, Righteousness is first of all imputed and then imparted. To teach "standards" in a Christian context is sinful and leads to terrible bondage. That's not because standards are irrelevant – it's because God's view of standards is radically different from ours. Standards are for all those living under Law, and *not* for those living under Grace.

Righteousness is imputed because God now calls us Righteous. What Jesus did on the Cross was so excellent that it broke down every barrier between man and God and dealt with every hindrance in such a perfect manner that God spreads a blanket covering of Perfect Righteousness over every Christian. He looks at us through the window of Jesus, and sees only Righteousness. "We *are* the righteousness of God in Christ" (2 Cor 5). Remember that God is outside of Time (see my chapter on that). What He is going to make us into is always and already a reality in His experience. What we are going to become we already are. We have the Righteousness of Jesus already in us. (That's why the Trinity can reside within us without difficulty). Therefore to strive after Righteousness when we already have it is both stupid and unnecessary. God does not need our help to make us perfect. In His sight we are already flawless. Therefore to try to improve on what God has perfectly accomplished in Jesus is actually to destroy God's work in us. Legalism in a Christian is wickedness. The Bible makes it clear that it is "Not by might, nor by power, but by My Spirit," and it is "not by works of Righteousness that we have done, but by Grace we have been saved through faith."

Paul goes to great pains in Rom. 4 to tell us that Faith = Righteousness. So excellent was the Righteousness of Jesus that faith in Him is the most righteous thing a Christian can do in this life. To have faith in Jesus *is* Righteousness. Having faith in Jesus makes us Righteous. That is, the base from which Righteousness is gauged has changed – it is no longer Law but Grace. No longer is it: "Have I done right or not?" It is: "Have I obeyed Jesus or not?"

A Christian's life-style is to be a copy of Jesus'. How did He live such a good life, tempted in all points like we are, yet without sin? How? - By Grace alone through Faith alone. He drew on His Father's resources, wisdom and direction all the time, and made it perfectly to the very end. If we do the same, live by Grace alone through Faith alone, God imputes Righteousness to us as we walk.

As we continue to walk with Jesus, simply obeying Him and doing what He asks us to do without sweat, He *imparts* Righteousness to us bit by bit. Having *imputed* Righteousness to us at our point of conversion, He now imparts Righteousness as we dance through time.

Focusing in on Jesus *is* Righteousness. Focusing in on Righteousness is sin.

How does it work out in practice?

God keeps us busy. Once we have cottoned on to how He talks to us (the major remit of this book), we just do what He says. There really is very little time for anything else. And doing His will is not irksome, because He gives the faith, the delight and the ability with every Revelation. One can therefore walk in joy and effectiveness without trying. How effective is my life? Who cares? That's God's problem not mine.

So what about Law? What about all those rules and regulations that the world is battering us with? Listen to Jesus. He will nudge us if there is one of them we ought to be observing right now. His leading is never in error. Remember the scripture that says, "Love is the fulfilment of the Law"? (Rom 13:10). If you *really have* to have a rule to live by, go for that one. But those Christians who search out rules in order to obey them are almost certainly in error, and will bring both themselves, their families and their businesses into enormous bondage. Didn't Jesus break the Law in Israel during His lifetime? He certainly did. But, He said, they were rules made by man and not by God. And were therefore valid to be broken if God had another agenda. We live today in a generation of the proliferation of unnecessary and burdensome rules, most of which we may take note of as advice rather than obligation. And if they disagree with any behaviour patterns or differ from those of the New Testament then ignore them – they are wrong. Legalists will find this paragraph very difficult to stomach. But it is New Testament life. And it is a freedom that legalists have never known.

But what about the Bible? That's full of laws, isn't it? Certainly – and Grace too. We need to *teach* converts *Grace*, and tell them to read their Bibles. Both. Then the Lord Himself will accrue in their minds all those rules contained in His Bible that He wants them to know. The trouble with today's Church is that we do it the wrong way round: we *teach rules and regulations* and assume that God might teach them Grace. That makes us all legalists. To teach Grace is the Christian way, and let's let *the Lord* open to each individual those rules that specifically apply to them for their lives.

So, Christians are set free from the obligations of the Law, and the Christian life-style throughout is to walk by the Holy Spirit, by Grace alone through Faith alone. So how can I tell if I am under Law? I'll give you one very simple key – criticism. If I criticise, I am a part-time or full-time legalist.

Criticism is judgementalism and condemnation of another person in the light of my individual set of Laws (which they would be completely unaware of) and in command of very few if *any* of the facts. If I criticise I am rejecting God's laws of grace and love, and I am a wicked legalist. *Assessment* of others only becomes criticism if I condemn that person in my mind. Jesus calls us to assess, but never to condemn ("By their fruits you will know them (Matt 7:20)."). Judgment, as in a court of Law, is different. There judgment is made and justice administered when in command of all the facts and in the light of Common Law. Criticism is the major key – although it is by no means the only sign that I am a legalist!

So what place does law play in a Christian's life – because it is still there, even if I am not under it? It is like the detective who always stands one foot behind a President. Law stands behind a Christian ready to kick-in when that Christian fails to listen to the Lord. If I go my own way or select a path not of the Lord, Law immediately returns as my supervisor. The moment I repent and turn back to the Lord, Law retreats back again and bows to a Superior Master.

<u>Righteousness for the Christian</u>.

So let me say firstly that a Christian's righteousness is not, repeat not, related to the Law. Or laws. Or rules. Or regulations. They have all been abolished for the Christian.

So what does it relate to? I have three Biblical perspectives on it for your consideration:

1. We are righteous as we live **According To the Covenant** we have made with the Lord. What covenant? When we first became Christians, we did two things: Firstly, we handed over our lives to Jesus. Secondly, we surrendered to the sovereignty of Jesus. That was our Covenant agreement

with Him. In exchange, He agreed to take on our lives into eternity, and be Lord. So far as He is concerned, we are righteous as we continue to keep our side of those agreements (our covenant). As I hand over my life today and yield to Jesus' sovereignty, I *am* righteous. This is Righteousness relating to Covenant. This is exactly the way the Old Testament tells us God operated with Israel.

2. We are righteous **As we Walk in the Holy Spirit**. Gal 5:16-18 tells us that walking by the Spirit overcomes the flesh and releases us from the Law. That is, Righteousness relating to obedience.

3. We are righteous **As we Believe** what Jesus is telling us to do. That is, Righteousness relating to Grace, but made effective by faith in the Now Revelations of Jesus. Faith = Righteousness (Rom 4).

These three can be summarised in one word – *Obedience.* Or, to put it nicer – Delighted Obedience.

Let me deal once and for all with Law. Firstly, those who walk according to the Spirit fulfil the Law completely (Rom 8:2). Secondly, the whole Law is summarised in this: "Love your neighbour as yourself". Therefore love *is* the fulfilling of the law (Rom 13:10). Thirdly, those who walk in obedience to Jesus *more than* fulfil the Law – they live a life-style that is *far higher than the Law.* That is why Jesus said, "Unless your righteousness *exceeds* that of the scribes and Pharisees, you cannot enter the Kingdom of Heaven." (Matt 5).

If we have *God's* Righteousness and approval, what else do we need? Surely that will bring us "into favour with God and men"?

There is one last thing we need to ask: "Where do the precepts and counsels of the Bible come in?" Surely if we read it, look at its rules and obey them, we will live a Righteous life, won't we? Well, you would if you could. But you can't. No one can because we are "weakened by the sinful nature" (Rom 8:3). Besides, even if you could, obeying the counsels of the Bible would not bring you into a relationship with God. So merely reading the Bible and learning its precepts and rules will never lead anyone into heaven. And so why read it? Answer: exclusively to enable the Holy Spirit to reveal Jesus to you and bring you into a personal relationship with Him. OK, so once we have that personal relationship, can't we stop reading our Bibles? *Never!* Every verse is an avenue to learning more about God. When will any of us ever come to the end of that? The Holy Spirit is so clever that He can guide us in a completely different direction from the one He did last week through the same scripture verse. There is a vast, untapped universe out there called "The heart and mind of God", accessed by the Holy Spirit through your Bible. So when Jesus said, "If you love me you will obey what I command," (John 14:15), He is referring to His Now *Rhēma* words to you. How do I know that? Because love is an active, present relationship. Therefore His words are active, present Revelations. It's present tense: "If you go on loving me, you will go on obeying what I command."

Wonderful Christian people – you have been set absolutely free. Enjoy your freedom. You are free from the demands and bondage of laws; you are free from the destruction of guilt and condemnation; you are free from the death of sin and sins. Righteousness (as God has redefined it) is simple, easy to accomplish and carries no burdens – walk with Jesus, listen to what He says, and do what He asks. Now *that* is a Righteous man!

The New Testament frequently uses the word "justify" when talking of Christian people. We need to remove the mystique from this word. It has neither a technical nor a theological definition. It means exactly the same as it does in normal common usage. Jesus justifies a Christian's life before God. How? Why?

"Continual faith in Jesus Christ" *perfectly fits* God's new definition of Righteousness. Everything else that we have thought, said or done that is outside that definition has been removed from the equation – it is not taken into account. All that "other stuff", the whole lot, is sin, and has already been fully dealt with eternally. Therefore it is irrelevant. Jesus now justifies our whole lives before His Holy Father. "This, my friend, trusted me implicitly, Father, and is therefore fit for heaven." "OK, Son."

So let's go back to the beginning. Righteousness (as mankind normally defines it) is impossible for man to achieve. Only God can fulfil the Law. His chosen way of accomplishing that is to abolish the Law along with its Rules and Regulations, and set up a totally different system of living for mankind. This new system, by Grace alone through Faith alone, *is* the Excellent way of life, *is* absolute Righteousness, is freedom, is effectiveness, is available to all ages from all tribes and nations on earth, does accomplish the will of God, is great fun and perfect freedom. Why strive after any other lifestyle?

Indeed, why strive at all?

SUMMARY

Righteousness in God's sight is not now related to Law. It is related to faith, is imputed and then imparted by Grace, and depends on our fulfilling our covenant relationship with Jesus. All Christians are already righteous, although still limited.

Chapter 9 GENESIS

We are all children of our time. Me too. We pick up the ideas and concepts of the generation and leaders in which we live. Very few people have original ideas, but when they do, and get them advertised, then the rest of us follow like sheep. So we have had movements to save the whales and the ospreys. "Green" became a serious issue in the late 20th century, and all political parties started to include it in their manifestos. Currently, Christianity is a political impoliteness, and Islam is acceptable because we mustn't marginalise a minority. It's all very hypocritical. Why can't people express what they think without getting trampled on? But all that is by the way. Since the publication of Darwin's "Origin of the Species" in 1859, Evolution has been the "in" way to view the origin of our universe. It's popularity coincided with a growing scepticism with Christianity, and the post-Victorian era saw an increase in that scepticism followed by an increased grip on the world by the Theory of Evolution.

When I was a lad at school, Evolution had escalated into full power, and a Genesis view of the origin of the Universe was marginalised to "myth". (A myth (apart from being an unmarried female moth) is a story that is not true in itself but contains a truth). This meant that what people want to make of the Genesis was up to them, and we are all very happy for them. But none of it could be eternally true.

So I grew up and joined the RAF, holding an Evolutionary world-view. We pretty well all did. Then I became a Christian. Suddenly the debate started to rage. I thought about it often, and all Young People's Fellowships in those days set it as the hot issue, and we all chewed it over a number of times. I did as much research on it as I could. The only stuff I could find was all from the Evolution lobby, with nothing from the Genesis lobby. (I was about to say "Christian Lobby," but no Christian that I heard at that time had a literalist view of the Genesis). The only conclusion that brought me peace and allowed me to be comfortable was the compromise one that a "Day" could also mean "An unspecified Period of Time" (and it can), the length of each Genesis Day being in God's hands.

A serious incident came when a Christian better versed in these issues than I and whom I trusted persuaded me that the whole Genesis story really was scientifically unacceptable, and should be discarded as a viable proposition. It was serious in that this thought hit me hard: "If I cannot believe one part of the Bible, how can I rely on any other part? If Genesis is seriously untrue, what about John or Acts or Paul?" This time I really struggled. It undermined the whole of my Christian faith. Was *anything* God wrote true? This conflict was so traumatic that the only solution I could find was to discard thinking about Genesis altogether, to shelve it as an unresolved difficulty, and go on with what I knew to be good in my Christian experience. I suppose my back-of-the-brain thinking reverted to the compromise solution I had previously embraced.

Some 13-14 years later I was flying Lightnings out of RAF Wattisham in Suffolk and fellowshipping in the Strict Baptist Chapel there. It was very Calvinistic, and it did me loads of good, challenging all my earlier Christian concepts. Indeed, you will see its fruit in much of what I have written in this book. One weekend Pastor Gordon Hawkins asked a guy called David Davies to minister. His message and the following Monday evening made me exceedingly angry. I was furious. He taught a Literal Genesis. I was so angry I was almost frothing at the mouth. I determined to expose this charlatan. How dare he question Evolution?

But I had a difficulty. Dr David was a Physics PhD and was head of the Science Department in a Secondary School. He had more scientific knowledge in his little finger than I had in the whole of my body. At question time on the Monday I dominated the meeting, bombarding him with difficulties that I had trouble with. The Pastor closed the meeting and I asked David if he was going to the Pastors' for supper, where we could continue this battle. He was. We did. At one point and sighing he asked: "Why are you so angry?" I paused and thought about it, because I was. Then I said: "Because you have to be right. I need a proper, scientific rationale for the Bible's Genesis, and I am fighting both it and you with 14 years of established "Christian doctrine." He sighed again. And we continued until I ran out of questions. He had given me loads of scientific reasons why the Genesis is perfectly acceptable as a literal explanation of the origin of the universe. He directed me to the Biblical Creation Society, and I became an avid reader and member. There very erudite Christians with loads of scientific degrees after their names wrote articles backing the Genesis story. The three most controversial disciplines of Geology, Biology and Cosmology were regularly addressed. For their help and that of the Creation Science Movement I will be eternally grateful. And I would like to use this opportunity of backing up a personal apology to David for giving him such a hard week-end. It has been life to me, all the way back to the early 1970's.

The rationale still stands: If I cannot believe the Genesis to be literally true, how can I believe any of the rest of the Bible? The Bible stands or falls together. I am so grateful that it does, and so grateful for those who have taken on the battle against the myth (!) of Evolution.

During the Charismatic Movement I did a study, not only on the Holy Spirit's work in the life of a Christian, but also on *Logos* and *Rhēma* (which you will find earlier in this book). In case you didn't read it, *rhēma* always and only means "a *spoken* word". So one of those scriptures was John 5:46-47. Jesus said; "If you do not believe what Moses wrote, how can you believe what I say (Literally My *rhēma* words)?" This verse pitches us immediately into Genesis, which Moses wrote. If I don't believe the Genesis, I will have terrible difficulty hearing God's voice. Wow! That's why this Revelation on Genesis is in this book; this book is all about Revelation and hearing God speak to us.

So, let me launch you into my children's version of how the Genesis hangs together. Please add to it, meditate on it, and develop it to your own satisfaction.

Day 1. "In the beginning God created the heavens and the earth." The word "Beginning" indicates that time started ticking then. "The heavens" mean that He created then what we now call "space". So from the beginning we have the space-time continuum. The earth was formless and covered with water. That gave God the opportunity to have Entropy lurking in the background, depending on Adam and Eve's choice of fruit-eating. I would be certain that there was no Entropy at the beginning. (I have a chapter on Entropy to save you finding out what it is). Rather, the creation was alive, fruitful and throbbing. "The heavens"? Angels in Heaven? The Bible does not give us any timing on the creation of angels, but clearly they were completed by Gen. 3 and the temptation.

Water? "The earth was formed from water and out of water" (2 Peter 3: 5). Water is the basic unit of life, and scientists spend much of their days trying to find it on other planets. No water, no life. The fact that the earth was covered with water meant that life was a probability on earth (fitting in with the scientific rationale), and that it could be completely covered again during the flood.

So where did "matter" appear from? I agree with mainstream theologians and Heb 11:3 that the creation was "ex nihilo" – out of nothing. That is, all "matter" was *created* from nothing through the mind of God. A simple acceptance of Einstein's formula $E=mc^2$ would show that the majority of "matter" is energy. That I can accept from the God that I know.

"Let there be Light". Presumably the *whole* electro-magnetic spectrum, not just the visible light frequencies?

Gravity? The water stuck to the surface of the earth, and didn't fly off into space. The earth was rotating, and water would have flown off if it hadn't been for gravity. Gravity has been there from the beginning. Sir Isaac Newton analysed the mathematics of the law of Gravity for us (32 ft/sec^2 on earth), but he didn't invent it. All scientific laws have been there from the beginning, and man has taken a long time before he has got round to quantifying them, analysing them and giving them named formulae.

This was and is the first Creation. This Creation is perfect, which ties up both with God's way of doing things and all the rest of Biblical Revelation. There are those who suggest that there have been previous creations, but their arguments are very thin, without evidence and based on a dodgy and controversial translation of one Hebrew word. Therefore rejected.

"The evening and the morning was the first day." A Literal 24 hour day, just like we know it. The Hebrew word can mean "an unspecified period of time" and an example of that is found in Numbers 7:12-84. Note v 84: "On *the day* it was anointed," representing 12 days, translated easier in KJV or NKJV. When that word "day" is preceded by a number, it always means a 24 hour period. You can see that from the same passage in Numbers.

The *first* day. God rotated the earth, so as to produce day and night. Presumably the Light came from Him, which is what it will do in the New Heaven and New Earth of Revelation 21:23. There was no sun. The evening and the morning indicates that on Day 1 Time had begun. Day and night simply measured it.

On Day 2 God separated water from water by an expanse of air. Note, not water *vapour* from water. There were no clouds. What many scientific Christians are suggesting (and I agree) is that God placed a canopy of literal water above the earthly atmosphere making earth a greenhouse (and I have expanded this in the next chapter). The temperature inside a greenhouse is constant all over, and the earth's temperature would have ended up (before the Flood) as tropical all over. No poles. No ice. And a meteorological high pressure area, as there is no record of rain or wind until the Flood. Indeed, Gen 2:5 specifically says there was no rain. The water layer above the "firmament" (that is, the atmosphere in which birds flew, Gen 1:20) would give protection from ageing factors that currently affect us – ultra-violet radiation, cosmic radiation and extremes of hot and cold. That would account for the prolific growth rate of the reptiles we now call dinosaurs. It would also account for the 900+ age of people. Even after the Fall of Genesis 3, these antediluvians lived in a tropical paradise, and barely appreciated any of it. Day 2 also saw the introduction of atmosphere we now call air (which is a remarkably chemical in its own right).

So God let the water remaining on earth drain away to reveal dry land. Gravity as we know it worked the same way then as it does now.

On <u>Day 3</u> God introduced vegetation. Plants cannot live without air. We can assume that photosynthesis kicked in immediately, and these new little green jobbies started sucking in CO^2 and spitting out O^2 to enable animals and man (and cars and all kinds of other internal combustion engines) to breathe. Meanwhile they grew through the "C" (carbon) that they retained from the CO^2. God gave each plant, in all their enormous variety, their own unique DNA. Each plant bore its own seed and/or fruit, the replanting of which reproduced that plant "after its kind". Man has been very clever in producing hybrids of most plants. But a rose is a rose is still a rose. You can't get a rose any other way than by using rose seeds or rose plants. The Genesis account is as true today as it was then. Every plant is "boundaried" and there is nothing man can do to change it. We can alter or destroy them. But we can't create them, make them or change them. It is worth stating that God made the plants mature (fully grown), as the animals and man started eating their fruit three days later.

<u>Day 4</u> saw the creation of the sun, the moon and the stars. The distance of the sun from the earth is perfect. A teensy-weensy bit nearer we would all fry. A teensy-weensy bit further away and we would all freeze. The other planets in our solar system bear

evidence to that. And the light and heat from the sun bring natural life to the earth. The moon is also perfectly positioned governing tides and bringing light at night. Its size and distance from earth is exactly right for man to view the sun at a total eclipse. How remarkable is that?

Each of the planets were presumably created and placed on Day 4, and each has a task to do in the solar system.

The sun and the moon were also designated to measure times and seasons, so God said. Aren't they still doing the same?

The stars? There are billions of stars in our Milky Way Galaxy. And there are billions of galaxies in the universe. We know the speed of light, and we therefore measure the distance of stars from the earth in "light-years". It's awesome. Genesis dismisses this enormous creative act with "He made the stars also." A kind of two-minute jobby. It was a problem I had with the Genesis: if stars were billions of light-years away, where are the missing billions of years that join star to earth with light if the creation is only around 10,000 years old? Genesis tells us. The stars were made "to bring light to the earth." So the light joining the star to earth was attached at the same time as its little sun was made. They all not only immediately worked but could also be seen. And they have kept the human race marvelling ever since.

The book of Job is reported to be the oldest book in the Bible, and I have no reason to question it. In it is the mention of three stellar constellations – the Bear, the Pleiades and Orion (Job 9:9 and 38:31). These are still with us today. God has fixed their locations and shape in space so that, even though we are told they might be whizzing around at breakneck speeds, they don't change in shape in relation to earth. How do I know they haven't changed shape? The three great pyramids in Giza in Egypt are an exact replica of the three stars in Orion's belt. All the angles and distances are precise. And the angles and distances of Orion's belt, measured today, remain the same as it seems they did in the days of ancient Egypt. Nothing has changed or apparently moved.

Day 5. God built fish and birds. Have you seen the extraordinary number and variety there are? In 2004 I watched a TV programme on the depths of the Pacific Ocean. There they recorded fish and sea creatures that no one had ever seen before. So the earth was made for man – for his enjoyment as well as his responsibility. And no one had ever seen these creatures before in the history of the earth. How amazing is that? What else are we going to discover that God has made that is right in front of our eyes?

So the birds flew in the "firmament" (KJV). That pitches where the "heavens" were – above the sea and land and under the water "up there". Being an aviator I know a little about flying. So, all the properties of air as we know it as a fluid today containing all the physical characteristics of pressure, temperature and density existed then in exactly the format we have now. (I guess it was less polluted then). But all the forces of aerodynamics that cause our aircraft to fly today caused birds to fly on Day 5. Air is a remarkable fluid. And it supports flight. It always has.

Birds are extraordinary. Their innate knowledge of aviation, with all its scientific intricacies comes naturally to them. Their structure, the lightness of their bones, the design of feathers, their songs and their innate manoeuvrability are all astonishing. Man has only been able to copy them and fly in the last 100 years. How extraordinary is that? There is a similar innate knowledge in man: how do we calculate balance in standing on two legs? We don't – we just do it. The mathematics are built into us, just like aviation is built into birds. The question: "Which came first, the chicken or the egg?" is a serious problem for an evolutionist. But not for a creationist.

The earth was covered with water from the start. Peter's statement that the earth was formed out of water and by water is a pretty accurate scientific truth. Certainly that would be true of the present earth as we now have it, being formed from the flood waters of Noah's day. Water is the most remarkable of chemicals. It is made out of hydrogen and oxygen, two of the basic elements of earth, and vital ones for life. Its three states of solid, liquid and gas are the most available of all elements and have excellent properties we use daily. Moreover, it is very unusual for a chemical to have its liquid form at room temperature. "Aqua-dynamics" were available from the start, and the fishes were created "aqua-dynamic". No one has been able to improve on either their lack of drag in the water nor their manoeuvrability. Man's inventions cannot compare with nature's excellence – rather, God's excellence. Professor Stuart Burgess has expanded the wonders and extraordinary intricacies of both water and air in his book "Hallmarks of Design". No life can exist without both.

Day 6. On the last day of creation God made land animals and then topped it with man. When man appeared, the whole of creation was complete. God made earth for man. Of that there is no doubt. All the animals, domestic and wild, were made for him. We use the animals in very different ways: domestic, beasts of burden, food, pets, study subjects, objects of beauty, observation, tourism, photography. The variety is immense. No human being can recall all the plants, insects, fish, birds and animals we observe on earth. And yet Adam was asked to name them all. That took remarkable intelligence, not just to think up a new name for each, but to remember it later. There are many who think that man's intellect is evolving. The Bible teaches the opposite – it is devolving. We are not as clever as our ancestors were. God gave man responsibility over the whole earth. That's why He gave man the opportunity to name the animals. We still have authority over the whole earth, as well as over the animals. What God said and did right at the beginning has not changed one bit.

So man was made in a different way to the animals. His body was formed, lifeless, from the dust of the earth. Then God "breathed" life into him, and instantly a soul and a spirit kicked in. Maybe God knew that this body would eventually have to die? For "Dust you are, and to dust you will return". So God made man in His own image. That same reference in Gen 1:26 tells us that God is plural: "Let *Us* make man in *Our* image." So Gen 1:27

says: "God created man in His own image, in the image of God he created him; male and female he created them." Moreover, the Hebrew name Elohim, used here, is masculine plural. Does "Image" mean Physically? Spiritually? Character-wise? Whichever, I think it is an immense and immeasurable privilege to be a human being. All animals have "being". They have awareness and God says He will call each of them to account (Gen 9:4). Just how much higher and more privileged is it to have "being" that is human? Ours is the privilege of walking and talking with God in conscious awareness on earth, and of living with Him in His heaven for ever. What future the animals have in heaven I have little evidence. But we do know what happens to humans – God has told us very simply and clearly. From those to whom much is given, much will be required.

One way in which man is made in the image of God is that we are a Trinity in Unity, just as They are a Trinity in Unity. We are spirit, soul and body. None of us can distinguish or measure the boundaries between any of those three parts. (Can you distinguish, in your head, which is brain and which is mind?). In the same way that we cannot separate our three parts, so God is Three in One and One in Three – inseparable.

So God made man on Day 6. He gave him full accountability over the earth. And He told him to replenish the earth. Both CS Lewis and Watchman Nee maintain that Adam was a really extraordinary human. Whereas now all our digestive, nervous, and replenishment systems are automatic, they reckoned that Adam had full control over every cell in his body. He was told to replenish the earth, which indicated that he was able to walk or run throughout the land area without getting tired or sweating. Sweat came in after the fall, when work became toil. By implication, it was not hard or toilsome before that. With his bodily control coupled with his intelligence, CS Lewis reckons that we would bow down and worship him.

God rested on the 7th Day, as He says we must. The creation was not only finished, it was "very good"; that is, perfect;

complete. How did God create all this? Who cares? It is mathematically, physically and chemically complete. It is so intertwined that it hangs together as One Thing. We all know this. Just how could non-intelligence produce stuff that human intelligence has yet to fathom, much less make?

We know where Eden roughly was – in the upper reaches of the Tigris and Euphrates, both of which are named as rivers passing through Eden, and are still with us today. Adam walked with God in the garden. They had an unrestricted relationship and fellowship together.

The first crisis came in that Adam was lonely. He was body as well as spirit. None of the animals God had given him satisfied his needs. So God anaesthetised him, took a rib from him and made woman. Now there is a strange mixing of words in Gen 1:27 and 5:1,2. Adam is referred to both as a "he" and a "them". And it's not referring to the Adamic race, because there was still only one of them, or two with Eve. My view is that God made Adam as One human being, containing all the characteristics of both masculine and feminine (not male and female, note). He was both genders in one being, but sexually male. When Adam woke from his nap, he knew he was only half there – feminine characteristics had gone from his personality. When he saw Eve, she was not only beautiful and female; she was also feminine. Into the female sex God had put all of Adam's feminine characteristics. This would be why Adam said, "For this reason a man shall leave his father and mother, and cleave to his wife, and the two shall become one flesh". He longed to be completed again by Eve just as much as she longed to be completed by him. They had been one. Now they were two. Together they made One again. Just like the three Persons in the Trinity, acting as One. Eve was "After his kind". She was bone of his bone and flesh of his flesh. (The Rib bone is the fastest to grow again in the body if removed.) This oneness was important to Adam in his tasks over the earth. It also became important when, later, he had to choose between God and Eve in the Temptation. Presumably, since Eve was both body and spirit, Adam preferred her to God, who was pure Spirit.

Now we need to talk about marriage. Marriage is NOT a man-made institution, as if it is just a legal and convenient form of living with someone of the opposite sex. It is *God's* institution. It was introduced before sin entered the world. The Bible goes on to say: if we are going to marry, we must be committed to one spouse for the whole of our lives. No compromise. No divorce. No affairs. No homosexuality. Committed faithfulness is God's norm. Remarriage is only permitted after death (Romans 7:1-3). Secondly, *marriage* is God's norm, not shacking up with your boy/girl friend. Couples should not be living alone together over a protracted period of time unless they are married. Married. Nothing less is good enough. That's not my view point, it's God's (see Mal 2:14-16). I'm only the messenger. Thirdly, sex outside of marriage is wrong. In the NKJV it is called fornication for single people, and adultery for married people. It means the same - sex is for marriage only. If people stuck to God's clear rules on sexual issues there would be no Aids, no VD, no teenage or unwanted pregnancies, no expensive divorces, no crippling compensations or alimony, no family break-ups and no despair, destruction of character or hatred between "Ex's". Moreover, children would be brought up with the stable norm of a Dad and a Mum. We live today in an unparented, promiscuous and unfaithful generation, and are consequently raising broken children. Our unbiblical behaviour is destroying our societies from inside out. What is more, God has provided us with every facility that would enable every Christian to keep His rules with joy. It's called Grace, and is freely available to all who are tempted.

In God's sight, having sex *is* marriage (see 1 Cor 6:16). But society requires us to confirm that private act with legally binding, public and lifelong vows. Hence the marriage ceremony. But the social requirements come before the physical – and this has been so in every society on earth from time immemorial, and therefore we can take it as God's will. Get married first – then unite physically. This is also the order that Jesus will take in the new heavens and the new earth when He gets married.

If you choose any other than God's perfect way, you choose disaster. And if you don't believe Genesis, the chances are that you are likely to believe the current cultural climate and do lustful and wicked things with one another. "Flee from sexual immorality (fornication). All other sins a man commits are outside his body, but he who sins sexually sins against his own body." (1 Cor 6:18).

The seventh commandment "You shall not commit adultery", although given many centuries later, was based on Adam's statement in Eden (Gen 2:24), and applies throughout time to every human being on earth. The testosterone hormone in man is not only the aggressive one – it is the promiscuous one. CS Lewis once pointed out that one man could populate a village in his life-time. I read a statement recently that one American man (apparently an accountant) had provided sperm to a sperm bank and had now fathered 1500 children. Men love generating babies, or simply having sex. They also love going their own way, abdicating from their responsibilities, and leaving their women abandoned, destitute and desolated, along with their children. Such is man by nature, and without the self-control and discipline of the Holy Spirit, men will continue to be promiscuous. The reason why AIDS has become an epidemic is simply due to sexual promiscuity, exposing on an international basis what people would prefer to keep secret. All promiscuity is sin. That is God's line, and very hard for a non-Christian to stomach. It also seems to make Christians spoil-sports. Actually, no. It makes Christians righteous, healthy, guilt-free and happy. Marriage is good in every way, and the best way a man and woman can live together. It carries with it God's blessing and enabling. I know that many are likely to disagree with me on that, particularly if they don't believe the creation account in Genesis.

Enter satan. There are a number of things we can know or assume:-

1. The angelic throng had already been created.

2. Lucifer, or satan, was the Spirit Being put in charge of earth, to act as God's go-between between Adam and God. Heb 1:14 tells us that the purpose of angels is to be ministers to those who are to be heirs of salvation. Their task has not changed. Even fallen angels, demons, are still ministering to human beings, and God changes their negative inputs to a positive effect (Rom. 8:28). So it was with satan.

3. Satan had already fallen.

In the cosmic state of things, satan called all the angels to side with him against God. One third of them did. Now satan, who had (and has) full and free access to earth, wanted God's finest creation to join his rebellion. There is an ancient Pharisaic teaching that satan was jealous of the importance God had placed on man, and that God's preference of man over him was one of the causes of satan's rebellion. The nature of Lucifer's rebellion was self-exaltation, the details of which can be found in Is. 14:12-17 and Ezekiel 28:11-19.

The temptation was clever, subtle, and effective. What is more, the account in Gen. 3 forms the basis for all temptations that we all experience today. How can it not have been literally true?

Adam was fortunate – he only had one command over which he had to make a choice – that one fruit from that one tree. It is a very helpful study to contrast the temptation of Jesus in the desert with Adam in the garden. Adam had a companion, who, it turned out, was little help to him. He was in paradise. He was not starving. Everything was for him and not against him. And still he fell. (Don't we all?)

It is uncertain whether Eve had been created when God gave Adam the commandment not to eat that one fruit. The account in Gen 2 of the prohibition came before Eve's arrival. It's quite possible that Eve had not been present when God told Adam not to eat from that tree. She therefore probably heard it second-hand. In the Temptation, satan subtly attacked Eve, not Adam, and she did not quote the prohibition accurately. She was therefore wobbly on the issue. Note that satan never confronted her with the real issue at hand – rebellion against God. He never does. But the real issue of temptation is *always* rebellion against God. In whatever form satan disguises the issue, rebellion is still the root matter. So Eve fell to the Temptation, took the fruit and ate. And there is no value in blaming her: every single one of us has followed her footsteps.

Now Adam was not tempted. 1 Tim 2:13, 14, specifically states that Eve was deceived: Adam was not. Satan scarpered when Adam turned up – although Gen 3:6 does suggest that Adam was present when Eve ate the fruit. Maybe Adam could not hear what satan was saying to her in her mind? It is a *very* important point that Adam was neither tempted nor deceived. He saw what Eve had done, and had to choose between following God or following Eve. God was absent, so the choice was clear, simple, unambiguous and unmistakable. He chose Eve. He ate the fruit she offered him. It is clear from the story that Adam was personally responsible for the decision he made and the law that he broke. As we are for all the decisions we make in the light of all the laws we know. But to him, as representative man, belonged the future of mankind and the earth for which he was accountable. Put simply, it was death. Death to the ground he trod on. Death to all the creatures over which he had been given leadership. Death to his innocence. And in the end death to God's Son Jesus. Their death was immediate, automatic and instantaneous – both knew they were naked. Not Eve first. But Both after Adam's choice.

There was a 4-way split possible in Eden that day:

- Adam and Eve could have said No.
- Adam could have said No, and Eve Yes.

- Eve could have said No and Adam Yes. (the least likely)
- Adam and Eve could have said Yes. (what actually occurred)

All four options were covered by God. All of the promises of the New Testament would have applied, but the pathway to accomplishing them would have been radically different. God said to Adam. "Because you have listened to the voice of your wife ... " So clearly, he did. And also clearly, he need not have done. God knows what was, what is, what will be, and also what might have been. Man's choice does not govern the eventual destiny of earth, but it certainly governs the way we get there. The curses that fell on all participants are still with us today. First, death to all. Second, death to the creation, and I have written about that elsewhere under "Entropy".

Then, death to Eve. (Adam and Eve were not cursed, just punished). She would bear children in pain. So far as I can tell, no animals bear their young in pain. Only human mothers. That has not changed. And it's amazing the number of women who try to reverse that. Then, woman was to be subject to man – to her husband in particular. Part of satan's rebellion is for women to try to reverse that too. But they fight their nature. Oestrogen is the submissive hormone. Women find their fulfilment in submitting to their man, and this travels through every aspect of a woman's life all the way down to sex. In addition, because of this punishment, women will always be tempted to reverse it and try to rule over their husbands and "wear the trousers".

The punishment to man was that the ground would become to him a toil and a labour. Hard work would characterise his life on earth. Thorns and thistles would be his inheritance, and sweat his method of achieving it. His labour would be hard work, his family would be hard work, and his prosperity would be hard work to come by. Therefore man's greatest temptation would be towards laziness – the abdication of any or all of his responsibilities. He will be tempted to abdicate from his leadership role, his responsibility towards the children he generates and the wife he marries, and from accountability in whatever job he takes up. How true that is still today. Fatherless families are today's curse on tomorrow's generation.

Have you noticed how both participants tried to abdicate from their responsibilities and blame someone else? And people call the Genesis story a myth – as if we don't all do it still?

The serpent was cursed. The earth was cursed. Man and woman were not cursed – only punished by the limitations of death.

So, the earth and the creation are young; 6000 years at the youngest, and 10,000 years at the oldest. All things were created mature.

How come the antediluvians lived such a long time? In Gen. 11, we read of people fathering children at age 30. If you halve that age to enable the top years to reduce to a recognisable size, people started bearing children at 15. That would reduce Adam's death from 930 to 465, still unacceptable in terms of our age–range. If you reduce it any more, it makes child-bearing ridiculously young. So why don't we simply accept the age as written, and work out a sensible reason why they lived so long?

Methuselah lived for 969 years, the oldest recorded human being. His name in Hebrew means "When he dies it will happen". His father was Enoch, a prophet who walked with God. Try adding all the ages of the early fathers together, and see what year you come out at. Then check the year that the flood came from Noah's age. You will discover that Methuselah died in the same year the flood came. So Methuselah lived longer than any other human being. Why? Because God delayed the flood as long as He could, giving the antediluvians the maximum opportunity to repent from their gross wickedness. Isn't that Grace? Noah and his wife and his sons and their wives were rescued "when it came", because Noah also had found grace in God's eyes. (Gen 6:8)

The flood covered the earth for a year. From the account in Genesis, God used the water from the sky and from underground, along with tectonic activity, to reshape the earth. It was covered with water to start with, and if dry ground was still going to occur, some heavy earth-moving was needed. Water, as I have already said, is a brilliant earth-mover. I do not find any scientific difficulty with the flood. It was "above the tops of the mountains to the depth of the ark". Those who propose a local flood in the Mesopotamian basin have to account for water finding its own level very quickly. You can't have a stack of water above the tops of the mountains in the Turkey area for a year and for it not be over the whole earth! In addition, most indigenous tribes have a flood account in their ancient traditions, so many as to make its rejection irrational. There are those who try to reconcile those ancient accounts, but every attempt has failed. There are others who have tried to make the Gilgamesh account the true one, and all others corrupt. And still others to give equal credence to all the accounts. But I put it to you that if God is God, and is both perfect and good, then the Bible account is the true one and all others corruptions of it. It even gives us the day, the month and the year that the flood came and left a year later. What could be more precise than that?

There is little dispute that Abraham was genuine, and little dispute that from him onwards the Bible is recording real history of real people in places that still exist today. So the only other disputed Genesis passage is Babel, where God created all the languages in the world in one fiat. All languages are very complicated. There has never been any evidence of a language where the grammar and vocabulary have "evolved". We are all conscious of language changing with culture and time, but the basic format does not change. Man does not "invent" language (apart from Esperanto, and that took men a very long time to get right). We learn it from our parents and take to it naturally.

Every Bible Translator can testify to the complexity of every tribal language.

But maybe the most significant thing about Babel is the observation God Himself made about language. "If as one people speaking the same language they have begun to do this, then nothing they plan to do will be impossible for them." (Gen 11: 6) Why is this significant? Because we have now returned to the pre-Babel era. English has become the globally common language. Therefore "nothing we plan to do will be impossible for us." We suddenly live in a very dangerous age.

Why this emphasis on Genesis? I have already said it from John 5:46-47 "Jesus said: "If you believed Moses, you would believe Me, for he wrote about Me. But since you do not believe what he wrote, how are you going to believe what I say?"'" (That is, Jesus' *rhēma* words). When we stop compromising with Moses, particularly the Genesis, the words Jesus speaks to us daily become much clearer and more lucid.

By writing as I have done about Genesis, I have given you a key. If you are having difficulty with guidance or with discerning the voice of God, make haste to find a rationale with which you are comfortable that enables you to accept Genesis exactly as it is written.

SUMMARY

God's creation fiat as recorded in Genesis needs to be received as written if anyone is going to hear God's Rhēma words clearly.

Chapter 10
THE FOUR EPOCHS.

According to Biblical history and prophecy, the life of Earth is in four phases, or Epochs. Each epoch is separated by a cataclysmic event from heaven. Each epoch has very different characteristics compared to the others. But the purpose of each is the same - to bring sons of Adam into God's kingdom to form part of the Bride of Christ. That Bride will consist of millions of people too vast for any person to count, and each epoch will contribute huge quantities of people into heaven. Therefore the major characteristic that will be the same for three out of the four Epochs is that the Earth will be full of inhabitants before each Epoch's cataclysmic end. Then God will begin again.

The Four Epochs are these:

1. The Creation to the Flood.
2. The Flood to the advent of Jesus (His first coming).
3. The First Coming of Jesus to the Second Coming of Christ.
4. The Second Coming of Christ to the end of the Earth.

<u>Epoch 1 - The Creation to the Flood</u>.

This epoch, so far as we can inaccurately calculate, lasted between 1800 years and 3800 years. I favour the former or thereabouts. The years, which are exactly the same as our years today, can only be calculated from the people listed in Genesis and added together. The difficulty in timing lies in translating a Hebrew word, which can either mean "became the father of" or "became the ancestor of". Hence the doubts.

The environmental characteristics of Epoch 1 were very different from that of today, and I wrote a bit about that in the last chapter. On day two of the Creation, God divided the water that covered the whole Earth horizontally into two, calling the bit in between "sky", and in which, on day five, the birds flew. So there was water above the atmosphere all around the Earth. The effect that this would have had on the earth would be to encase it in a greenhouse so the atmosphere would be stable throughout the Earth, with none of the high and low pressure air masses we now know trundling through. There would be no convection and therefore no clouds. Therefore no rain. In Genesis 2:5-6 it tells us that in Eden there was no rain, and plants were watered by mist, rivers and springs. There would be no rain throughout this Epoch until the Flood.

The temperature would be tropical throughout the Earth, and there would therefore be no ice caps. This is confirmed by coal seams found in the Arctic and Antarctic, which are all formed from tropical forest. The temperature variation would be daily as the sun came up and went down. But it was never large enough to create convection in the stable global high pressure situation.

For the same reason there would be little or no wind. Nowadays, wind is caused by pressure differences in air masses caused by temperature differences across the surfaces of the Earth. But the Coriolis Effect means that the wind cannot go in a straight line from high pressure to low pressure, but goes round in circles due to the rotation of the Earth. In the northern hemisphere, the wind blows anti-clockwise round a low pressure, and clockwise round a high. But in Epoch 1 there were no vast temperature differences, no high or low pressure areas, and therefore no wind. The first mention of wind in the Bible is after the flood when God introduced today's weather systems.

Now Epoch 1's weather pattern had a significant effect on the earth. All the things that bring ageing to man, plants and animals today were almost absent in those days. Cosmic radiation from the Sun today is bombarding us all the time. Like the gamma radiation from nuclear fission, it decays the body, and is the most significant facet of ageing. Take a Geiger counter outside and you can hear the radiation bleeping at us at about two every second.

But the water canopy will have filtered most of that out. In addition, the canopy will have filtered out the majority of the ultraviolet radiation coming from the Sun. Ultraviolet burns and ages the skin and is a prime source of skin cancer. Thirdly, the canopy created a constant temperature throughout the Earth, with only a few degrees daily variation from the Sun's heating of the land mass. Today human bodies have to cope with temperature ranges of, on average, minus 20°C to plus 50°C, depending on what part of the Earth one lives. These three major ageing factors of today's living beings were absent in Epoch 1.

Consequently, we read of 900+ years being the normal age span of antediluvian (pre-Flood) man. There is no scientific reason why this should not be true, given the environmental conditions. People have tried to argue a different length of day and year, but none of them work according to the record in Genesis. Skeletons of dinosaurs that grace our museums today would indicate huge ages for these creatures. Even today I am given to understand that reptiles never stop growing. If that was still true pre-Flood, then it is not surprising to see dinosaurs of such huge size, and, I would think, created by such huge ages.

One can still see a pattern of this in the Amazon or any tropical forest. There the tree canopy also shields the life beneath it from all the radiations, and one finds butterflies as large as dinner plates and Anacondas 20 to 30 metres long. Enormous.

Now, if human beings lived for 900+ years, just how many children could they "beget" in that time? We have no record of numbers of offspring, only that they had "sons and daughters". I favour the length of Epoch 1 to be more towards the 1800 year mark than more because there would have been a population explosion. If couples started producing children at, say, 30, and stopped, say, at 700, having one baby every two years, each couple could have 335 children in their lifetimes (a conservative estimate). Clearly brothers and sisters married in the first few generations. If we did that today we would find genetic anomalies occurring, but in those days the gene pool would be strong and the genes robust. It is constant interbreeding that causes the anomalies, as we find today with dogs and horses. So what am I saying? That the Earth would be full of people in 1800 years - up in the billions. I speculate that one of the reasons why the Flood came (from above!) was that the world had become overpopulated and God needed to change the population by bringing a paradigm shift.

The reason given in the Bible was the wickedness of people. "The Lord was grieved that he had made man on the Earth, and his heart was filled with pain" (Genesis 6:6), because "the Lord saw how great man's wickedness on the earth had become, and that every inclination of the thoughts of his heart was only evil all the time." Very sad. So God destroyed the earth and all the animals and people except Noah's eight and the animals in the Ark.

So why was man's heart only evil all the time? Surely they saw how wonderful the Creation was, and therefore their Creator? Apparently not. They lived in a tropical paradise; were they not grateful? Apparently not. Was there nothing to restrain their wickedness? Apparently not. So what does restrain wickedness? That is the $40,000 question!

There are two things that restrain evil, according to the New Testament. What are they? The Holy Spirit and Law (see the chapter on Righteousness).

In Epoch 1, few listened to the Holy Spirit, and all those who did are recorded in the genealogy of good men in Genesis 5, ending up with Noah, who "found grace in the eyes of the Lord." In his generation he was almost the only one. He was "a preacher of righteousness", and had 100 years of opportunity as he built the Ark. When he told people that it would rain, they, perfectly understandably, had no idea what he was talking about. There had never been any rain in living memory.

So what about Law? Galatians tells us that Law restrains evil. So wasn't there Law in those days? Only one. And that had been broken by Adam and Eve in Eden. So there were no laws, no rules, no guidance for good and evil behaviour, no restraints. The result? Anarchy. Everybody did their own thing, and the inclination of the thoughts of their hearts was only evil continually.

So God destroyed them all, bringing down from above the water that He had separated on day 2, so that the whole Earth was once again covered with water as in Genesis 1:2. He then used water and tectonic energy to reform the land. He had to scoop out the oceans and plonk mountains on the land mass so that Noah and his three sons had land on which to start again. Remember – Water is a *very* efficient earth mover. One cubic metre of water weighs a tonne!

One has to ask how many people God was able to claim from this period for His Bride? Only those good ones mentioned in Genesis 5 and Noah and his three sons and their wives? That would be very few from the billions that must have filled the Earth by the time the Flood came. There seemed to be nothing that would encourage them to come to God. Even Noah, righteous man that he was, was ignored and ridiculed. But we have a window in the New Testament. In 1 Peter 3 we are told that when Jesus was in transit between his death and resurrection, He went and preached to those who had been alive in the days of Noah (and obviously still alive in spirit). So these people are the only ones I can find in scripture who were given a second chance – as I have already pointed out. And, hopefully, preferably, there will be many from Epoch 1 whom we will have as companions in the Bride other than the dozen or so nominated as good and godly in Genesis.

Epoch 2 – The Flood to the First Coming of Christ.

The environmental conditions of Epoch 2, so important and different from Epoch 1, were what they are today. The collapse of the water canopy enabled God to change Earth's environment. This released the cosmic radiation and other ageing factors to reduce the life span, first of all to 120, then to 70 (Psalm 90). So we had a situation where fewer people inhabited the planet, and the population increased far slower.

Even though Noah and his three sons were righteous, godly people, their nurture had been in Anarchy. It would certainly not take satan long to stimulate them again to selfish acts of violence and wickedness. Therefore God had to introduce a system into the new Epoch that would restrain the evil. Having promised never to flood the earth again, God could not allow man to be 100% anarchical. So what did God use to slow the wickedness down? It was not yet time for the Holy Spirit to be fully released onto mankind. So God introduced the other restraining agent. Law. Rom 5:13 is so very clear: "For before the law was given, sin was in the world. But sin is not taken into account when there is no law."

One of the first things God did to the eight as they emerged from the Ark was to give them rules to live by. Genesis 9:1-6 were the first. And since all human beings came from Noah and his three sons, all were "under the law" from then on. The history and development of the nations is lost in the mists of antiquity, but when they emerged (represented by their histories recorded in writing), every nation had its own law code and its rules and regulations. Law governed mankind from the Flood onwards. Eventually God gave Moses a perfect set of laws through Israel, but a general set of Laws were incorporated into all cultures from Noah, as was the universal principle of Law.

So how does Law restrain evil? Very simply, through guilt. God built a conscience into every person, and that conscience is stimulated by law. Law sets a perfect standard for behaviour. Because no human being is perfect, the breaking of the Law generated guilt. One of the Holy Spirit's tasks is to convict men of sin (John 16). Before Law came in, the Holy Spirit had nothing to bite on. Now He had. It could not have been long before authorities also recognised this brilliant method of controlling their population, and it would not have been long before they used it as a lever of control and introduced punishment. "You will not drive faster than 30 miles an hour in a built up area, but if you do we will fine you and knock points off your licence." So not only would guilt control people, the fear of official reprisal would also bring restraint. All of us from our earliest childhood are conscious of Law as the overriding and controlling authority over our lives. It started after the Flood.

The New Testament comments on the purpose of Law. It says there are four purposes:

1. To expose sin. "Through the law comes knowledge of sin" (Romans 3: 20).

2. To restrain evil. "We were held prisoners by the law, locked up until faith should be revealed." (Galatians 3: 23).

3. To enable wrath (God's anger). "Law brings wrath." (Romans 4: 15).

4. To lead us to Christ. "So the law was put in charge to lead us to Christ that we might be justified by faith." (Galatians 3: 24).

It is *so* important for us all to realise that Law can never make a person good. All it does is condemn, and thereby restrain evil. This fact is beautifully and succinctly encapsulated by Paul in Galatians where he says: "For if a law had been given that could impart life, then righteousness would certainly have come by the law." (Gal 3:21).

But that was not known throughout Epoch 2. The consequence was that because Law was so condemnatory and men couldn't stand it, some tried to align themselves with it. By human effort they attempted to become righteous according to the Law. This culminated in the teaching and behaviour of the Pharisees of Jesus' day. It was as if God had planned the very worst people to be present when Jesus was around. We now call this approach to righteousness Legalism.

But there are some things that need to be said about Law that are good. Associated with Law are four other things. There is Authority, Justice, Punishment, and Righteousness. Without Law there would be none of these four. These four make up the legislature of every nation today. It seemed as if there was no one in authority in Epoch 1. But in Epoch 2 nations emerged (particularly after the creation of different languages at Babel), and they formed their own societies with their own structures. No Law, no structure. But with Law came Authority and Rulership. With Authority came a legal system. With that system came accountability. With accountability came Trial, Righteousness according to their Law and Justice.

So how does Law "lead us to Christ?" Let's see how it works for the good of the Gospel - and it still does. If the Justice is fair and impartial, then the nation lives in peace. People are then free to worship Jesus. If the Justice is unfair, corrupt, too harsh, or too weak, it breeds rebellion and discontent in a nation. If that prevails, people will turn to Jesus for help to endure it or combat it.

If the Legal system is good, then Righteousness according to the Law prevails. Everyone breaks that Law at different times, some deliberately and some unintentionally. Whichever way it is, God uses it through conviction of sin through conscience to enable the Holy Spirit to draw people to Christ.

If the Authority is good and fair, then people are free to worship Jesus. If the Authority is oppressive, dictatorial or corrupt it will drive people to Christ. In communist Russia in the 20th century the oppression of that atheistic regime, instead of destroying the Christianity they hated so much, actually promoted it. Moreover, it was that same Christianity that destroyed their communism by peaceful means.

So, Christian parents – bring your children under Law. Bring them under fair, reasonable and consistent rules, because Law is the schoolmaster that leads them to Christ. And pray that the Father will draw them to Jesus. To bring them up under Grace releases them into anarchy. To be too strict with them leads them into legalism. Both lead to rebellion against all authority, including you. But good, fair, consistent law with clearly defined boundaries and prayer lead them to Jesus. There is no other way.

So, whichever aspect of Law one takes, all of it is used by God to bring people to Christ. But Christ was not available in Epoch 2 (although one can still see the principal working through the righteous and Godly Daniel, bringing the tyrant Nebuchadnezzar to God).

So, with the slowing-down of population growth and the advent of Law, Epoch 2 lasted from the Flood to Christ. Its major characteristic was Law leading to Legalism.

Epoch 3 – The First to the Second Coming of Christ.

God never repeats himself; He doesn't need to. So what He has done in the Third Epoch is to bring to birth a world within a world. We are still living in Epoch 3.

The world of Epoch 2 was successful in that it curbed Anarchy. Also, the population increase was slow enough such that God did not need to erase mankind and start again. It would continue to grow until the end of Epoch 3, when the land will once again have to be cleared of people so that God can start a new population drive. It is almost as if God has divided Epoch 2 down the middle by the advent of Jesus.

So, the Rule of Law still applies in Epoch 3 - as we well know. All the advantages of Law still exist and also still apply. But now there is a spiritual infusion into the Rule of Law. Law works well to curb Anarchy. But it leads either to despair or Legalism, depending on the character and stability of the individual. So Law is good, but it fails: it cannot bring Life.

The cross of Jesus was remarkable in every way, and I have written much about it elsewhere. For this chapter, therefore, I will examine only its bare bones. What Jesus did was to offer to all mankind the potential to be released from both the bondage of Legalism and the obscenity of Anarchy. Jesus introduced a "parallel universe" such that people living in the same bodies and in an unchanged environment may be freed from the burdens brought on by being born a human. The Church, magnificent concept and creation that she is, is being brought into existence soul by soul from the mass and mess of humanity and under the very nose of satan. He must be furious! And it was partly his own fault, for if he had known what would have happened, he "would never have crucified the Lord of glory." (1 Corinthians 2:8).

So what is God's new doorway for Christian living in this third Epoch? What is this new lifestyle? Very simply it is: "By Grace alone through Faith alone." The *whole* of our salvation (past, present and future) is by God's Grace alone, and man *cannot* add anything to it. Grace was the great Revelation that Jesus brought, and I have already written about it. It is appropriated, according to hundreds of statements in the New Testament, only by Faith in Jesus Christ.

This creation, the first creation, was "inch-perfect" and microscopically complete. The New Creation will be as accurate and as perfectly complete as this one was. Not even God can improve on perfect! Therefore the New Creation will, of necessity, be *different* but still perfect in its differences. That perfection includes the redemption. So Jesus has begun His New Creation by dealing with the problem of the old creation – man. Then one day He will build a new cosmos around the New Man He has redeemed, when once the Bride of Christ is complete. The provisions Jesus has made for the New Man who will run God's New Creation are therefore perfect. He has erased every barrier - all sin, all Law, all death, all separation from God. He has established a perfect New Way for the New Man to act perfectly and completely, in peace, without strain or hassle and with ease. That New Way is "By Grace alone through Faith alone". Or by the Holy Spirit's Revelation received by faith. (It's the same thing). And this New Way will therefore be the new and permanent lifestyle of the New Creation from now until it is finally completed and then on into eternity forever. Man Mark 2 is a new man after the model of Adam Mark 2 - Jesus (see 1 Corinthians 15:45).

So let's skip to the end of this Epoch.

Satan's fury knows no bounds. At the end of Epoch 3 he is going to emerge from the shadows and bring devastation and disaster to mankind, because he hates God and his Church, and "because he knows his time is short." His exposure will emerge in human form, and that person the Bible describes as the Antichrist will be satan in human flesh, a demonic parallel to God in human flesh - Jesus. The entire world will worship him, and the entire world will "believe the lie" (whatever that will be). All, that is, but the Christian Church and the Jews. For both of those, either protection or extreme persecution is prophesied, and then the end will come.

Many biblical students, as well as many others on earth, have an addictive fascination for the things of the future, and the things leading to the Second Coming of Jesus. Me too. It was the first thing I seriously studied as a young Christian. After many years of trying to piece it all together, I came to the conclusion that the "What" was mainly obvious, but the "When" was hidden from us. All the way through, the *sequences* of events were unclear. God has hidden them until the time when Revelation will be needed, and He will teach those living then how to interpret correctly the signs of the times. The best and least speculative book I have read on biblical prophecy of the end times is by David Pawson, and is titled "When Jesus Returns". I commend it to you as a beautiful analysis of every Bible student's speculations, and a clear analysis of what he thinks the Bible steers us towards best. I agree with his conclusions, and have done so from my earliest studies all those decades ago. If you want to know my position, read that book.

Before looking at that Second Coming, it is worth pointing out that both Legalism and Anarchy are in our genes. In every human being, Christian or other. Mankind has had a non-stop existence since Adam, and therefore the perceptions of our ancestors are incorporated in our psyches (souls). Every single one of us will find rebellion based on Anarchy very easy to come by. We will also find Legalism - Righteousness by self effort - a very common way of life. Both are the two mainstream ways in which self-centredness expresses itself in human behaviour. The only alternative lifestyle to these two is surrender to Christ, and to live under the shadow of the Almighty (see my chapter on Righteousness). Jesus is the only person who can curb self-centredness in human beings. No other philosophy or religion is able to deal with its root inside. Christians also need to beware - the vestiges of Anarchy and Legalism take a lifetime to eradicate from us, and we will meet them both, not only throughout the Christian Church, but particularly in ourselves.

People talk about Adam being a myth. But think about this: where did the sin in all mankind come from? Where did death in all mankind come from? How come 100% of humans are born with both? Apart from Jesus, can anyone find another source of humankind than procreation? If a monkey mutated into a human being, wouldn't there have to have been two? Or more? And if procreation is the only known, scientific way of producing human beings, shouldn't there have been a first pair? And a pair in which both sin and death were inherent, and which 100% of their descendants has inherited? So why is it so difficult to believe in a real Adam and a real Eve?

Now - I accept that there are many "interpretations" of the chapters in Revelation and other books on the Second Coming and the Millennium. What I have written is a skim across the top and is my simple acceptance of how I see what it says. If you disagree with me, please don't get up, throw this book into the bin, consider me an idiot, and spread negatives about me from then on – as is the habit of some Christians. I think you will agree with the "what", but you might disagree with the sequence. So please don't lose the major thrust of this chapter or this book because you disagree with my position!

So let me be bold and invite disagreement. I have space here to say that I believe Christians will go through what is commonly known as The Great Tribulation, through the reign of Antichrist and through mega persecution, where they (we) will either be martyred or "kept". As I see it, that time is not the time of God's anger, but satan's. Then they will be "Raptured" at the very coming of Jesus. If I am right, I (and you?) will be prepared for it. If I am wrong, and we are raptured before that persecution, then goodie – it will be very good to have been wrong. But if I am right, then I will not be taken unawares by bad events. Moreover, whichever position we hold as to the timing of it all, *none* of them are absolutely watertight. Hence the debates. So adopt the "interpretation" that will enable you consistently to walk confidently with Jesus, *regardless* of what happens. Isn't that a wise position to hold? Did He not say, "When the Son of Man comes, will He find faith on the earth?" (Luke 18:8). Yours?

The Second Coming of Jesus will be catastrophic. It will be sudden, unanticipated and immediate. Jesus will appear in the clouds of heaven in great glory and every eye will see him, and He warned us it will be when we least expect it. He comes with all his angels and all the redeemed. The first thing that happens is that all God's people who have previously died will receive resurrection bodies, instantly manufactured from Earth to join their owners in the sky. The second thing, immediately after the first, is that Christians (and some Jews?) still alive on earth will have their earthly bodies transformed into resurrection bodies, and they will fly up to join their fellow Christians in the sky. The third thing is that Jesus will destroy the Antichrist and all his armies with the sword that comes out of His mouth and with the brightness of His Coming. He will then descend to the Mount of Olives outside Jerusalem from which He ascended 2000+ years before. There will be all kinds of geological rearrangements made to the Jerusalem area, and Jesus will enter through the (now sealed) Golden Gate to rescue the trapped and besieged remainder of the Jews as their Messiah.

Jesus' Second Coming marks the end of Epoch 3. The vast majority of the world's population will have been removed by it - either into heaven by resurrection or into the lake of sulphur.

Epoch 4 – The Second Coming of Christ to the end of the World.

The 4th Epoch lasts 1000 years, and is often known as the millennium. The population will be changed once more, as will the environmental conditions. So will the spiritual atmosphere. Let's look at them one at a time.

Who will be living on earth then? One bunch has flown upwards; a second bunch has zoomed downwards; so who are the bunch that are left? Ordinary human beings who were living in Epoch 3. They will not have been Christians, nor will they have joined the army of the Antichrist. Their commitment will not have been either to the good or the bad. The whole of their condition is given to us by Jesus in Matthew 25, which is *not* a parable. It is often called the Parable of the Sheep and the Goats, but it is a prophecy of reality. Firstly, Jesus sets the scene. "When the Son of man comes in his glory, and all the angels with him, he will sit on his throne in heavenly glory." That makes it unambiguously clear when this scenario is going to be played out – right after His Second Coming. The division between sheep on Jesus' right hand and goats on His left is made specifically clear in explicit detail. During the persecution of the Antichrist against Christians and Jews here described by Jesus as his "brothers", the sheep are those who surreptitiously helped those persecuted - hungry, thirsty, estranged, naked, sick, imprisoned. The goats are those who had the opportunity to help them, and chose not to. The goats are banished into hell, and the sheep are given a further chance. Because they helped those distressed Christians they will be granted the privilege of living on the earth for 1000 years more.

Let's move to the environment. The present environmental system is entropy - everything decaying to chaos (see chapter 12). But in Romans 8 and there only, God tells us that when the Sons of God receive their resurrection bodies, then also the creation will be set free from its bondage to decay. Entropy will disappear. Not only will the creation be prolific in its growth, but the human beings will also be prolific in their growth. They will grow up but not grow old. All the present decay we now see in old age will be absent. Indeed, the "sheep" will all last 1000 more years. There will be no death. The Utopia that many people have longed for and dreamed about will at last be here. The scientific details of how God will accomplish this is a matter of conjecture.

The spiritual atmosphere will also be radically different. Firstly, satan will be banished to his bottomless pit until the end. That means no temptation and no sin. Fantastic! What an era that will be! Secondly, Jesus will personally reign from His throne in Jerusalem. Thirdly, all Christians with resurrection bodies will have access to earth, and, presumably, be able to walk through walls like Jesus did. This is particularly true of Christian martyrs (Revelation 20:4). Because there will be no fear, wickedness or secrecy among any of the old-style humans, the intrusion of a Son of God will presumably be welcomed. That is my speculation. Suffice it to say that many completed Christians will have access to earth and its people. It will be paradise.

What about the people? They will work as we now do, but under the Benevolent Government of Jesus, in righteousness and prosperity. And the population? That will increase to Earth's capacity over the 1000 years. See this - if the earth could be filled in 1800 years in Epoch 1 by people living for 900 years, how exponential will the population growth be if people lived for 1000 years, their capacity for reproduction never decayed, and there were no deaths whatsoever? There will be no wars, no sickness and no deaths caused by natural disasters.

It seems to me that in three of the Epochs, 1, 3 and 4, the end is roughly gauged by the fact that the Earth's population will have reached saturation for Earth's capacity to support it.

Now these people in the millennium, apart from the "sheep", will not have known temptation. Their allegiance to Jesus will be total because they will know no other. But for His Bride, Jesus will always require choice. So, somehow, these people in Epoch 4 will need the opportunity to choose between good and evil.

That choice will be given them at the end of the 1000 years. Satan will be released from his bottomless pit, and will tempt the people. There is only one scriptural section for this (Revelation 20:7-10), and it tells a little of how he will do it. But then fire will come down from heaven and consume satan and his new army.

Then will the end come. Earth will be burnt up by fire (2 Peter 3:7), and the heavens rolled up like a scroll. God will create new heavens and a new earth. Judgment will take place for all people through the Epochs from Adam to the end. There will then be the Marriage Supper of the lamb. And, I presume, Time will then be no more.

Then the Real Story of the universe will begin. The four Epochs of this Earth's history is the pre-run, the school, the preparation for the Real Thing that God has in mind. The Bride of Christ will reign over the new universe alongside her Lord and King, Jesus. Who can tell what wonders God has planned into eternity for those who love Him?

SUMMARY

The whole history of earth is divided into 4 epochs. The single purpose of the earth's millennia is to be the womb in which God is conceiving and forming the Bride of Christ.

Chapter 11
DEATH.

The real mark of genius is, in my view, the ability to be able to put the most complex things simply. People who have a full appreciation of a subject, can see through the minutiae, go to the root and describe it such that a child can understand it – that is genius. God is the best at it. This is why His words to us are so short and pithy, but contain everything necessary for us to know at that point in time. Thus God's summary of the universe (the whole purpose of the creation and the working of it all) can be summarised in one word – Jesus. The Bible tells us that everything was made by Jesus and for Jesus. He is the first cause of all things, is holding all things together, and will complete all things (Col 1). The universe *is* Jesus. Jesus *is* the universe, and much more besides.

That is by way of saying that, because I am not a genius, this chapter is likely to be confusing to all who read it. I do pray that you will get something sensible out of it.

When God (through Jesus) created the earth and its cosmic wrapping, He created it perfect and perfectly good. There was not one negative thing in it at all. Lucifer became the focus of negativity in the heavenly places when he wanted to be bigger than God. Even then, negativity still did not enter the created order – only the heavenly order.

God's command to Adam and Eve in Eden not to eat the fruit of the Tree of the Knowledge of Good and Evil contained one single consequence – Death. Because Adam decided to eat of it, it was he who introduced negativity into earth and its cosmic coat. That negativity is summarised in this one word Death. Most would agree so far.

So what is Death? My simple definition is Separation. That definition will help us to understand it easier. Otherwise we arrive at the following complicated concepts: Death parts us from life but not from existence, parts us from God but doesn't, parts us from ourselves but doesn't, parts us from each other but doesn't, and does not mean what people normally take it mean.

So what do people normally take it to mean? The normal definition of death is "cease to exist". There are many philosophers who have come to that conclusion, and have broadcast their views onto the general public. This is why the majority of people find that physical death is such a disaster. People think that this world is all there is, and when we die, existence gets snuffed out altogether. Therefore to lose a loved one is a mega disaster, and bereavement (good and healthy that the process is) can be permanently terminal. But that view is part of the negativity of this world.

The Bible view is very different. Physical death is merely a separation of the person from their body. Their soul and spirit move on into the realm of the Spirit, because the chain that held them to the earth (their bodies) has ceased to function. The body dies. They don't. They do not cease to exist; they have simply moved to another country where we can no longer contact them. Jesus said that between us and them "a great chasm has been fixed so that those who want to go from here cannot, nor can anyone cross over from there to us." (Luke 16:26). But let me not minimise physical death, as if it is a small thing. It is not. Jesus said "Greater love has no one than this, that he lay down his life for his friends." To view death as immaterial is a terrible thing. Imagine how you would feel if your life was cut short in your prime. All those things that you dreamed you would do on earth will have gone for ever. Life is indeed very precious and there is an instinct built into every human to preserve their lives. There should also be an instinct in everyone's life to preserve other lives also. (Please note that the digital games children play today that involves killing hundreds of humans just for fun breeds an attitude of inconsequence to killing and death. That kind of input is *very* dangerous, especially to the young).

But death is not the end. Heaven is the end. There is more beyond earth that we can only dream about, and we do best to carry with us on earth the promises of those who have insight into such matters, and particularly of Jesus. Why Jesus? He went through physical death and came back again. In my view, that makes His philosophies more valid than anyone else's in the world. Neither Mohammed nor Buddha nor Confucius came back to earth after they had died. Jesus is unique – the only one. Therefore He needs to be listened to more than everyone else in the universe.

So, what exactly did God mean when He said to Adam in Eden "In the day you eat of it you will surely die"? We, perfect in retrospect, know now that He meant spiritual death as well as physical. What is that? Spiritual death means to be cut off from the Life of the Spirit. Yet it cannot mean that completely. Why? Because human beings are spiritual creatures as well as physical. Adam didn't "cease to exist spiritually" when he ate the fruit, but he did die spiritually. The beginnings of *physical* death started then, and 930 years later that came to completion. But he died spiritually then too. That is, he was cut off from that intimate fellowship with God that he had enjoyed in the garden. They were separated.

The fact that we have inherited all of Adam's Sin means that we have also been cut off from God from birth, but not cut off from being spirit beings. We cannot stop being spirit beings, any more than we can cease to be humans. We are who we were born to be. So we are spiritually dead but spiritually still existing. (Spiritually dead but still spiritually alive!). (This is why I say that we need to get our definitions and distinctions right).

So, we are physically dying and destined for bodily death, but still alive. How does that work out? It means that we have to define the base from which we are talking. Death relative to what? Life relative to what?

If we look at death as a separation, then we can see that death relative to the separation of body from soul means that we can define death from that perspective. So to say that we are dying means that we are all moving towards the day when that separation occurs. We are a dying species and I am a dying person. Separation from our bodies also means separation from all that is tied into that body – earth. So physical death separates us from our bodies and from this earth.

Taking that base then, Life is defined as union with this body and the earth. That makes sense. Life is union, death is separation. I am alive relative to earth and all that it contains so long as I remain in union with my body. That is, so long as I have not yet died. That is straight forward enough.

So let's retain that principle and talk about the spirit realm. Death would then be related to the Life that is in that realm. What is that? So far as I read my Bible, *zoë* Life comes from God and is God (*zoë* is the Greek word for God's kind of Life as opposed to biological life *bios*). So everything that is in union with God is Life, and everything that is in separation from God is death. More of which in a moment.

But do you see that, by that definition and that base, Life and death in the spirit realm differ little from life and death in the physical realm because neither define the realms themselves. They only define our relationship with each of those realms. That is, in relation to this earth I am alive or dead as I am in union with or in separation from it, and in relation to the spiritual realm I am alive or dead as I am in union with or in separation from God. Being alive or dead in either case in no way affects either the existence or the reality of either realm.

I find it very interesting that human beings are fascinated by the spirit realm. They are addicted to it, and we can see the extent of that as we look at the Sci-Fi market. People love dreaming about "What is out there". Moreover, they are spiritual addicts, and every tribe and nation on earth has a tradition or practice of religion of some kind or other, ranging from the fully pagan, through the demonic to Christ. (Even Evolution is a religion). Does that not tell us that the spirit realm certainly exists, and although it is full of mysteries, it cannot be destroyed or ignored? Indeed its mysteries serve to make it more juicy and addictive. People long to know for sure "What is out there", and I think Jesus has the only sensible and confirmed answer. Indeed, that is why He came to earth – to tell us what Heaven is like and how to get there.

Back to this relationship in the spirit realm relative to God. That the spirit realm exists few query. There is no other way in which to account for man's fascination with it. Here on earth we can fill our minds and our days with many things that have no relationship with God at all. We therefore think that it will be the same in the spirit realm. But I think not. So far as I can read, *everything* in the spirit realm is God related. He is the fullness of it and nothing in it falls outside His jurisdiction, knowledge and influence. He fills every nook and cranny, and no one can escape from Him there. I think that is why, in that realm, angels are either fully good or fully bad. They are either in union with God or in separation from Him. That is, they are either dead or alive. (You will note that that does not mean that the dead ones do not exist, or that the spirit realm in which they live does not exist. It means that they are fully evil, and have no vestige of good in them whatever).

If that is so (and the Bible assures me it is), then what of man when he gets there, when his soul separates from his body here on earth? Immediately the choices that his soul made while here on earth kick in 100%. They polarise. If, while here on earth, he lived in union with God, however thinly, then the union becomes 100% Life as he separates from his body. If, on the other hand, he lived in separation from God while here on earth, then the separation becomes 100% Death up there as he loses his body. Choices on *earth* matter in the spirit realm because we are spirit creatures, and we will be the same persons up there as we are down here. We will polarise 100% either way when we get there, but we are still the same people all through our existence from the day we were born on earth.

So, when we get to the realm of the spirit, we will find ourselves instantaneously Dead or Alive. All the philosophies of earth, intriguing though they might be, become useless and nonsense in the spirit realm. The only thing that matters is whether we have a relationship with the God who has revealed

Himself in Jesus. No other God will do. Why am I so exclusive about Jesus? No other god has dealt so absolutely with the sin that separates us from the beginning from a good relationship with any god. Only Jesus. I have fellowship with the real and true God as I access Him through Jesus. The Bible is very clear about that.

That definition of death and life applies here on earth too. If I have a living relationship with the God of Jesus here on earth, I have Life. If I don't (which state every human being is in from birth), I am dead. From birth I am alive as I relate to the earthly realm, but dead as I relate to the spirit realm. There are millions of people walking this earth today who remain in their birth position, and are both alive and dead. There are others (I feel we are a minority, but I cannot be certain of that) who are alive and alive.

Even entropy is a kind of death. It is a separation from energy, and from all that is whole and ordered.

So God ordained death as a result of Adam's choice of disobedience.

Now see this wonderful thing, God *uses* Death as a means whereby Life can be restored. God has a secondary use for the death Adam chose. This comes in two forms.

The first form is in Jesus. God used the death of Jesus as the means whereby a relationship with Him can be restored to any man who is living in death. The death of Jesus neutralised and removed the barrier that divided man from God, so that, in principle, every single human being on earth has the opportunity for his relationship with God to be restored. God used death to defeat death.

The second form is in man. In order for the death of Jesus to become effective in a person's life, they have to die. Not physically. But to themselves. I have to die to the sovereignty I have over my own existence. That is, I deliberately, as a matter of personal choice, separate myself from the responsibility of ever making any more decisions for my own destiny, and hand that over to Jesus. Handing it over to Jesus brings me into Life – that is, I come into a personal relationship with God through Him. I yield to Him in all things and for all things. As I continue to do that, my existence becomes one of constant Death and constant Life – constant death to myself and constantly appropriating the Life of Jesus.

This makes sense of many of the words of Jesus, which otherwise would be nonsense. For example:

> "He who believes in me will live, even though he dies; and whoever lives and believes in me will never die. Do you believe this?" (John 11:25-26)

> "I tell you the truth, a time is coming and has now come when the dead will hear the voice of he Son of God and those who hear will live." (Jon 5:25)

> "If anyone would come after me, he must deny himself and take up his cross daily and follow me. And anyone who does not carry his cross and follow me cannot be my disciple." (Luke 9:23, 14:27)

Or see the writings of Paul:

> "For we know that since Christ was raised from the dead, he cannot die again; death no longer has mastery over him. The death he died, he died to sin once for all; but the life he lives, he lives to God" (Rom 6:9-10)

> "For if you live according to the sinful nature, you will die; but if by the Spirit you put to death the misdeeds of the body, you will live." (Rom 8:13)

If you catch the point I am trying to make about death being relative to different things, and that there are two kinds of Life and two kinds of Death, then all these scriptures make perfect sense.

The Bible makes much of death, and many of its statements relate to the spiritual death experienced outside a healthy relationship with God in Jesus. Let us see the sequence of logic that the Bible makes clear.

Death is the consequence of sin. Sin is the consequence of Law. "The sting of death is sin, and the power of sin is the law. But thanks be to God! He gives us the victory through our Lord Jesus Christ." (1 Cor 15).

The majesty of the redemption brought by Jesus is that it delivers us from the bondage of the law, the awful separation caused by sin, and from the disaster of death. All three.

But there is another death that we need to observe. It is less important but just as valid. It is our relationship with other people. In the same way that death to myself opens the door to a relationship with Jesus called Life, death to my own selfishness opens the door to a good relationship with other people. Indeed, I cannot have a good relationship with anyone else unless death to my selfishness is involved.

It is the key to a happy marriage – I have to die to my selfishness if I am going to keep my marriage beautiful. It is the key to opening up myself to others; every time I stop and talk to someone I have to die a little bit more to my own agenda. Every time I invite someone into my house I have to die to another selfish agenda. If I want friends on this earth, I have to die to my self-centredness. To cling to myself is to become poor indeed. To die to myself is to become rich indeed. It is another application of the thing Jesus said:

> "For everyone who has will be given more, and he will have an abundance. Whoever does not have, even what he has will be taken from him." (Matt 25:29)

That statement applies to myself (Do I want Life or am I happy living in Death?), applies to my relationship with God (Do I want heaven or hell when I die?), it applies to earth (Do I want to retain my existence or lose it?), and it applies to friends (Do I want friends in my life or do I want to live an isolated and lonely existence?). If we want what is the best in each case, we have to die to get it.

Adam chose death and bequeathed it to us all. Physical death has become the dread of all mankind, and it is what the Bible calls "The last enemy" (1 Cor 15:26). God has done this extraordinary thing: He has taken Adam's terrible choice and has transformed it into the pathway to the most blessed and delightful thing mankind could have. God uses death as the pathway to Life – but take care that you know in what senses you apply that statement.

It is through death that we gain life – each death relating to its individual form of life. Paul says that he dies daily. Through it he gains life daily. So let us follow his example.

SUMMARY

Death is separation, not annihilation. Life is fusion. Death separates man's spirit/soul from his body. It separates man from God and from other people. God used death in its various forms to be the channel for bringing Life to mankind through Jesus. Life is fusion with God.

Chapter 12
ENTROPY

Ken Pollard used to be a Physics teacher in a Secondary school. He now does DIY locally in Scunthorpe. I consider him famous for building and crashing his own aeroplane. He is a Trustee of the Peace and Hope Trust, working in Nicaragua with Mike Cole OBE, my friend.

We were ensconced together in my tent in a place called La Barra del Río Grande, at the mouth of that large central river in Nicaragua that drains into the Atlantic/Caribbean. We were demolishing and rebuilding the clinic that had been constructed by the Government some 6 years earlier. I was casually remarking how quickly things deteriorate in the fierce tropical climate. He casually replied "Entropy." This started a useful conversation and Revelation I have never forgotten. It was Revelation to me because although I had heard of the word I had no idea what it was and what it meant. He told me. It is the tendency of everything in the universe to decay and degrade to chaos. The dictionary definition is hopeless, so here is my friend Tony Langmead's: "In a closed system without an input of energy, disorder tends to increase. (That is, Entropy increases)." Entropy can only be slowed or stopped (but not for long) by the injection of energy. The scientific community has accepted that the whole universe is running down. Christians would add "to the disorder and chaos it was at the beginning".

This brought me to contemplate the degree of energy that God must have put in to change the chaos of Gen 1:2 to the order and beauty of Gen 1:31, where God saw what He had made and called it "very good". The atomic bomb would confirm to us that Einstein's formula $E=mc^2$ is correct. Energy = mass x the square of the speed of light, which goes on to tell me that the energy God put into the creation must have been unbelievably phenomenal. Science knows no effect greater than its cause, so

God must have energy much greater than the creation. If the present theories of cosmologists and physicists are correct, then our sun is a continuous chain reaction of nuclear fusion and fission. And, presumably, the billions of stars in our own Milky Way Galaxy, and the billions of galaxies in the universe are the same. The energy involved in all that creation is beyond our wildest dreams and way beyond our wildest calculations. How phenomenal therefore is God's restraint to hold Himself back toward us on this earth, enough to hide His immensity? But I digress. The creation cannot have had entropy. That which was perfect in every respect cannot have incorporated a law which deteriorates everything to decay and chaos.

So when was Entropy created? Hmmm. I'm not convinced it was actually "created". It's a bit like evil. I wonder if evil is not merely an automatic antithesis to good? That is, if good is absent, evil is inevitable, and takes the equal and opposite form of the good it replaces. So untruth is an inevitable opposite of truth. And deceit of integrity. Thus, if someone is not a person of integrity, they will automatically be deceitful. It can't be avoided. I recognise that Is 45:7 quotes God as saying "I create evil". But I wonder if what God actually created was opposites, such that everything in His creation was in balance? Like North and South poles of magnets? Or High and Low Pressures in Meteorology? But it's only a thought, and I wouldn't base a doctrine on it.

So where did satan get his evil from? Is 14 tells us exactly what happened to him; it is a succession of I, I, I, me, me, me. Ez 28 tells us that he was "The Guardian Cherub," and admired his own beauty and capabilities causing him to "go solo" and set up his own empire to try to replace God's. The cherubim are fearsome creatures (see their description in the first 10 chapters of Ezekiel), and are guardians of God's Throne. Lucifer was the chief. So he was the greatest created spirit being in the universe. Fearsome. Where did his evil come from? Well, my view is that God is a Trinity, a family. And all good and godly things flow from togetherness, unity, Oneness and family. So when someone breaks that unity and oneness and decides to "go it alone", the opposite of who the Trinity is, then the opposite of goodness kicks in. And because all the angels are perfect, then the opposite of goodness must have kicked in absolutely, instantaneously and perfectly with Lucifer, changing his name to devil – the accuser. One third of the angels thought he was the "bees knees" and joined his rebellion against God, which indicates they have choice like we do. So I think that satan "became" evil in a moment of time, transformed into The Devil immediately by rejecting God's perfect ways.

So where does this leave Entropy? I guess it came in at Genesis 3, with the fall of Man. But before I get there, I need to look at the authority structure God instigated on earth. It seems that God has placed an angelic being in charge of each heavenly body. He calls the host of heaven all by name, and calls the stars by name. He calls both stars and angels His Host, and each are named. I conclude that each star and each angel are intertwined. Nevertheless, what is very clear is that satan is the heavenly being in charge of the earth. He is the "Prince of the Power of the Air", and "god of this world." So God put His greatest created heavenly being in charge of His most important heavenly body – earth. Satan was supposed to be the liaison between man and God. According to Heb. 2, all angels are "ministers to those who are to be heirs of salvation." So man was designed to listen to satan and liaise with him.

Man, on the other hand, was given responsibility and rulership over the earth. He was to till the ground and subdue it. He was given rulership over the animals, hence God's requirement that he named them all, more of which in a moment. God warned Adam that if he was to eat the forbidden fruit (giving him and Eve choice), then death was inevitable. I put it that way because when they did eat it, they realised they were naked. That is, "other than perfectly good" kicked in automatically. (Have you never wondered why animals are not embarrassed about being naked?) So did guilt, and they hid from God. That is, death began to affect them immediately and automatically. It was an inevitable result of "non-goodness" and "other than family". Evil is the automatic antithesis of good.

Of course, satan deceived Eve. Deception is the inevitable result of self-centredness. And, of course, satan knew no other kind of temptation and negativity than that which he had himself embraced. This is why all human sin emanates from self-centredness. There is only one opposite to God and His (their) good life-style, and that is what both satan and man have embraced. Man loves wickedness and is addicted to disaster. So does satan. They both love it together. And that is what God calls "death". Everything that is the opposite of God and His life-style of love and togetherness in unity is death. So, when God confronted Adam and Eve with their wrong choice, He also gave them all sorts of other restrictions; woman would be subject to man and would bear children in pain; man would till the ground in sweat; the ground would produce thorns and thistles so that work would be hard from then on. And because man had been given responsibility over earth, when he sinned he brought death into the whole area of his responsibility – that is, earth. So death entered earth. And this, I believe, is what the scientists call "Entropy". Everything tends to decay, death and chaos. And if I have read it right, man's choice of sin affected the whole cosmos; everything, all creation, is running down towards chaos.

All the stars are decaying and running down – so cosmologists tell us. This tells me that both the heavens as well as the earth are subject to entropy. So we can presume that the entropy that kicked in to earth at the Fall also kicked in to the cosmos. The Lord gave me understanding on this. The first creation was made perfect in every way, and was designed to house a perfect Bride for Jesus. Everything God does is perfect and complete. It failed because Adam failed. At that very point, then, God downgraded this whole creation, to dump it eventually into the trash can. The whole environment having failed in its primary object, it was relegated to a temporary arrangement because of its imperfection. Man and his environment are One. A perfect man needs a perfect environment; an imperfect man needs an imperfect environment.

It still has to produce a Bride for Jesus, but now through the dual gateways of Decay/Death and Redemption. When the Bride is complete at the end of time, God will erase this whole creation and produce a second perfect one in which the Bride can operate in an environment like God originally intended. God is never lost for initiative. But this plan is pretty extravagant!

I guess because man is God's greatest created physical being, along with man goes all his choices. Certainly, all the problems on earth other than natural disasters are man-made. They don't come from trees or animals: We humans are still responsible for earth, and God holds us accountable, not just for everything we individually do with our lives, but for the whole earth too. We are its boss. So having thought through that background, we now come to the really interesting bit.

The way to reduce Entropy is with the application of energy. So, cars and aircraft need to continue to burn fuel to keep going. If you take your foot off the accelerator the car slows down; - Drag and friction = Entropy. You don't have to do anything at all for dust to accumulate on your mantelpiece – Entropy. But you have to inject energy regularly to clean it. And up at our La Barra clinic termites eat away at wooden structures and the fierce sun and rain rust out the corrugated iron. I have seen it, and calculated that gap at 9 years – a very short space of time. So, if we do nothing, death and decay are inevitable in everything we do and are. Even in our bodies Entropy is evident: we lose teeth, hair, vision, sound, muscular ability and power. God has said some important things against laziness and idleness, especially in Proverbs. On the other hand, God has made us workers – even as He is a worker. He has given us food and drink and sleep to renew our energy, and He says that diligence receives a reward on this earth.

Now – a salutary tale. When I was a cadet at Cranwell, the Assistant Commandant was Gp. Capt. (later Air Chief Marshal Sir Neil) Wheeler. He gave us an illustration from the aircraft we then flew at the College, the Vampire. If the (jet) engine quit, there was no point in trying to relight it above 30,000 ft. The density of the air was too low. Wait until it had descended to about 15,000ft and then relight it. The lesson he got from that was: - "There is no relight over 30." He then made the point that the pattern of our lives is established below that age, and there is no relight above it. If we establish diligence and hard work as a habit below that age, we will continue to be diligent and hard workers all through our lives. (And I can testify to the truth of that). On the other hand, if we let our lazy bodies take control of us before that age, we will be lazy people all our lives. So our task, Christian or non-Christian, is to inject energy into this earth in the areas for which we are gifted, and we will be battling against Entropy – decay, death, chaos – all the days of our lives. If there is to be order on this earth, then man has the responsibility to bring it about and the responsibility to do it. *We* bring order into chaos. Which leads me to another tale.

The story goes of a man wandering round a National Trust property. It was beautiful. He stopped at one of the gardeners and said, "Hasn't God made this garden beautifully?" The gardener tilted his cap back, rested his foot on his spade and said slowly. "To be shore, zur. But 'ee should 'a zeen it wen 'e 'ad it orl to 'isself." That's right. God gives us prolific abundance on this earth, but the partnership He has made with man is that man should subdue it into submission and bring it into order.

This applies to everyone in everything they are doing. From the humble maid dusting the furniture to the President of a nation – all are bringing order. Have you ever wondered why maids can never cease dusting the furniture, and Presidents never find final solutions to the difficulties they encounter either nationally or internationally? Entropy. Death, decay and chaos is the inevitable direction everything is travelling in, and doing nothing is the worst possible option. How we all long for a quiet life. "Eat, drink and be merry, for tomorrow we die." But if we take up that life-style, we will die a lot earlier than we expect or need to. Entropy can kill.

Have you ever thought how excellent Entropy is? If it wasn't for Entropy we wouldn't have anything to do. The house your grandfather built has deteriorated enough to be rebuilt; the house your father left you has to be maintained or redecorated. Every work on earth is altering and changing such that there is always more work to be done. Every new generation has work because Entropy has decayed the last generation's work. Or even yesterday's work. Isn't that good? How would we ever earn an income without Entropy?

The energy of *goodness* needs to be exercised continually to slow or stop the entropy of evil and wickedness. That is, the norm for all mankind is the entropy of sin. To combat it one has to inject the energy of goodness. Entropy applies in the moral realm as well as the physical realm.

It also applies in the spiritual realm. The norm for every human being still living on this earth is sin – even for those who have been redeemed. Satan is the god of this world, and the prevailing pressure is always downwards. As in the physical realm, entropy in my spirit can only be combated by the input of energy. That energy takes the form of personal choice. I must *choose* Jesus all day long every day of my life, and that choice overcomes the natural tendency to godlessness and self-direction. It is much easier to go my own way than to ask Jesus for His. And, do you see, to *do nothing* is *automatically* to decay my relationship with Jesus? As someone so cleverly put it, "One week without Jesus makes one weak"! Those of us who are spiritually sensitive will recognise that, even in one day, we can feel shoddy at the end of it if we just haven't bothered to communicate much with the Lord during it.

My charity called SIFT is injecting solutions into many of the conditions of the poor in Nicaragua. Will I ever get to the end of it? I'll certainly get to the end of each one of my projects because I am a finisher as well as a visionary. But I will never run out of projects. Would that half the UK and USA would inject energy into lovely Nicaragua with me!

I have diverted again. So the next question to ask is: "Will Entropy ever come to an end?" You might as well ask: "Will sin and evil ever come to an end?" because they are interlinked. Well, the answer to both is a resounding "Yes!" When Jesus deals with sin once and for all, then the inevitable result is that Entropy will disappear. We know precisely when sin will be banished from the earth – at the 2nd Coming of Jesus. There Jesus will appear in the clouds of heaven in power and great glory, accompanied by all who had previously died. Then both those and we who remain will receive resurrection bodies, all those who did not serve Jesus will be collecting a non-stop frying in a lake of burning sulphur (I hate even talking about it) and satan will be imprisoned in his bottomless pit. There will be no more sin for 1000 years, and Jesus will reign from Jerusalem with justice and righteousness. Now let me quote Rom. 8:21- 23:

> ".. in hope that the creation itself will be liberated from its bondage to decay and brought into the glorious freedom of the children of God. We know that the whole creation has been groaning as in the pains of childbirth right up to the present time. Not only so, but we ourselves, who have the first fruits of the Spirit, groan inwardly as we wait eagerly for our adoption as sons, the redemption of our bodies."

The whole creation groaning? Yes. The earth dislikes Entropy as much as we do (and we caused it!) The "adoption of the sons of God"? That's the moment we get an eternal, resurrection body. And the Creation? "Set free from its bondage to decay." There it is! Entropy gone for ever. It's true.

So, work hard, bring order, wait in confident expectation for that Day of Great Rejoicing to come, and hasten the day of the Lord. Work to get earth free from the chains we gave it.

SUMMARY

The whole cosmos is decaying to death and chaos (entropy). It can only be slowed by the injection of energy. At the Second Coming of Jesus, entropy will be erased by God.

Chapter 13

PLAYING WITH TIME.

I keep (and have kept) some scrapbooks. Lots of little Christian philosophies and revelations that God has given to others and that I couldn't possibly remember, I either copied them down or cut them out and pasted them into my books. I now have four, and I graze them irregularly. I would recommend this practice to all Christians; things that bless you as you read them are worth keeping, because they will bless you again in time to come. I learnt it from the Pastor under whom I was converted, and would like to pass on the practice to my readers. If you have never done it before, start today and keep alert for those little blessings in a literary form that enhance your life day by day.

That's by way of saying I copied down the following little ditty which I have modified a bit:

> In vain we call old notions fudge
> And bend our conscience to our sham;
> For our wasness will not will be
> If our isness is not am.

I admit I had to read it a couple of times before I understood it. But when I did I thought it was a corker, cut it out and kept it. It set my mind a-thinking. Some time later I came across 2 Corinthians 6:2 "Now is the time of God's favour, now is the day of salvation." The result of these two discoveries has produced the following meditation on Time.

At once I need to apologise; no language on earth has a vocabulary that covers timelessness. All our words are timed - past, present and future. Therefore I am going to struggle to convey, and you are going to struggle to understand exactly what I am getting at.

So let's start at the beginning.

God is outside of time. When Moses at Sinai in Exodus asked God what His name was, He said "I AM." That was the best way God could convey timelessness to mankind. Later in John 8 Jesus told the Pharisees, "I tell you the truth, before Abraham was, I Am."

Although the Bible says that God was, God is and God will be, and that Jesus is the same yesterday, today and for ever, it is using a human perspective of Time to give us understanding of timelessness. "Eternity" is *not* an awfully long time. Eternity is without Time - it is timelessness, and therefore unmeasurable, and is not describable from a timed earth. So let me give you a definition of eternity based on the above: "Eternity is the ever-present now."

Now this is a tricky paragraph. So sorry. I hope you get something sensible from it. Back in Genesis, God *was not*: He was I AM. At the end of the world, He *will not be:* He will still be I AM. When God spoke the heavens and earth into being, He AM. When He called Abram to be irresponsible and "go south and don't stop until I tell you," He AM. He is the same I AM that dreamed up 12 creative plagues for Moses to play with in Egypt, and to survive 2,000,000 people impossibly in deserts for 40 years. He's the same I AM that enabled David to defeat all those grotty Philistines. He's the same AM that enabled Solomon to be the wisest man who ever lived. He's the same AM who gave the prophets impossible prophetic insights into the future, and gave Daniel diplomacy. He's the same AM who filled 120 common people at Pentecost and thereby change the known world in their generation. He's the same AM who gave light and understanding to the Apostle Paul. He's the same AM who will wrap up the heavens and deal with all rebels with power and great glory at the end of time. He's the same AM who lived on earth in the form of a Galilean carpenter. He's the same AM who has spoken to you, and now talks to you daily. He's the AM who never changes, and because He AM, He's the AM who will ask you to do wild, irrational, irresponsible (in the eyes of sensible, level headed, sane and reasonable people) things. How foolish is it to commit yourself to a course of action for which you have no funds, little ability, little agreement from sane people, and based only on a word given exclusively to you personally by Jesus heard in a secret and private chat with Him? Irresponsible? Certainly. Wild? Certainly. Anyone else ever done that in the history of time? Never. So why be so foolish? Because you are a son or daughter of God, and you've caught the family likeness. "Though none go with me, yet still I'll follow. No turning back. No turning back." Faith of this irrational kind comes from the I AM who has galvanised irrational acts throughout time. He's not going to change. So how about you changing and saying "You bet, Lord!"? Or are you going to be a wimp and run the rest of your life on fear?

When God decided to create the Earth and the cosmos, He had to make a decision based on the choices that man might make when he lived here. As I have pointed out elsewhere, there was a 4-way possibility in Adam and Eve's choices concerning the fruit of the tree of the Knowledge of Good and Evil. So God had to design earth for every scenario that might possibly occur. Thus he designed time.

Time is merely a measurement, and is strictly limited to earth. One "day" on Mercury or Jupiter is very different from that of earth. But time describes events occurring in sequence - one after another. God decided that none of the creatures He was going to create to live on His new earth would be able to cope with all events occurring simultaneously. We can presume that in eternity, the ever-present now, all things happen at once. (Don't get misled by "at once"; it's a timed word and there is no other I can use). Someone pointed out that you can add to *heaven* (like humans who are dying on earth), but not take away from it. *Eternity* would be added to by babies being conceived and born on earth. No angels are being born - only humans. So everything that has happened before is always permanently there and Now. But God knew that even his greatest creation, man, could not cope with all that. So He made time. In time, events occur in sequence. Nothing remains. Past decisions get superseded, even if they have been written down. Past "permanences" like buildings, cars or empires all decay and get replaced. Change is permanent in time.

Moreover, the future is unobtainable. The future is the place of plans and dreams - and, for some more vulnerable humans, fears and anxieties.

Has it ever occurred to you that the only Time we can live in is "the ever-present now"? We are aware of the past; we plan for the future; but we live only and ever in the present. Now isn't that exactly the definition of eternity?

What we are doing is living permanently in eternity. The extraordinary miracle that God has designed is to "stretch" eternity by putting events in sequence instead of bundling them all together at once, which is where He is. Nevertheless, we all actually live where He lives, in the ever-present Now.

That has far reaching consequences.

Firstly, it means that Now is the only place where we can talk to God. Now is that one point, if you like, where the tangent of heaven touches the circle of Time. If you prefer it, the only point of communication between God and man on this earth is that moment when both can say "I Am" together. We may be able to recall the past and prayers of the past. But we cannot live there. We can repeat them in our present Now, but we cannot recover them. Now is the only place of communication with heaven. We think that if we talk to God in the morning and ask His blessing on a day all will be well. But no. If that's all we do, we have abandoned the Lord for the rest of the day. We've moved on and we have left Him behind in our yesterday or this morning. No. The only thing we can logically do is to keep in tune with the Lord every moment of our waking day. We have to carry our vertical relationship with us all the time. *Now* is the only place where we can talk to God and He with us. So if we call ourselves Christians, then the only realistic choice we have is to live our lives in continual fellowship and communication with Jesus. Without Him, all we do is self initiated - which is what we have been delivered from. If I am not getting a Now decision from

God, who am I getting it from? No wonder Paul wrote: "*Now* is the time of God's favour."

Paul's addition of "Now is the day of salvation" would indicate that if I access Jesus and His *Rhēma* words in my "Now's", then His deliverance and prosperity (salvation) impinge in every "Now" moment onto my life. That's the only way to be spiritual in my life and to continue to receive His salvation – to be being saved.

And secondly, what about the choices we make? Every choice we make is a new Now choice. Therefore it is eternal. It is an eternal decision made in eternity. God heard; God saw; God recorded. God may have *influenced* that decision, but He always leaves us to choose our behaviour and therefore our destiny. We may well forget decisions of the past, whether good or bad, but they are all recorded for ever simply because they were made in eternity and that's where we, God and the angels live. Nothing is forgotten in heaven. Why? Because heaven is always and only Now!

Thirdly, when we die, we will plunge instantly into Eternity. But hang on – aren't we already there? Certainly. But at death we will be separated from Time for ever. So, actually, we will arrive in heaven *on the same day* as Adam, Abraham, our own grandparents and our great grand children (if Time lasts that long). Think about it! On that same day will be the acquisition of everyone's resurrection bodies, the Great White Throne of Judgement and the Marriage Supper of the Lamb. For those Christians already "dead", all is permanently Now, permanently beautiful and permanently sinless.

If you are not happy with that concept, let's play with Light for a moment. Our sun is 93 million miles away. It takes light travelling at 186,000 miles per second nine minutes to reach us on Earth. So when you watch a sunrise or a sunset, and see the first or last peak of light on the horizon, the Sun itself has already moved nine minutes further on. Or take the nearest star, Proxima Centauri, which is 4½ light years away. I said in my chapter on Genesis that God constructed the light from each star at the same time as He created its star. So the light was joined to earth from the beginning. Nevertheless, the light we *now* see from Proxima Centauri is $4\frac{1}{2}$ years old. Therefore there is a record $4\frac{1}{2}$ years' long stretching between Proxima Centauri and Earth of everything that has happened on that star.

Reverse it. "Someone" on that star could be observing right now what you did on Earth $4\frac{1}{2}$ years ago. And every second of your last $4\frac{1}{2}$ years is recorded in a line of light joining Earth and Proxima Centauri, and is being played out detail by detail to any observer on that star.

Let's go deeper into space. However old you now are, there are lines of light stretching out in all directions from Earth carrying a full and perfect record of every moment of your life. When you die, your living line of light will be cut off. But going out is an indestructible record of your life from the day you were born to the day you die. If you thought that no one would remember what you did when you were seven, or see all those things you have surreptitiously done in secret, then you would be wrong. Anyone with the right technology can access your life story and examine it detail by detail. They would, of course, have to travel around at the speed of light, or site themselves at a point in space where your story unfolds; but in heaven that should be a normal thing to be able to do, especially for God. The Bible tells of books that have been written of our lives. There are many ways that we can recognise that nothing we do and have done can ever be erased - even if *we* have chosen to forget it.

There are many things we do in life that are not retrievable, and the spoken word is one.

> If you your lips would save from slips,
> Attend five things with care:
> Of whom you speak; to whom you speak;
> And how, and when and where.

The cross of Jesus Christ took place in Time. We are eternally grateful for the cross. But it also took place in eternity. That one single act in Time was also a Now, eternal act, and introduced the song and the reconciliation of redemption that spreads backwards in Time to the beginning and forwards in Time to the end. It was an eternal act. Thus we read in Revelation of "the lamb slain from the creation of the world." (Revelation 13:8). The heart and character of the Lord have been the same yesterday, today and for ever. Sometimes I have heard Christians desperately pleading for God's mercy and forgiveness. But we have no need to do that. He is "semper idem" - always the same. Forgiveness is His nature. From the beginning He was what He is now, and the future will add nothing to His character. He is. Before Abraham was, Jesus is. How unlike Him we are!

How easy it is for the Lord to prophesy and predict the future. In the same way that He knows every detail of the past, He knows every detail of the future - He is already living there. That sounds mighty like predestination, which truth terrifies many Christians. Does God's predestining take away our choices? Or predetermine our eternal inheritance? You can answer that yourself. Ask: is my choice limited today, Now? Do I feel myself oppressed by a God who is forcing me into a mould I do not like? Of course not! And the freedom of choice I have right now is the freedom I will always have. The key scripture is in Romans 8:29:- those God *foreknew*, God predestined. He influences us in love (how can He change?), but all the choices in every Now moment are ours. All He is doing is watching, observing what we decide, and granting us an inheritance that is 100% appropriate to all our decisions. In time we change and grow. In eternity we always were what we will end up to be. We are adding to eternity by the good choices we make right now. And God has placed us in an environment that enables us to be tempted; that is, to be offered the real choice in any Now moment to do God's will or our own ("Satan savours the things of *man*.")

So why is God constantly forgiving us? Because the Cross is constantly operating. God does not have to screw Himself up every time we sin, and force us to extract forgiveness from a reluctant Saviour. He was crucified from the beginning. In

Revelation we read of a lamb in the centre of the throne of God that looked as if it had been killed - in the beginning, at the end, and all the way through. And the earth and the sky fled from the presence of the Lamb (Rev 20:11). His heart is a crucified one, and always has been. He is the innocent, gentle, humble, completely unthreatening Lamb. Of all the creatures God has made, it is astonishing that He should choose a lamb to represent His character best. Yet there it is. His approach to us is and always will be lamb-like. That's because He *is*.

The redemption is perfect and complete. Now that we have been converted and become Christians, the final redemption is having to be worked out in Time in our lives. That word "final" is a Time word. In heaven our destiny already is. The final is, and always has been Now. We are permanently forgiven. Our sins and bad choices are permanently paid for and forgotten - the cross is eternal. So how could that affect us? We could eat, drink and be merry! But if we did that, and presume upon the grace of forgiveness and redemption, making selfish choices in every Now moment, on what good choices and actions would God give us a reward and a good destiny? Every bad and selfish choice is another opportunity lost for doing good. I know many Christians who are not now walking with God. Can they lose their salvation? Terrifyingly, the scripture says so, and warns us to be on our guard lest we do. The Bible certainly says: "Once saved, always saved." But it also says, "Lest I myself should be a castaway." Both are possible and these opposites sit uncomfortably in human logical minds, but not, apparently, in God's. We just need to keep sweet with Jesus in all our Nows. "He that endures to the end will be saved."

I went to the Keswick Convention in the early 1960s. Two things stood out from that visit. The first was John Stott's masterly Bible studies on 1 Corinthians 1-5. The second was George Duncan's talk "Stale Grace Stinks." He may not have called it that, but that's how I remember it. His point was that yesterday's Grace is not good enough for today. Like the manna kept overnight by lazy Israelites who didn't want to go collecting the following morning, it turns to worms and stinks. (As a piece of irrelevant information, "Manna" means "Wot is it?"). Why does yesterday's Grace stink? Because yesterday's Grace was yesterday's provision for yesterday's situation and we now live in today. So for today's situation there is an appropriate supply of new Grace to enable us to overcome and be more than Conquerors right now. If we are running (or trying to run) on yesterday's Grace, all our choices and resources revert to human ones, and we abandon the Lord. We cannot top up on one day, and run on a tank-full for a week. God can only be found and accessed from eternity, from our "ever-present Now".

Thirdly, Time is an illusion. It is a very strong illusion and we are bound by it. We have no language to express life outside of Time where Time does not exist. So how is it possible to think in a Timeless way? Very difficult. But the reality is always heaven, or where God lives. All we see and know in this creation is a sub-reality - stretched and thinned eternity. After all, physicists tell us that, in all matter, the molecules are spread so far apart that most matter is space. That doesn't enable us to walk through walls, because the mathematics that hang our bodies together (with just as large a space between the molecules), is the same as that of the walls, and we go "boing" if we try. But walls didn't restrict Jesus in His resurrection body. He used the spacey bits and walked right through them. Which tells me that the realm of the spirit possesses a different mathematics, far more sophisticated than any we know, and for which we have no key. One of the reasons why so many scientists do not believe in Jesus is that there is little or no evidence for the existence of the spiritual realm. Because they have no handle on its mathematics they believe it doesn't exist. But the major reason they don't believe in God is not a scientific one at all - they just don't like the idea of being accountable to a Higher Authority, and having all their secret decisions scrutinised and finally exposed. They are no different from us lesser human beings. Their unbelief is a matter of sovereignty, not intelligence - just like yours and mine.

Time is an illusion. It is a temporary arrangement and not the reality. So, have you ever thought about praying backwards? After all, all our yesterdays are as Now to God, just as much as are all our todays and all our tomorrows. But why should we? Surely yesterday is set in concrete, and cannot be changed? True. So what about our *tomorrows*? Are *they* set in concrete, or can we alter them by prayer? If we couldn't, we wouldn't pray! So why shouldn't the past be influenced (it's not changed, you will note) by our prayer of today? Let me give you the illustration that pitched me into this freedom. One of my lovely teenagers asked me to pray for her exams - the taking and the results. Because I loved her (I love them all, both genders), I said I would. But I forgot. So there I was reneging on my promise, and I was distraught. What could I do? That's when I learnt to pray backwards - that God would give her peace and prosperity in both the taking and the results. So how did that work? God, who is outside of Time, saw my prayers of tomorrow, took them into account, and gave the lass peace in her exams. Why shouldn't God take into account prayer from the future, which He already knows we are going to make, and influence somebody's Now moment? If He can do that for prayer from time past, He can do that from Time to come. It works - so long as, when we remember the thing we had forgotten to pray for, we actually pray; whether it is forwards or backwards. So why did she have peace taking her exams and prosperity in the results? Because I prayed backwards, she and others prayed forwards, God took all the prayers into account, and she prospered in every respect.

It is interesting to see how people use Time. One of the most astonishing and "unhuman" chapters in the Bible is Luke 12. It starts with a crowd of many thousands thronging Jesus and tramping on one another. But Jesus ignored them and continued to teach his disciples. In verse 13 someone butted it into that scenario, and Jesus dealt with it graciously. Immediately, Jesus returned to teach his disciples all the way down to verse 53. In verse 54 He turned to the crowd, gave them only a few choice thoughts, most of which were "hypocrites" and rebuke, and then walked off. If I had been Him, I would have capitulated and given in to the crowd right at the beginning; the disciples could wait until later. But Jesus was God-centred every moment of his earthly life. Only to do God's will and nothing else - that was His use of Time.

Another incident springs to mind. Mark 7. In verse 24 "Jesus withdrew to the region of Tyre and Sidon..." from Capernaum and the Sea of Galilee. That's an awful long way to walk. What did He do there? Apparently only one thing – deliver the daughter of a Greek (non-Jewish) woman from a demonic spirit. And that seemingly reluctantly. In verse 31 He left there and returned to Galilee, not to the Jewish side but to Decapolis on the east. That's also an awful long way. So what did He do during those walks? It must have taken him days, maybe even a fortnight, but there is no record of what He did. Did God just ask him to tramp all that way to deliver a Greek woman's daughter? Seemingly so. To my Western mind, where Time is money, or Time is precious, that's a very inefficient use of it. But God is God. And we have to become like Him. Thus, recently, in Nicaragua, I spent some $100 flying to Bluefields and back for one day only to give Shakira Thyne, a 15 year old girl an eye test for a pair of glasses because four months earlier I had seen her on a Sunday, and the opticians had been closed. That's what God had said, so that's what I did. And I had Jesus' example to follow as an inefficient use of my Time and money.

So how do we use Time?

The first and most important thing is to live in heaven. We are living in eternity anyway. But we need to make every *eternal* Now a *heavenly* fellowship opportunity with Jesus. Sometimes we have to force ourselves into heaven, because "the crowd" or "things" are demanding our attention. If we live in heaven while on earth, we pick up heavenly characteristics. We don't get fazed by interruptions. We find infinite patience. We pick up the joy and the singing of heaven. Christians living in heaven on earth are happy, carefree people. People and things matter to them, but none of them are an anxiety to them. Remember the parable of the Sower? What thorns choked the plants? "The anxieties of this world, the deceitfulness of riches and the lust of other things."

I have noticed, too, that a Nicaraguan view of Time is very different from mine. I plan my day. I am an achiever - I want to get things done. I work hard and try to fulfil the scriptural injunction: "Redeem the Time, for the days are evil." Or to follow another little ditty from my scrapbooks: "Make Time in Time while Time lasts; all Time's no Time when Time's past."

But not Nicaraguans. They are indeed probably the most hard-working of all Latin Americans, so they are not lazy people. But they don't plan ahead. They come to me to ask for help while I'm in the middle of something else (I'm always in the middle of something else!) and if I cannot fulfil their request now, that's OK. They are prepared to wait till tomorrow or next week or four months later or next year. What is a day? Only an opportunity to find and do the will of God. And in Nicaragua I have found a strength and ability to handle interruptions with grace and courtesy, ditching the plans I had in mind without being frustrated by it. It seems to me that that was what was happening to Jesus throughout his three years of ministry. And if He wanted to plan ahead and get something done (like finding a room to eat his last Passover), He had to do it secretly and surreptitiously.

We must all be, to quote the title of Demos Shakarion's book, The Happiest People On Earth. The only way I can see of doing that is to be accessing heaven - or, better, chatting with Jesus - Now. Truly, "*Now* is the Time of God's favour; *now* is the day of salvation."

Life is real, life is earnest
And the grave is not the goal.

"Dust thou art, to dust returneth"
Was not spoken of the soul.

Lives of great men all remind us
We can make our lives sublime.
And, returning, leave behind us
Footprints in the sands of Time.
(Longfellow)

SUMMARY

Time is an illusion. Eternity is the ever-present NOW, which is where we all live. NOW is the only place where we can access God.

Chapter 14
BIG C

Today I want to introduce you to the most astonishing, the most amazing, and the most stupendous thing that God has ever invented. It's the reason why He made the universe. It's the reason why He made the earth. It's the reason why He made all the animals, birds, fish, vegetation and rocks. It's the reason why the sun, moon and stars were made. His plan is beyond belief (almost) and beyond imagination. What was the reason? The CHURCH!

God made the earth for His Church. He made His great sacrifice in sending His very own Son so that mankind could belong inside His Church. His redemption of mankind will bring about a total transformation in the earth itself, and, later, the whole cosmos. Then His Church will reign with Him for ever over a new heaven and a new earth which will be full of a variety that we cannot even dream. "No eye has seen, no ear has heard, no mind has conceived what God has prepared for those who love him" (1 Cor 2:9). He has made it all for ***us!***

So what is the CHURCH? Certainly not a building! Jesus' Church consists of all people who have put their trust In Him, and have been redeemed by Him from all the centuries past, the present and from the future.

So where do we find evidence of this? "God has appointed Jesus to be Head over all things for the Church." (Eph 1:23). That is, Head over ***All*** things ***For*** the Church. The whole purpose of the whole creation is to locate and unearth the Church. People might ask if there are any other creatures in outer space? Surely there cannot be? If God has chosen to make His Son a human being, and the whole cosmos was created for human beings, and when the full number of Christians has been gathered in the cosmos will be rolled up, then surely man is the centre stage of the creation? There cannot be any other creatures in the cosmos.

In addition, this whole world and the universe are for us. Made for us, the Church. Made for our pleasure. Made for our control. Made for our authority. Isn't that why the prayers of God's people are so globally effective?

God's one single purpose in creating is to bring into His companionship for ever all those people who want to be there. For them, His Church, he is planning a New Home and Rulership over His New creation. Moreover, God Himself will change His address and come down from heaven and live with them.

The Biblical description that best reveals God's intention is THE BRIDE OF CHRIST. The Bible *Verse* that best describes it is: Eph 1:23,24 – "And God placed all things under His feet and appointed Him to be Head over everything for the Church, which is His body, the fullness of Him who fills everything in every way."

Just think for a minute: *WE ARE* the fullness of Him who fills *everything* in *every* way. That's what we are, what the Church is. Isn't that just beyond our imagination? We are the fullness of His grace, the fullness of His love, the fullness of His kindness, the fullness of His reconciliation, the fullness of His power, the fullness of His wholeness. The Church is Jesus in human flesh, just an expanded and multiple version of the Jesus in One Body who lived 2000 years ago in Israel. We are Jesus in One multiple Body. And His fullness. This revelation from scripture is astonishing.

One day, The Church is going to add a fourth dimension to the Trinity: Father, Holy Spirit, Son and Bride. How do we know this? Because we have the guarantee of the Holy Spirit living inside us to bring to fulfilment all the promises of God (Eph 1:13, 14). (See the Bible Study chapter on the Bride of Christ).

The Church will reign with God over the new Creation for ever, acting out God's will from the vantage point of God

Himself. We will be seated with Christ together on His throne in the heavenly places.

We will be complete. Complete, that is, in Being. Every cell will be in place, and none of us will lose our individual identity in the mass of humanity, any more than we lose our identity in God's salvation scenario today. Complete also in righteousness and holiness. The redemption of Jesus will then be over, and His plan is to make us all perfect and flawless. Complete also as human beings – along with resurrection bodies to complete our perfected souls and spirits. And, to crown it all, married to the Son of God, whose name is above every Name in the universe. God's invention of the Church is amazing, stupendous, extraordinary, and beyond our wildest imaginations. **What God dreams, God accomplishes.**

What an immense privilege it is to be:

- A human Being. All creatures have Being. Any of us could have been born as a donkey, or a bird or a bug. The imagination boggles what Beings we could have been. But God ordained that we should be *Human* beings. What a privilege. What a humbling concept.
- A Christian. It is a privilege to be a human being; it is quite another to be a Christian. What a privilege to have been sought and found by Jesus. What a privilege to have been caught up in His arms of love, and to know His reconciliation with His Father. We are the purpose for the universe, and here we are, all totally undeserving, wrapped up in the immense plans of an immense God. Wow!
- In at the Beginning. Those who think that the cosmos has been going for billions of years have no faith in God's revelation of the way He made the world. Billions of years are a requirement for evolution, not for Creation, and a figment of imagination. We are in at the beginning of all things. We live in a universe that's only 6,000 – 10,000 years old. CS Lewis said something like:

> "The whole history of this earth is like turning over the fly leaf of a book. We have not yet arrived at the title page, much less started on what the story is all about."

****

So that's something about what God has in mind for the future of His Church. So let us turn now to His plan for that same Church on Earth right now. So - what *is* the Church on earth now? It is the very same Bride of Christ, but *in embryo,* in *foetus* stage, still in the womb. She remains such until her birth at the Second Coming of Jesus. That event is what the Bible calls the Adoption of the Sons of God (Rom 8).

There are many who tell us that the Church has come of age. I fear not. We will be persecuted, discouraged, oppressed and be in a battle until we die, incomplete until the Second Coming of Jesus. We have to think of ourselves as *developing* into "Christ Likeness". And as soon as we individually have cottoned on to what God has in mind for us, it's time to go home. The world will continue in its wickedness and sin until the full number of the saints has been gathered in, and every new generation learns for itself the things that every older generation learned, but sited in their own unique environment in their own unique century.

We all grieve when a friend or relative dies. But do not grieve too hard. "This world is not my home; I'm just a-passing through." Right now we are in embryo stage, forming inside God's womb until it is time to be born. That's why the church on earth is so limited, underpowered, ignorant, ineffective, and nowhere approaching the likeness of Christ or the promises that God has for her. We make many claims, but we don't have the performance. You discover a good preacher and they leave for heaven far too soon, and long before you feel their work is done. We cling to earth wrongly, as if it was the only thing in the universe. What folly. Run heaven-bent.

A foetus is an undeveloped human being. The church of today is the undeveloped Church of the New Heavens. The Bride of Christ will join the Godhead as joint-heirs with Christ. She is now *still being conceived* (in the sense that new humans are joining the Bride of Christ every day), but not yet born (in the sense that the Bride of Christ as One Being is still incomplete), and definitely not yet fully formed.

A foetus is nowhere near like the adult human being. Moreover, it's pretty incapable; and why not? It's still in the womb. You don't expect it to run 100 metres in 10 seconds. Not yet. That's exactly what the Church is like on earth today. In the womb God is shaping a real human being, but doing it gently and carefully as Psalm 139 reminds us. The Church is being shaped as the Bride, slowly and carefully. But not yet born.

See, a foetus is a real human being – only underdeveloped. From the moment of conception it is fully human. You cannot get a human any other way. But that way it is human from the moment that little seed enters that egg. It is the same with each Christian. From the moment that Jesus entered our lives we became a part of the Bride of Christ – fully spiritual, fully conceived, fully Bride. Only underdeveloped. We sometimes think ourselves so marvellous. But we are not. Not yet. While on earth, we are *being* formed. Nothing more.

How do we know we are still in foetus mode? By the limited, decaying body we live in right now. This body is made for earth only, not heaven. This earth and all that is within it is destined for destruction. When we get a resurrection body, *then* we will have been born together and come of age. Gen 3:19 reminds us that "dust you are and to dust you will return."

This theme of development will continue all the days of our lives. My wife's Bible Principal Mrs Jock Habermann said: "We are all made of the same common clay." I put it this way: "We are all squelching through the same syrup." That is why Encouragement is perhaps one of the greatest attributes we can acquire and hand out on our journey heavenwards. We are all grossly under-talented in the majority of ways, and will remain so until we die. But be encouraged - we *can* learn about Jesus, copy His wonderful ways, and become Christ-like in every way. One does not need intelligence, talent, or any of the accolades that men revere or worship in others; all we need is faith and obedience, and God will be set free to develop that part of the embryo which is you until you reach to the full measure of the stature of the Son of God.

There's no doubt whatever that marriage between Jesus and the Church is intended. It seems from Revelation 19:7-9 that it's not just an illustration. It seems to be a reality.

If you really want a Big Bang to replace the mythical Evolutionary one, try this one: God exploded His character into trillions of little characters, placing one unique but mini combination in each human being. So that, at the end of time, these trillions of little characters would combine together to make One Being with a character like that of Jesus Himself – and therefore fit to be His Bride.

But, you may ask, what about the losses? There are probably more human beings lost to heaven than gained, and each a unique representation of one aspect of Jesus' character. I cannot fully answer that. But I would point out that God is enormously extravagant. Just how many acorns fail to germinate from one year's fruiting from one tree? Yet still the ones that do become oak trees are sufficient for the world. Or the seed of animals? At one time only a dozen puppies are produced from billions of seeds. Acorns have other uses, but the seed of animals has no other use. Those that don't germinate are all discarded – like, unfortunately, human beings in whom the seed of the Word of God finds no good soil. But in the end God will not be thwarted. Even though many characteristics of God are lost in humans who never want to come to Jesus, the rest of us will make up the Bride perfectly. God has diversified into us all so that we will merge together again to form One Perfect Other Being – the Bride. And then to explode in another new way through us, the completed Bride.

Countless billions, whom no man can number, are going to be welded into One Unit – One person, One Being, and together we are going to be married to Jesus. It's called the Marriage Supper of the Lamb. When The Church is complete and the song of redemption has reached its climax and is over, then there's going to be a party. Wow, what a party that's going to be!

All sorts of other things implied by marriage are stated in scripture.

- The Bride will be pure. All contamination will be removed for ever from her. That will have to be a sovereign work of God, because every cell of the Bride has a diseased beginning.
- The Bride will be a virgin. How God is going to achieve that is anyone's guess, because none of us are. We have all been "married" before to the world, the flesh and the devil.
- The Bride will be fully prepared.
- The Bride will be clothed in a beautiful, pure, white wedding dress, which are the righteous deeds of the saints.
- The Bride will be given a gift – a new home in which to live. It's called the New Jerusalem, and is part of the new heavens and the new earth that God has planned for that time and from then on.

What will be the consequences of this marriage? One thing is certain: we will reign with Jesus eternally (Revelation 22:5).

It is with and in a new resurrection body that we will be ruling over the universe with Jesus. At present all the stars are ruled over by the angelic host. In the New Creation, whatever God makes out there will, I guess, be ruled over by us.

****

So, for a time, God has a number of provisions that He has made for the embryo stage, and I have expanded this in the next chapter.

All God's work pivots round the local church. (Of course, people differ as to what constitutes the local church. It does not have to be those who meet in a building called a Church. It may be as simple as those who meet together in a home).

Cut off a branch of a vine and it withers (John 15). Every Christian *must* belong to a local church. Pull a coal out of the fire and it dies. No Christian can survive outside the fellowship of a local church. A Head can only work through its body, and Eph 1:23-24 tell us, among other places, that we are Christ's body of which He is the Head. The metaphor fits exactly. Beware the Christian who sits alone. Beware the Christian who cannot mix with God's sub-standard saints here on earth. There is definitely something wrong with them and their Christianity will soon die if they don't integrate.

Worship is best in the church. We go to church throughout a week to contact the Lord. Of course we talk to Jesus throughout every day (I hope). But "Where *two or three* are gathered together in My name, there I stand in the middle of them." (Matt 18). And "Let us not give up meeting together, as some are in the habit of doing," (Heb 10:25).

Life can only continue through a body. That is obvious physically. But what we fail to notice is that it is also obvious spiritually. God does not work outside the Body of Christ. You may quote some examples of where He has, but look at the long term view – the Oneness and Unity of the One Bride of Christ. Moreover, there are things that God wants us to know that He has incorporated into the framework of local churches.

Unity. There should be unity among all the denominations in a local area, as well as inside each local church.

Acceptance of all. If God has chosen to save an individual, who are we to reject them? I did not choose any of the people who worship in my church to be there; God did. If I had have chosen people to belong in my local fellowship, who would I have chosen?

Love and Unconditional Forgiveness. Loving people means eventually coming to like them too. We love them into liking them. Love is from God; liking is from man. We belong to each other and we are *commanded* to get on with each other, regardless of how odd they are.

Communication. God illustrates the Christian Church with the metaphor of the Body. How does the human body hang together? Eph 4 says "Ligaments". How does that fit into the Body of Christ, and what are those ligaments? That same passage tell us it's Love. *Love* binds the body together. But how does the human body operate so effectively as one unit? Communication; God has built in a nervous system that operates at the speed of light. If it does not communicate (as it doesn't with Multiple Sclerosis or Leprosy), then bits get damaged and die. How much more is communication truly needed for the church? "If we walk in the light ... we have fellowship with one another ..." (1 John 1:7).

Submission. We are to be servants and slaves of one another, just like Jesus was, and is, our servant, even though He is Lord of all. Voluntary slavery is an attitude of heart that is in the centre of God's character.

All these five are characteristics of the **Bride of Christ.** They are also characteristics of a **human head and body.**

We all have to grow out of our natural (demonic), self-centred, individualistic ways of behaviour, and grow into "Bride Likeness," which is "Christ Likeness". Note the communication bit – "Secrecy is the Author of Gossip", said Rick Warren. God wants us to be open minded and open hearted people. No one can misunderstand an open person, but anyone can misunderstand a closed or secretive person. If you don't want to be misunderstood or misrepresented – you know what to do.

The metaphors BRIDE and BODY describe two different phases of the One Being, The Church. BRIDE describes where we are all going. BODY describes how we get there in the phase of living on earth.

Let's look at some scriptures:

- Romans 12:5. "So in Christ we who are many form one body, and each member belongs to all the others."
- 1 Corinthians 12:12. "The body is a unit, though it is made up of many parts; and though all its parts are many, they form one body. So it is with Christ."
- 1 Corinthians 12:27. "Now you are the body of Christ, and each one of you is a part of it."
- Ephesians 4:12. "To prepare God's people for works of service, so that the body of Christ may be built up."
- Ephesians 5:23. "Christ is the head of the church, his body, of which he is the saviour."

So – the Greatest Invention that God has ever dreamed up, far above all the wonders of Creation, is His Church. Everything else in God's heart and mind, everything else in the whole cosmos, is secondary to this one single purpose – to draw out from earth's millennia of years a Bride for His Son.

God's Church, whether on earth or in our dreams of Heaven, requires:

- Our Maximum Appreciation.
- Our maximum Expectation.
- Our maximum Participation.
- Our Maximum Integration.
- Our Maximum Confidence.

We need a VERY BIG view of the Church. We need to honour it and respect it, and all the members of it. We are to be One, because we are One.

Someone has asked: "Does the Church have a future?" Silly question. It is better to ask another question: "Does this earth and this universe have a future without the Church?" ***NEVER!***

SUMMARY

God is creating something new as time goes by. The Church is His new creation, is excellent and wonderful in the extreme, is the Bride of Christ, and is the only purpose for the continuation of the earth.

Chapter 15
LITTLE C.

There is Church (big C) and there are churches (little c). This meditation is mainly about the latter.

By "churches" I mean the expression of Christianity that appears in multiple forms in millions of small groups dotted around the world. Some have big congregations, some small. Some have big permanent buildings, some meet in homes. And every format in between.

The Vital Importance of Local Church.

First, the New Testament in Acts reveals One Local Church in each locality. We could argue that, at the beginning, when there were only a few converts, and when those converts all came from the same source, there would obviously only be one local church. But hold on. God's best is *always* found at the beginning. Regardless of any rationale that might explain it away, *one* local church in any town is the New Testament requirement; *the* saints in Corinth, in Ephesus, in Lystra etc.

What is the Local Church? All the Christians in that locality. Those who now belong to every Christian denomination. In the New Testament there was no such thing as anything other than a local Church. We must not get confused here. The fact that God has chosen to use denominations today and in time past does not mean that He necessarily approves of them. The best form of church on earth is found at the beginning of the New Testament. So the faster we can return to New Testament practices and have one church in each area, the better. Or, those separate denominational churches must club together and work as "One Thing".

God's plan for the evangelism of the world is through local churches. That may seem rather a narrow thing to say, but look at the New Testament. *All* God's activity was focussed towards local churches and through local churches. There were no exceptions. The Apostolic letters (most of the New Testament) are to local churches with the odd exception to an individual. And where they were written to individuals, it was because those individuals were having trouble with and in their local churches. Paul wrote to local churches, and Peter to those scattered abroad, but serving in their local churches.

Someone could argue that the situation in the 1st century AD was different from the sophisticated, multi-media, technological situation of today. Of course. But the Lord determined that both the doctrines *and* the patterns of His plan for the evangelisation of the world should be encapsulated in the writings of the New Testament (backed up by the Old). The pattern set up by the Holy Spirit to the Apostles was the very best that could be achieved. Eph 2:19, 20 says: "Consequently, you are no longer foreigners and aliens, but fellow citizens with God's people and members of God's household, built on the foundation of the apostles and prophets, with Christ Jesus himself as the chief cornerstone.." And Eph 3:5 adds: "which was not made known to men in other generations as it has now been revealed by the Spirit to God's holy apostles and prophets." Still today we are based on what the Apostles wrote.

In the early church (New Testament version), all Christians met in one often non-religious place in one city/town under leadership that was elected from among them. During the week they met in homes. And *that* church flourished – they took the known world in one generation.

The reason why local churches are so important is that Church is the Body of Christ. The Head only moves through His Body. Whatever Christian activity happens outside the local church is guaranteed not to be blessed – or for the blessing not to last. If, say, a youth work (all of which tend to be extra-church) does not integrate its converts into a local church, those converts are likely to die. The blessing flows through the church, like blood flows through veins and arteries that are attached as parts of one body, or sap runs through branches. Cut off any of those, and the life dies.

The local church, however inadequate, is an expression of The Church, the Big One. It's all about people Jesus has redeemed being together, worshipping together in the place where they live. Churches are all defective from a human perspective, but not from God's: it is in the local church that God invests His blessing and His power. The key concept here is "Belonging". For how is it possible for the Head to communicate or bless a member or group of His Body that is not joined to His Body? So how does this apply? I have met many instances in my Christian years.

A mission is one. An itinerant evangelist holds meetings or a beach mission. People or children get converted, the mission leaves, and the converts are not fed back into the local church. (Often it's because the evangelist thinks the local church too rotten for his new chicks to grow in). The consequence? They are cut off from the life-blood of Jesus. Those converts who are never committed to a local church will die. The Head and the Body are One, and that is the channel through which the Life of the Spirit will flow. Pastor Cecil Radford once said, "Mix the young and old together".

I have even met this division inside a local church. An innovative, energetic and successful youth leader fires up a good youth group and kids get converted. If they do not belong and are not filtered into their own local church to worship together with the others who meet there, they will die. It's the seed that fell on rocky ground – full of early enthusiasm but wither when the going gets hot. Without the support and prayers of the local (flawed) church, converts cannot and will not survive. I have noticed too that children whose parents belong and go to church stay the course far far better than those whose parents don't. Conclusion? Get the adults first, preferably the Dads, and the whole family comes under the blessing and influence of God.

The deposit of Biblical Truth is normally held in local churches, rather than in denominations. The larger the organisation, the more off-beam it tends to get. Today we see that in denominational headquarters where political correctness and unbiblical theology have taken the place of Biblical Revelation. Someone asked me the question the other day, "How long will it be before we have a female lesbian Archbishop?" "You can't fool the common man" said someone else. That's why God puts the deposit of truth into the local church where the common man is.

The New Testament leaders were not professionals. Constantine introduced professional Church leaders – Jesus didn't. So we need to return to the New Testament, where leaders come up from inside, not in from outside, were anointed by the Lord for the task of leadership, and were called to that position. I do not object to professionals, provided they are anointed by the Holy Spirit and called of God into the positions they hold.

Things which cripple Churches from being New Testament Ones.

There are three inheritances donated by Christians in time past which hinder today's churches from being New Testament ones – the first was given by Emperor Constantine, the second by the Reformation, and the third by the great missionary wave of the 19th century. All of these were wonderful in their day, but their descendants did not move forward with Jesus' visions – they moved forward in their parents' visions. Today we are therefore still contaminated by them.

Constantine put a spoke in God's wheel. He was not only a Christian but a very shrewd politician. He introduced a Professional Priesthood. He decided to unite the vast and disintegrating Roman Empire he inherited through Christianity. How? He set up hundreds of Christian buildings (funded by the State), and trained hundreds of Christian priests both in literacy and Doctrine (funded by the State), who ministered loyalty to Christ and, of course, loyalty to Caesar to an illiterate Empire. The priesthood united his Empire, and we now use the historically later word Christendom (the spiritual empire of Christ on earth) to describe what he did. Very effective.

But that way they lost the concept of meeting informally in homes. They lost their local leadership appointments. They established "State Religion". They lost the leadership of divine appointment and substituted a "professional priesthood" appointed from officialdom – so only those who had done the course could minister as priests. Most tragically of all, they lost the spontaneous breath of the Holy Spirit. All the major Christian denominations still retain the trappings of Constantine (beautiful permanent buildings, robes, professional priests, fixed times of services, fixed forms of services, tradition, liturgy etc. [contrast modern styles with the New Testament style of worship in 1 Cor 14:26-31]) perpetuated and dragged into every Century from 300AD. Didn't Jesus say to the Sadducees, "Your traditions have neutralised the word of God."? When will we get back to the New Testament? Have you noticed that, even today, when the church "goes underground" it multiplies exponentially? Why? It's so obvious and so simple - it returns to the New Testament *pattern*.

Who wants professional Christians? The Gospel spread faster in the first generation through common people gossiping the Gospel than it has spread since. Not even Paul was a professional. He was an Apostle – a divine and not a human appointment and designation. It was simple people whose hearts God had turned from darkness to light who couldn't keep their mouths shut. Brilliant.

The <u>Reformation</u> introduced Intellectual Christianity. I have tried to analyse the difficulties with that in chapter 1. All the denominations (that is, divisive separations) have arisen since then – as a direct consequence of the inheritance that the Reformation bequeathed to their successors. What was that? That every Christian and church should have the foundation of their faith laid on Doctrine. Methinks we may have lost our way here. Denominational division cannot possibly be a scheme of the Lord's. In addition we may have lost our way on the issues that unite us. Many Christians think that Doctrine *should* be the unifying factor. I fear not. Indeed, Doctrine is the major *dis*uniting factor in Christian churches. And the problem there is that opposite doctrines may sit comfortably in God's lap, but never in ours, because we all have limited capacities. Therefore there will be many things that one person agrees with but another doesn't. That causes division and, yes, heat. Moreover, God possesses all knowledge of everything. We limited human beings struggle to grasp the details of practically everything, and then forget what we had once grasped. Some people try to fathom all God's mind. But they fail. We can see that no Doctrines will ever be complete, and therefore they will always divide – if we insist on the centrality of Doctrine as the basis of either our Christianity or our unity. Am I therefore saying that Doctrine is unimportant? Of course not. How silly. But it cannot *(must not)* be allowed to be the central issue around which our Christianity stands. If there is a central pivot, it has to be our common relationship with Jesus. His Doctrines are *infinite*, and He can accommodate all lesser ones in peace. We can't.

Now I need to come to the vexed question of para-church activities – generated so beautifully in the great Missionary wave of the 19th Century. Things like Missionary societies and Christian charities. The first question to ask is whether they should be part of a local church? The second question is whether there is any Biblical precedent for them? If the body is One, and the local church is an expression of that One body, shouldn't all Christian activities come out from, be under the covering of and report back to a local church? Shouldn't accountability be invested in a local body? After all, every para-church organisation has their HQ sited somewhere. So shouldn't that "somewhere" dictate the covering and accountability? Clearly, if we take the Biblical pattern, it should. There is no New Testament precedent for para-church organisations, and methinks the perfect way to operate is found in the New Testament, and cannot be bettered.

So what about Paul's Apostolic Team? Surely they were para-church? They were indeed. But they never formed "organisations". The Apostles were the Reference Point for all local Churches in the New Testament. (Actually, they still are, if we run by the New Testament). In the New Testament, it was the Apostles who stopped local churches from going off beam. Thus Paul visited them again and again. When he couldn't, he sent his Apostolic Team to supervise, oversee, correct and encourage. They never stayed long. When that became too difficult to maintain, he wrote them letters to keep them on track. We now have all those letters gathered together in one library called the Bible. The New Testament era had the Apostles and Prophets themselves. We have their writings. Both were God's provision to stop us *all* going off beam. And so we are still being "built on the foundation of the Apostles and Prophets, with Jesus Christ Himself as the chief cornerstone" – provided, that is, that we base our Christianity on Jesus and on the Bible.

We need to see that Paul's Apostolic Team were never resident in any one place. Timothy was sent to Ephesus (1 Tim 1:3), and Titus to Crete (Titus 1:5). But see 2 Tim 4:10–13: "Crescens has gone to Galatia, and Titus to Dalmatia. Only Luke is with me. Get Mark and bring him with you, because he is helpful to me in my ministry. I sent Tychicus to Ephesus. When you come, bring the cloak that I left with Carpus at Troas, and my scrolls, especially the parchments." So, according to the need, Paul's Team travelled throughout the Middle East to help churches. None of Paul's team ended up resident in any one place.

For nearly 30 years I was involved in a Christian Conference Centre. We saw people saved, transformed, healed, delivered, empowered and all good New Testament things. I was the main Bible Teacher, and we had the freedom to "do God's thing" without restriction or restraint. We were accountable to each other and to God. The Trustees were distant and did not interfere because they could see God's hand at work blessing the things we said and did. There was an earlier time when we got so fed up with the inactivity and death of all our local churches that we seriously considered forming a local church of our own – a temptation facing many vibrant works of God. But because we had made a rule that we would all be in agreement with every decision we made (one in heart and mind together with Jesus), we ditched the idea – not all agreed. So we all went back to our various local churches, supported them, and, over the years, watched life grow there as well (albeit not through us particularly).

I now run a charity, which has the remit to transform the lives of particular poor people and areas in Nicaragua. Therefore God has directed people from the local church that I go to as my co-workers. Thus the work of our para-church charity belongs in house in a local church. I rely on local people for prayer backing, and many of the local Christians are supporting the work financially. In addition, I report back to the fellowship what we have done and are doing out there.

But, here is the difficulty; it doesn't stop at the local fellowship. Because we are a charity, we have to have Trustees. None of my Trustees live locally. They are all Christians, but are drawn, if you like, from the wider body of Christ as found nationally. They are the ones to whom I report mostly and to whom I am directly accountable. I spend more time talking to my Chairman of Trustees than I do to my Pastor about the work of SIFT. Moreover, the Trustees are accountable to the Charity Commission, a non-Christian, secular body set up by the British Government. Secular, not Christian. Paul in Romans 13 says that all Government is God appointed, so I suppose I should be content with that "thin" association with the Divine. At least it is legal and fully compliant with the law of the nation. But dodgy Biblically.

So why are we a charity anyway? Why not go it alone, by Grace through faith, out from the local church? Finance is the major consideration. Should it be? Well, the remit the Lord has given us is jolly expensive. We are building schools, clinics, supporting families etc etc, and all that costs a bundle. The local church cannot provide that, so I have to go to the wider Body for the greater financial support for the work. Then there's Gift Aid. I have to pay my workers. Without taxback the charity couldn't survive, or we would have to dilute funds meant for the poor to pay the rich in the UK a small but necessary wage. All that requires us to belong to more than the local church. I guess in this day and generation with communication so abundant, both in terms of transport, telephone and computer, it's inevitable that we belong to a wider group than the local church. But is it Biblical? No amount of rationalising will make it so. However, God told me that our missionary style is based on that of Nehemiah. He got State funding for the rebuilding of the walls of Jerusalem. So I am happy about that parallel.

Some might argue that Paul and his Apostolic team were para-church, mobile and communicated in the best way possible in those days. But Paul belonged to the church at Antioch. He was a leader and teacher there when God called him out, and he reported back to them at the end of his journeys. And surely we should do the same? If, as a missionary, any charity can be regarded as an "Apostolic Team", then we are Biblical. But if we are, then both the local church and the wider church need to recognise that, and pray for us accordingly. Nowadays few, if any, are. They are just missionaries, and no one bothers to check if they have a Biblical structure or remit. We have moved a long way from New Testament principles and patterns.

For me, a missionary living a long way past the great wave of missionary activity of the 19th century, submission to the wider body of Christ in the form of my Trustees, *and* to my local fellowship is an inescapable and delightful duty. Whatever my predecessors may have felt and done, for me the grace of submission is the pathway to power and effectiveness in my/our ministry. With joy – and not through clenched teeth! But I am still not convinced it is Biblical. Has God adjusted His plans to fit in with the current church situation? Is that the perfect pattern He has planned, or is He just shrugging His shoulders and bowing to the inevitable? (Sorry, Lord). As I said, it is a vexing question.

The Concept of Unity.

Unity is so important that I have written a whole chapter on it. But still I need to explain it a little more. God has made it very clear that His plan for Christians is that they should be One. "I will remain in the world no longer, but they are still in the world, and I am coming to you. Holy Father, protect them by the power of your name—the name you gave me—so that they may be one as we are one." (John 17:11). "I have given them the glory that you gave me, that they may be one as we are one:" (John 17:22). One in heart, aim and purpose.

So what should be the catalyst for unity? I think the New Testament makes that very clear – love. God's kind of love. I have written another chapter on that, but enough for me to say here that I define *agapē* love as "Unconditional Acceptance". Doesn't that neutralise *every* source of division? "A new command I give you: Love one another. As I have loved you, so you must love one another. By this all men will know that you are my disciples, if you love one another." (John 13:34, 35). "Love covers over a multitude of" doctrinal disagreements – often called sins.

When churches come into unity together (regardless of denomination) then Psalm 133 leaps into action – "How good and pleasant it is when brothers live together in unity! For there the Lord bestows his blessing, even life forevermore." (vs 1, 3). Christians down through the centuries have found that the blessing of the Lord following unity is second to none. Revivals have sprung from it, as have every other kind of goodie heaven can throw at us.

The Imperfection of Local Churches

Let me say from the outset that all churches are sub-standard. You'll not find a good one anywhere in the world. All local churches are criticisable. We can criticise the décor, the layout, the people, their clothes, the leader, the preacher, the worship, the sermon, the prayer and its style. Everything is substandard in every church, and most church things will sit very uncomfortably inside our prejudices and preferences. Surprising? Not at all. Every foetus is sub-standard as a human being. We are in foetus condition so that we can learn the character of the Bride and change into her likeness.

Some churches you might think are better than others you have known, but that's a personal and individual view-point: they suited your taste better than the rest.

Why are they so flawed? Because they are populated by imperfect people who are on their journeys towards perfection (or towards Jesus if you prefer it) and not one individual has got there yet. Just like you and me. Therefore we are as yet all incomplete. We all still sin – some less than others, some more than others. Therefore the one thing you can guarantee is that, among the delightful things you can find in every church, there are problems and difficulties in every single one of them. You'll find rivalry, jealousy, party factions, anger, resentment, insularity, lack of co-operation, revenge and all sorts of nasties. Just hang around for a little while in one you think is good and you'll get a taste of the flak that lies under cover. Criticism is a biggy – especially of the leadership.

I'd like to add here that limitations are not sins. I have a whole chapter on sin elsewhere in this book. Limitations are gifts from God to enable us to be humble, know there are things we cannot do, and offer our place to someone who can. That blesses them and uses them. Limitations are just as much gifts as talents. But none of them are sin: sin is using them out from our own initiative, not from God's.

Attendance and movement across denominations is a very fruitful experience, and brings us into the place where "Unity of the Spirit in the bond of peace" can be an actual reality. I need to belong to all denominations regardless of their abominations. I am the one who has to change first.

Don't you think it is immeasurably gracious of God to use the denominational structures despite them being alien to His leading in the New Testament? What a kind God we have! Despite the inadequacy of every local church, God is still committed to bringing His blessing to people through local churches.

At the latter end of 1 Cor 11, talking about the Lord's Supper, there is a strange and significant set of verses:

> (v27ff) "Therefore, whoever eats the bread or drinks the cup of the Lord in an unworthy manner will be guilty of sinning against the body and blood of the Lord. A man ought to examine himself before he eats of the bread and drinks of the cup. For anyone who eats and drinks without recognising the body of the Lord eats and drinks judgment on himself. That is why many among you are weak and sick, and a number of you have fallen asleep."

What does it mean – "without recognising the body"? I am convinced that it not only refers to the physical body of Jesus which lived on earth and died on the cross. It also refers to the spiritual Body, The Church – Jesus' Now Body. So, if I eat and drink at the communion "without recognising the body", I eat and drink judgement on myself. For this very reason some Christians are weak, some are ill and some have died. Wow! A major cause of distress and difficulty in the local church. A self-inflicted injury too.

So what does it mean? I think it is talking about unity. Are we not *One* Body, *One* Bread, *One* Bride? Thus if I have a squabble or grudge against *any* other Christian, past or present, in this fellowship or in any other, and I come to the communion not having put it right, then I eat and drink "not recognising the body", and I plunge myself straight into the soup. Confession and forgiveness are the key elements here. Eph 4:26-27 says that I am allowed to be angry, (but not in a sinful way), *but I must not let the sun go down on my anger*. Deal with it *today*. Jesus also said that if we are bringing a gift to the altar and remember that another person has a grudge against us, we are to leave our gift at the altar, and go and get reconciled first (Matt 5:23, 24). Our task, as

Paul said in his trial before Felix, is to have a conscience void of offence before man and before God (Acts 24:16). See, it is not enough to confess our sins to God. "Recognising the body" means confessing our sin to our fellow Christian, and getting it cleared. Let me end this thought with a personal testimony: I think the Christian life can easily be defined as one of "non-stop repentance from beginning to end". At least, that's one aspect of how I have been able to survive for the decades I have – and how I have come to love people so much.

The Difficulty of Leadership.

Poor people, our leaders. Fancy volunteering to be in charge of a group of people you didn't select, deal with issues the individuals should have dealt with ages ago and resent you intruding, and try to weld a group of self-determining individualists into a common direction to do a common task.

Democracy, as John Stott has pointed out, is the best form of National Government there can be in this sinful era. In it, everyone is accountable to everyone else, and it stops dictatorships, corruption, irresponsibility and greed. But Democracy in a local church is appalling. It breeds opinionated people, party factions, criticism and rebellion – all of which stink in a Christian setting. Local churches should be *Theocracies*. That is, Dictatorship by the most Benevolent Dictator in the universe – Jesus. Everyone needs to submit in gladness and peace to Jesus and His plan for each church. We must not get contaminated and diluted by worldly thinking or worldly methods. Democracy in church kills the work of the Holy Spirit. Read that last sentence again – and stop doing it. See this: we have to wrench the control of a local church out of the hands of people and put it back where it rightly belongs – into the hands of Jesus. People are going to resist that with all their might, because they like to be in control. But sinful human beings always make a mess of everything they do, and dump the Holy Spirit into the trash can.

So how does leadership occur in a Theocracy? Leaders are appointed by God. How do we know who they are? It becomes obvious – they pop up to the top like corks in water. Everyone gets the witness inside that he is the person who should lead. That's why it is so important that leaders are appointed up from inside, not in from outside. They have done their apprenticeship in the full sight of the rest of the congregation, who then accept the Lord's anointing on their lives. Often it is the man himself who hasn't seen it, and some get the job kicking and screaming against it. Which is very good. It means he is not full of his own importance. None of the human accolades for leadership – presence, talent, ability, care, knowledge – apply. God's appointing carries God's anointing, regardless of every other consideration. The only qualifications are Godly ones and are recorded for us in 1 Tim 3:2-10 and Titus 1:6-9.

So now I am going to tread on lots of toes. I don't mean to offend, so please don't take offence. I agree with David Pawson and the Roman Catholic Church – Leadership is Male. That's not just my opinion; it's the New Testament pattern. With the odd exception, the world agrees with it too – look at the few ladies there are in international leadership positions. There are many roles for women in every church that completely fulfil and satisfy their gifting. They can be appointed to those positions without hindrance, as they were in the New Testament (e.g. Rom 16). Why, then, the considerable number of women whom God has used since the 19th century? Missionary ladies have been the lifeline of evangelism in leadership roles, and many still are. Why? I think my answer would be God's Grace. Where the Biblical norm and the best solution (men) was not available, God has used those who were available, and we honour both Him and them for the amazing spiritual and effective work they have done and are still doing. But like denominations, that does not necessarily mean that it was ever God's best. Neither am I disparaging *in any way* ladies who are at present in leadership in the denominations. I have met some excellent ones, and I honour them as much as I honour men in similar positions. I only ask all of you to consider the scriptures and to ask how closely we are following God's revealed guidelines. For both men and women, the key for everyone in leadership, it seems to me, is that every one has to be "under authority", and, in some way, that authority must be male.

Next, leadership is collective. Every church leader *must* have a group of contemporaries round him to whom he submits. In the New Testament they were called Elders, and there were more than one in each assembly. A man who cannot submit to his peers is a very dangerous man, and should not be in any leadership position until he has got rid of the sin that drives him or divides him. The Elders acknowledge the Leader's anointing, and the Leader acknowledges the Elders' spiritual inputs. Jesus sent out His disciples two by two. Paul always took a companion on his missionary journeys. A husband and wife combination is not acceptable – there must be a minimum of two men together. This applies to all Christian works, not just churches. Leadership is collective. But don't get me wrong – there must be *one* main leader. But he must be in submission to fellow elders.

Personally I think that only those church leaders who have been in a fixed location for some 20 years have effectiveness. That is the only way to stem criticism, build disciples, and see through to the end the visions they have begun. Happy is the church leader who has more than 50% of his congregation with him and supporting him with enthusiasm.

What do you make of the four-year leaders – those who stay in one place for a short time and then move on? How can they possibly have an effective ministry? Is it a career they are looking for? So what then would be their calling – into a professional priesthood? So what are they doing now – *practicing* on a congregation? Surely leadership in the Church should be intertwined with people, not careers, shouldn't it? Just asking, that's all. But I think that is why God's New Testament plan was to elect leadership from among the local converts, to have people in leadership that "come up from inside", not "in from outside".

I cannot see that leadership of a local church "in from outside" is Biblical. There is still too much influence from Constantine.

<u>The Self-Centredness of Spiritual Butterflies</u>.

What are Spiritual Butterflies? People who flit from church to church to find "one that suits them". I am privileged to live in a generation and in that part of the world where we can commute Sunday by Sunday to a church of our choice. People in the 1st Century AD could not and the poor of the 21st century AD cannot. "Bloom where you are planted". Belong! It does not matter if there are people or leaders there you don't get on with, belong! There will always be people we don't get on with. And I am certain that God deliberately positions difficult people together, just so that we can rub the corners of wickedness off each other, and learn just how much love and grace must be brought to birth in our hearts.

Think of it – those who can't stand a particular church and flit like butterflies will never find one to their liking until they end up in their own church of one. Themselves. Have you ever met Christians – born again, water baptised, Spirit filled, got-all-the-goodies Christians – who cannot fit into a normal local church? I know lots. (Maybe I'm their problem?) There is something very wrong with a Christian, *regardless* of their testimony, who cannot mix with the weak, the poor, the ignorant, the difficult, the normal common people there are in every church. I would call it extreme self-centredness. Which, you will read me writing, is the root sin of the universe. Satan has got them – very subtly, very cannily, but very certainly. And very tragically. Have you ever considered the *details* of Matt 7:21-23?

So let me try to deal with two more troublesome issues: Membership and Tithing.

<u>Membership</u>. Should Churches have a written membership system or not? Certainly there are many advantages - particularly for the leadership. To have a membership system would give the

leader a list of those he could rely on, those he would need to visit regularly, and those who "belong". For the member, it gives the advantage of security, commitment, consistency and involvement. All churches have casual visitors, and rightly so. But those "casuals" who live locally and are not committed into one particular place of worship (i.e. are not members of any church) have probably got something wrong with them. They prefer the freedom of flitting between churches, or not going anywhere at all. "By their fruits you will know them." Some churches (Baptist in particular) use membership as a voting right; no membership, no vote. But these churches tend to favour democracy as a base for their operations, and I have already noted how unbiblical that is. So, we could argue that churches should establish a membership system.

However, I don't think that arguments or points for debate are the issue here. The real issue is, "What guidance does the Bible give in this matter?" Answer - none. Or very little. Membership was irrelevant in the New Testament Church. Nor is it an issue in today's world where the church is persecuted or marginalised. Where it could cost you your life if you belonged to a church, a written membership system is totally unnecessary. It's only in a decadent, woolly, comfortable Christian environment, where people can please themselves what they do and where they go that a written membership becomes an issue. But, again, what guidance does the Bible give? Probably the most relevant is in 2 Cor 3:6 "He has made us competent as ministers of a new covenant - not of the letter but of the Spirit; for the letter kills, but the Spirit gives life." This applies to membership as well as ministry, I think. That which is of the Spirit brings life - even though its boundaries might seem ragged. The letter always kills. That is, rules and regulations always bring bondage, and will always be inadequate. I therefore conclude that, to have a "membership" of any kind - other than simply being a born again Christian - is to take a church away from the fluidity, and therefore the life of the Holy Spirit. Having said that, I do accept that it can bring both the church leader and the individual

Christian into security and commitment of belonging. But I have to ask whether it is really necessary, or of the Holy Spirit.

Tithing. A tithe is one tenth. It was an Old Testament requirement and Jews brought to God one tenth of their income - often of their produce. That tenth belonged to God, had to be the best, and was not theirs to keep. It went into the temple - or their central place of worship - mainly for the provision of the priests and Levites, who had no land inheritance among the tribes of Israel. Over and above the tithes came the offering, which was a voluntary gift beyond the obligatory tithe. All this was part of the Law.

So what about the New Testament, where the Law has been superseded? There are those who say that there is no mention of tithes in the New Testament. But they would be wrong: there is one. It came from the mouth of Jesus Himself in Matthew 23:23. "Woe to you scribes and Pharisees, hypocrites! You give a tenth of your spices - mint, dill, and cumin. But you have neglected the more important matters of the law - justice, mercy, and faithfulness. You should have practised the latter, without neglecting the former." Which means, "Continue with your tithing." Do both.

However, Hebrews 3 and 4 give us an interesting principle in relation to the law on the Sabbath. In the Old Testament one day in seven belonged to God, and the rest belonged to the people. In Hebrews 3:7 - 4:11 it tells us very clearly that in the Epoch of Grace it is no longer one day in seven that belongs to the Lord, but *seven* days in seven. The "Rest" of God is that no days belong to us. The Sabbath day has been cancelled and extended to a week, month, year and lifetime. This principle also applies to all our income. No longer does a tenth belong to God; in the New Testament ten tenths of our income belongs to God! None of our income belongs to us.

So I tried to put this into practice. I tried to live by the Holy Spirit in what I spent on my family and myself, and what I gave to God and to others, making a careful note of all my expenses.

Over a period of two consecutive years, living "by the Spirit" revealed that I was well short of a tenth of my income going directly to God through my local Church. "Surely," I then thought, "would living by the Holy Spirit ever cause me to give away to God less than I would give under law?" Of course not! So I realised that I had got my guidance screwed up (it must be my fault, not God's). I also realised that, so far as money is concerned, nearly everyone gets it wrong, and the tendency is to err on our own side rather than God's. That is, there's always something I desperately need to use my money on - now. In addition, I remembered the words of Jesus from Luke 16:11, "So if you have not been trustworthy in handling worldly wealth, who will trust you with true riches?" So I came to the decision that I would go back under Law in this matter. I set up a Standing Order at the bank that took one tenth off my monthly income (before tax) and sent it straight to my local church. All my other giving came under the heading of "offerings". And that way I got peace with God, for I was "not neglecting" the tenth that was God's minimum right, and that Jesus Himself commanded us to do. If you're not sure whether you are giving God the tenth of your income (via the local church you attend), do the same exercise that I did. Then read Malachi 3:8-12. Do you want God's blessing to be poured down on you without measure? Then bring your tithes into the Storehouse, for the blessing of the Lord makes rich and adds no sorrow with it. I tell you, if every Christian gave a tenth of their income to God there would never be any shortage of funds to spread the Gospel far and wide. Nor would any of our church leaders be poor. The sums are simple. Ten Christians giving a tithe means that a church leader can earn the average wage of those 10 people. That means that if they can live without poverty, he can live without poverty. Twenty tithing and that church could fund a missionary or youth pastor. And so on. It seems to me that giving one tenth of our pre-tax income straight to God via the local church we attend is the minimum we should be accomplishing in this Day of Grace.

Church.

"Church" is God's word, not man's. It means "The Called out Ones". *We* are The Church. *It* is merely a building. We The Church can meet and worship anywhere in any numbers and do not need towers, spires, bells or consecrated buildings to be who we are and do what we must. The Church is a living, throbbing, united entity, called by God, redeemed by Jesus, united by the Holy Spirit, made up of *people* of every tribe and tongue and nation.

We are the Bread of Christ. We are the Body of Christ. We are the Bride of Christ.

But there are many local churches that need to see that a Body without its proper Head is also dead. Why go on pretending we are doing Jesus' thing when the evidence is that He is nowhere to be seen in what goes on? He is Spiritual, supernatural, and does things like changing lives, doesn't He? So if those things are not happening in our church, have we not cut ourselves off? If we find ourselves cut off from God, guess who moved? (I quote another). Life is too short to be associated with dead churches. Or, as another has said in answer to "Should I move or should I stay?" "It's like sitting on a block of ice. If it freezes you, get off. If you melt it, stay." We can easily tell if the place in which we are worshipping is a good place – we will have living fellowship with Jesus there and living fellowship with other members of His Body.

By way of another aside, let me tell you how you can tell which attitudes in our hearts are from God and which are from satan. Any attitude that divides person from person or people from people is from hell. Any attitude that unites person to person is from heaven. (I am not talking here about sexual love). Kindness, gentleness, generosity, encouragement are all attitudes that unite people together, and are characteristics of God. Anger, bitterness, resentment, rejection, control and hundreds more are attitudes that divide people, and are characteristic of satan. It's that simple.

And it's a key for discerning people. Divisiveness breaks the principle of the Body of Christ, because it breaks unity.

I used to have a fear. As I read and meditated on the enormity of The Church (The Big One), I feared that I would get absorbed into the Big Thing, and become as insignificant but possibly as useful as a washer or nut in a huge machine. But the more I have walked with Jesus, the more I see that a relationship with Him makes me bigger - bigger than I ever imagined I could be and certainly bigger than I could ever make myself. What Jesus does is to *complete* us. We were very rough material when we first gave our hearts and lives to Him. But years and experience refine and hone us, reshape us and introduce divine characteristics and attitudes within us and transform us into Sons of God – warriors in God's Kingdom. People of significance. We don't lose anything but our sin. We gain. We become perfect and complete individuals (we were all unique from the start), and lose our independence. So, because God is consistent and does not (cannot, will not) change, what is true of His dealings with us on earth will be true of His dealings with us in heaven. We will never just be one mini cell in the huge Body and Bride of Christ. We will all be significant and very important. I have already quoted CS Lewis writing that in heaven the inside is bigger than the outside. Similarly, I see that in the Body of Christ, every individual is bigger and more important than the Whole, and the Whole is bigger and more important than the individual. Both. We will never be "absorbed" and disappear.

That is also true of churches. In my local church I become less important but more significant. Less important because I submit to everyone else; more significant because my contribution is more Christ-centred and more Christ-timed. Moreover, I become part of the glue that holds my local fellowship together as an effective unit. That glue (or the sinews of Eph 4) is love, unconditional acceptance of *everyone* and encouragement. Without my support, where would my local fellowship be? And where would I be without them?

So let me pull this all together.

How do local churches fit into The Church? The glory of the Holy Spirit is that, like the Father and the Son, the Trinity are everywhere at the same time – not limited by geography. So every local fellowship, of whatever abomination, is part of The Church and is a complete representation of the Whole Body, but in a unique way. The five-fold ministries of Eph 4:11 will all be represented there (with the possible exception of Apostle. Apostles are sent out by the local church to others elsewhere. No Apostle *from* that church has an effective ministry *inside* that church. Didn't Jesus say, "Only in his hometown, among his relatives and in his own house is a prophet without honour." God will supply a Leader, Elders and Deacons (or whatever the denominations have renamed them). Each will function individually and uniquely (which is why there are no job descriptions in the Bible for Elders or Deacons – only character requirements). And the variety of style represented by every local church, of whatever size, is typical of God and a joy to every Christian who belongs.

I need another little aside here. In Eph 4:11 the five-fold Christian ministries are listed: Apostle, Prophet, Evangelist, Shepherd and Teacher. The word "shepherd" is regularly translated "pastor" in this passage, and I cannot find a reasonable reason why. The Greek word "*poimen*" is used 18 times in the New Testament. 17 times it is translated "shepherd", and this once it is translated "pastor". Why? It's a wrong translation. It confuses. And it has led to much misunderstanding. Everyone knows what a shepherd is and does. No one knows what a pastor is and does (although anyone with any knowledge of English will know that it means the same thing). Consequently, a Pastor can do what he chooses because there is no definition anywhere as to what he should be doing (a bit like Vicar or Rector). No one seems to understand that his primary role is to shepherd Jesus' sheep.

God delights in His people. We all have a significant place and a part. So the local church has been designed by God to be the central hub round which every Christian functions, to which every Christian belongs, and through which every Christian receives the vital flow of Spiritual Life that transforms him from darkness to Kingdom Light (or from one degree of glory to another). We may yet be only the embryo, but *WE ARE* the mighty and eternal Bride of Christ.

SUMMARY

All God's work on earth pivots round local churches. People are saved and nourished through them. It is in them that we are discipled into Bride-likeness. We learn to belong together as One Body.

Chapter 16

CHRISTIAN INITIATION.

God has made some very clear provisions for when people first become Christians. Those provisions are so that the entrance into our new life in Jesus can be smooth, sweet, safe, secure, effective and without hassle. My observation of today's Church is that practically all but one of those divine provisions are unused or delayed. The result is that Christians born again by the Holy Spirit don't last long in the kingdom, or have a mighty struggle to remain consistent and hassle-free. I place the blame for the failures among new converts squarely onto local church leaders. Woolly Christian leaders lead directly to failed Christian disciples. So what are these provisions? There are four.

They are rebirth by the Holy Spirit and not by man's choice; Baptism in water; Baptism in and filling of the Holy Spirit; and joining the local church. Let's go through them gently, and see what God provides through them.

<u>New Birth</u>.

The New Birth is a sovereign work of God. Jesus is the person who does the "wooing", and He has a run-up whereby He starts to reveal Himself to the individual inside. This is often accelerated by prayer, which itself will be promoted by the Holy Spirit in the heart and mind of another Christian. Nowadays we tell those who are seeking that they must give their hearts and lives to Jesus, and ask Him to come into their lives. Neither of those can be found in scripture. Where that process might be close to the truth, the real truth is that they need to yield to Jesus' sovereignty. They have to abdicate from the Rulership of their own lives and allow Him to be Sovereign over them. Jesus is *Lord*, and must become Lord to each individual. There are those who give their hearts to Jesus, pressurised by well-meaning and zealous Christians, when neither the time nor the initiative belongs to God. Babies who are premature and born before their terminal time are born weak and fragile. It is the same with Christian New Birth. When *God* does it, the timing is perfect and complete.

There are those who join a church, and see that as becoming a Christian. It isn't. Indeed, there are many substitutes devised by man whereby people "join the club". But none of them work, and people who "become Christians" in any other way than the biblical way of New Birth by the Holy Spirit will neither last nor find heaven. If a person does not come into a personal relationship with Jesus, they are not a Christian. It is worth my repeating here that Christianity is not a religion, it's a relationship. People who "get religion" don't get Jesus. Therefore they've got a substitute which is hollow in substance and will lead nowhere valuable, even though it may feel nice at the time.

The Total Package.

Even when someone today is born again by the Holy Spirit, the Christian Church fails to complete the job, and leaves them defective and under-developed. It is the fault of the Church - new converts know nothing. Why do we not read our New Testaments and do what the early Church did?

What did they do? Acts is the book that tells us. They got the new converts baptised in water as soon as possible. As they came out of the water, they prayed for them to be baptised and filled with the Holy Spirit. And then they joined the body of believers. Let's have a look at the Bible passages first and then make observations.

> Matt 28:18-20. "Then Jesus came to them and said, "All authority in heaven and on earth has been given to me. Therefore go and make disciples of all nations, baptising them in (into) the name of the Father and of the Son and of the Holy Spirit, and teaching them to obey everything I

have commanded you. And surely I am with you always, to the very end of the age.""

Acts 2:38. "Peter replied, "Repent and be baptised, every one of you, in the name of Jesus Christ for the forgiveness of your sins. And you will receive the gift of the Holy Spirit.""

Acts 8:12-13. "But when they believed Philip as he preached the good news of the kingdom of God and the name of Jesus Christ, they were baptised, both men and women. Simon himself believed and was baptised."

Acts 8:14-17. "When the apostles in Jerusalem heard that Samaria had accepted the word of God, they sent Peter and John to them. When they arrived, they prayed for them that they might receive the Holy Spirit, because the Holy Spirit had not yet come upon any of them; they had simply been baptised into the name of the Lord Jesus. Then Peter and John placed their hands on them, and they received the Holy Spirit."

Acts 9:17-18. "Then Ananias went to the house and entered it. Placing his hands on Saul, he said, "Brother Saul, the Lord—Jesus, who appeared to you on the road as you were coming here—has sent me so that you may see again and be filled with the Holy Spirit." Immediately, something like scales fell from Saul's eyes, and he could see again. He got up and was baptised."

Acts 10:44. "While Peter was still speaking these words, the Holy Spirit came on all who heard the message."

Acts 10:47-48. "Then Peter said, "Can anyone keep these people from being baptised with water? They have received the Holy Spirit just as we have." So he ordered that they be baptised in the name of Jesus Christ."

Acts 16:14-15. "One of those listening was a woman named Lydia... The Lord opened her heart to respond to Paul's message. When she and the members of her household were baptised, she invited us to her home."

Acts 16:31-34. "They replied, "Believe in the Lord Jesus, and you will be saved—you and your household." Then they spoke the word of the Lord to him and to all the others in his house. At that hour of the night the jailer took them and washed their wounds; then immediately he and all his family were baptised. The jailer brought them into his house and set a meal before them; he was filled with joy because he had come to believe in God—he and his whole family."

Acts 19:2-6. ""Did you receive the Holy Spirit when you believed?" They answered, "No, we have not even heard that there is a Holy Spirit." So Paul asked, "Then what baptism did you receive?" "John's baptism," they replied. Paul said, "John's baptism was a baptism of repentance. He told the people to believe in the one coming after him, that is, in Jesus." On hearing this, they were baptised into the name of the Lord Jesus. When Paul placed his hands on them, the Holy Spirit came on them, and they spoke in tongues and prophesied."

You will notice that every single one of these incidents differs from the others in details. Sometimes the order of events is changed. Sometimes the timing is different - that is, there are sometimes gaps between the New Birth, the Baptism in water, and the Baptism in the Holy Spirit. Why is it not consistent? Because, simply, *every* Christian New Birth is unique, and the Lord caused those incidents to be singled out from the thousands that took place at that time to tell us two things: the first is that every part of the New Birth is essential. The second is that every new Birth is different from all the others. The *parts* are essential. The *pattern* may differ.

So what are the common factors?

1. That every New Birth was followed by Water Baptism.
2. That every Water Baptism was done as soon as possible after the New Birth. There was no option for new

converts. They were virtually frogmarched to the nearest water and dunked (more of which later).
3. Every Water Baptism in Acts was done in the name of Jesus or into Jesus, rather than the Trinity.
4. Every Water Baptism was followed by prayer for the filling of the Holy Spirit.
5. Every filling of the Holy Spirit was accompanied by some supernatural phenomenon or sign - speaking in tongues, prophecy, healing etc.

Those are the common factors. Where it was possible, all those events took place *on the same day*, or as near as possible. So let's look at these events in a bit more detail.

<u>Water Baptism</u>.

There is considerable controversy among Christian denominations about the method of Water Baptism, and I am bound to tread on a few toes by coming down on one. But it seems to me that Romans 6 paints a picture that can only be interpreted in one way. "We were therefore buried with him through baptism into death in order that, just as Christ was raised from the dead through the glory of the Father, we too may live a new life." This paints the picture of total immersion. And there I will have to stick. The picture is definitely one of death, burial and resurrection, and, of all the methods of Water Baptism used in Churches today, total immersion fits that symbolism best. The new convert comes into voluntary Death to Self, is buried by others as a picture of its completeness, and is brought back up out of the grave by a power not his own (symbolised by the person doing the Baptism) to start a new life with Jesus as Lord over Him. That's the New Testament picture.

As I have mentioned, it was done on the same day where possible. Those Churches who practise total immersion today leave the decision for Baptism to the candidate, as to "whether" and "when". The New Testament never gave new converts those choices, and the kind of delays we have today, for whatever reason, are unbiblical, and leave the new convert "undressed" and ill-equipped to live a new life in Christ.

Why? Let's see what the New Testament teaches that Water Baptism does.

It's a cut off. It initiates a supernatural severance of the bondages to the world, the flesh and the devil, all of which the convert has been plagued with all his life so far. It's supernatural because Jesus personally does it. And it cuts the ties of sin through those three channels to which every non-Christian is addicted.

The major Bible text for this is Colossians 2:11.

> "In him you were also circumcised, in the putting off of the sinful nature, not with a circumcision done by the hands of men but with the circumcision done by Christ, having been buried with him in baptism and raised with him through your faith in the power of God, who raised him from the dead."

Here Paul sees the Old Testament Covenant of circumcision being the perfect picture of "flesh" being cut off. In the New Testament this represents "flesh" or carnality being cut *out.* And that is done personally by Jesus – as the verse clearly states. It is a supernatural event, regardless of what it "feels like" to the new convert. Moreover this severance is *only* connected to Water baptism.

The second picture is separation from the hooks of the world and the devil, and we have to turn to another Old Testament occurrence to see it. Moses brought the children of Israel through the waters of the Red Sea by Divine power. Egypt represents the world, and Pharaoh represents the devil. Having gone through the waters of the Red Sea, Israel would never see those two again. In the same way, but miraculously, Jesus severs the ties of the world and the devil from the new convert by "going through" the waters of Baptism. The New Testament scripture for these last two is 1 Corinthians 10:2: "They were all baptised into Moses in the cloud and in the sea."

There is yet another Old Testament picture given of Baptism in the New Testament. In 1 Peter 3, Peter likens baptism to Noah and his family being rescued from God's wrath by the Flood, a picture of the cut off from the world through water and a cut off from God's anger and punishment.

So Water Baptism is not just a *symbol* of being cut off from the world, the flesh and the devil: it is the occasion when Jesus *supernaturally severs the ties* to those addictions in the soul of the convert. Now just imagine the struggle new converts would experience in their new life with Christ if these three addictions were not cut off! That's why it is essential that Water Baptism is done immediately or as soon as possible after conversion. It is a command of Jesus to His Church to do it (Matthew 28) - not a choice of the Convert. It was 3 days between Paul's conversion and his Baptism. Today's Church expands that to 3 years or 30 years! How very, very foolish we have become.

This supernatural cut off by Jesus is, if I read my Bible correctly, *only* done through Water Baptism. I don't read of it happening *any other way* or at *any other time*. So a Christian can live their lives in Christ without it, and the internal stranglehold to the world, the flesh and devil will always be there, regardless of how good and holy the individual may appear to be. They will struggle all the days of their lives. No Baptism, no cutting off. No other way.

Surely, you may argue, every Christian has trouble with the world, the flesh and the devil all their lives? Absolutely true. But those *without* Baptism remain addicted to all three and to their old life from inside out. Those *with* Baptism fight them from outside in. The latter are invariably the more victorious - the Velcro has been taken away from inside them, and the little hooks coming from outside don't stick so well, or even at all.

Now let me talk for a moment about children. Many Christian denominations today practise Infant Baptism. This was a practice that came in around 300 to 400 AD, and was initiated because many children were dying in infancy because of the huge infant mortality rate at that time. Where the scripture says that if we believe and are baptised we will be saved (Mark 16), Christians thought that they could not influence an infant's belief, but could influence their Baptism. So it became the common practice for infants to be baptised in case they died in childbirth or childhood.

So what does the Bible say about Infant Baptism? Regrettably, the Bible is silent about it. It actually does not specify children any way. What is very clear and absolutely certain is that the New Testament practice was Water Baptism of *BELIEVERS*. And no one else. But, you might ask me, what about households? For example, Lydia's household, Cornelius' household, and the household of the jailer at Philippi were all baptised when the head of the house was baptised. There is considerable debate amongst denominations as to who would be qualified to belong to a household, and I do not want to enter that debate. It is enough for me to say that whichever argument one uses using those illustrations, the argument is from silence. Arguing from silence is a dangerous affair. One can argue in many ways, and each way is just as valid as all others. It is therefore better not to use silence at all as a proof of any behaviour pattern. So what can we conclude about Infant Baptism or the Baptism of children? We should not argue it in any way. However, we can say for certain that if a child has been born again by the Holy Spirit and is a believer in the New Testament sense, they should be baptised in water just like any adult.

There have been a number of (good) books written justifying infant baptism (e.g. J.C. Ryle "Knots Untied"). But if the basis of their argument is from the Bible, then they only have silence and implication to argue from. And as I have just written, one can argue many ways from silence, and therefore it is better not to argue from it any way at all.

Again, the common practice of many churches nowadays is to delay Baptism (or Confirmation, which, again, is unbiblical) until Christian children have reached the age of about 12 or 13. From a Biblical perspective, this is completely unjustifiable. If a child has been born again, they should be baptised immediately just like any adult. People, and particularly parents, might argue that a child needs to be a little bit more grown up before they get baptised, because "they do not understand what they are doing." It is worth my pointing out that not even an adult who has just been born again knows what they are doing! It is the responsibility of the Church leadership, who know the significance of Baptism, to make sure that every new Convert goes through the waters of Baptism as soon as possible. Remember too, that becoming a Christian is not a matter of intelligence or understanding, but of Revelation from God himself. If God chooses to regenerate a child into the kingdom, then that is His affair, and we have no authority to water down or manipulate the pattern that He has established.

So how do we handle infant baptism or christening? God is gracious. Even though it is the dodgiest of the practices of baptism (Biblically), God still uses it as His sovereign will foreknows. Some people I know feel so strongly that they should not get baptised twice (once as a child and once as a believer) that they accept their infant christening by faith. That is their choice. I was baptised twice – once as an infant (so I have been told) and then after I came to Jesus. So long as we are in peace with God about our actions, then all will be well.

Many churches who teach Believer's Baptism also hold "Baptismal Classes." Where do they get that practice from? Certainly not their Bibles! If a person is born from above by the Holy Spirit and baptised immediately on his confession of faith, then there is no time for "classes". Do you see what has happened? By abandoning the New Testament pattern, we have to make up all sorts of other practices to cover our tracks. Things like Infant Baptism, Confirmation, Baptismal Classes, giving choices to the convert etc – all stem from our ignoring what God taught New Testament Christians to do. Pleading reasonableness and common sense still does not justify our disobedience to what God initiated and continues eternally to recommend.

Baptism in the Holy Spirit.

Alongside Water Baptism is the Baptism in the Holy Spirit. The pattern was set by Almighty God Himself with his Son Jesus. As Jesus came up out of the water at His baptism, the Holy Spirit descended on Him in bodily form like a dove. There is no way one can argue that Jesus did *not* have the Holy Spirit before His baptism. So this was another anointing. If you read Luke 4, words like "full of the Holy Spirit", "in the power of the Holy Spirit", "being led by the Spirit" are used of Him after His baptism, where those expressions had never been used of Him before His baptism. And from then on wonderful things were done through Jesus. Listen - if it was necessary for *Jesus* to be baptised in water *and* filled with the Holy Spirit, *how much more* do the likes of us need both? Thus in Samaria in Acts 8, with Paul in Acts 9, with Cornelius in Acts 10, with the Ephesian church in Acts 19, all were filled with the Holy Spirit, either before or after their Water Baptisms. With that filling went some supernatural manifestations, many of which are listed in 1 Corinthians 12. It is not enough to be *born* of the Holy Spirit: we also have to be *filled* with the Holy Spirit. The New Testament tells us that that should happen immediately after Water Baptism. There must have been thousands of converts in those days. But the Holy Spirit has highlighted those specific incidents in Acts to enable the rest of us to follow the pattern He initiated at the beginning. Not to understand it is human. Not to follow it is rebellion. Not to do it is to be a Christian cripple.

To be born of the Holy Spirit is *for* the new convert. To be filled with the Holy Spirit enables God to work *through* the convert. That's the difference. That's why it had to happen like that to Jesus. And therefore us.

As a matter of passing interest, a "Baptism" is an initial and one-off event; a "filling" is a subsequent and frequent event, and can (should) happen many times.

Joining the Local Church.

Very little emphasis is made nowadays on the fact that new converts must belong inside the local church - whatever denominations they may be. Why should they? I have already written that the local church is the embryo version of the Bride of Christ, and the New Testament describes it as the Body of Christ. We are all aware that a local church is only part of the Body of Christ, and every church is inadequate and fallible in many ways. But it is still the Body of Christ, of which Jesus is the Head. In a human being or an animal, cutting off a head brings death both to the head and to the body. The life of Jesus courses through His Body, the local church, simply because He is its Head. In Romans 2, Paul talks about the Christian Church being grafted into Judaism; we have been attached into God's tree, from which our life, existence, and fruitfulness receives its nourishment. In John 15, Jesus talks about the vine. Only a branch remaining in the vine receives the nourishment that it needs to produce grapes. People who join and belong to a local church are those who receive the nourishment of Jesus on a regular basis. Those Christians who, for reasons best known to themselves, cease to attend a local church, cut off the very flow of life that God has provided to keep them whole, faithful and clean. That's why new converts *must* be committed permanently to their local church fellowship.

What about church membership? I have already written on this subject. Many churches have a legal format for this. This invariably involves regulations, obligations and privileges. However, I do not see that system as being biblical. An individual needs to be committed to his local church, and the local church needs to be committed to that individual. Am I a member of a local church? We qualify by being born again. Does anyone *need* to have it in writing? Or to be excluded if it's not in writing? To enter into rules and regulations is to bring bondage, is part of democracy, and should not be seen in churches. In 2 Corinthians 3, Paul says "For the letter kills, but the Spirit gives life". It can be helpful for the Leader to welcome new people officially from the front. That introduces them to the congregation and the congregation to them. Then they "belong", and should take care that their belonging becomes a commitment.

Someone has pointed out that what every new convert needs is friends. Church members need to bear in mind that new converts immediately start to "belong" when they make new friends. That is very important to their remaining in the Body of Christ.

Have you noticed in Acts 2:47 that "The Lord added to their number daily those who were being saved."? What a strange sentence. Isn't it obvious that that is what happened? But its significance is that those who were being saved *actually joined* the Christian family. None were independent and went off and did their own thing.

Let me try to summarise the situation. Before we become Christians, Jesus lives outside us and the hooks of the world/flesh/devil live (reside, abide) inside us. When we first become Christians, both Jesus and the hooks of the world/flesh/devil continue to live together inside us. Water baptism removes the hooks and pushes the world/flesh/devil out of our innermost beings; from then on they work on us from outside in. The Baptism in the Holy Spirit fills us full with Jesus, and He needs to be continually filling us from then on, because, as D.L.Moody said of himself, "I leak."

My Church Leader Robert Spiller says this of the baptisms: Each one has an element, a baptiser and a candidate. In water baptism, the element is water, the baptiser is another (maturer?) Christian, the candidate is the convert. In Spirit baptism, the element is the Holy Spirit, the baptiser is Jesus, and the candidate is a Christian. In the body of Christ, the element is the Christian Church, the baptiser is the Holy Spirit, and the candidates are Christians (see 1 Cor 12:13 "For we were all baptized by one Spirit into one body—whether Jews or Greeks, slave or free—and we were all given the one Spirit to drink."). All three baptisms are essential for every Christian, and we need to see that the Holy Spirit needs to *baptise* us into the Body of Christ.

So why these necessities for Christian Initiation?

If I am not born again by the Holy Spirit, I am still in my sin. The redemption of Jesus does not apply to me, and never will until I come into a personal relationship with Him. The result of not having a personal faith in Jesus is that I will therefore personally carry the consequences for all my wickednesses - eternally.

If I am not Baptised in Water, my soul and spirit are still plugged into the modem of sin - and the world, flesh and devil have permanent and unrestricted access to me inside. I am on the broadband highroad to sin. I will *never* be free from those addictions and hooks.

If I am not Baptised in the Holy Spirit, I am not empowered to live the life of Jesus on this earth. I will have to struggle with living a Christian lifestyle with the strength of man, not the strength of God.

If I don't belong to a local church I cut off the regular flow of divine input from God, and fellowship (support) from other Christians.

Is it any wonder that so many new Christians struggle nowadays? If any of these four are omitted the new Christian will be still locked into sin, live an underpowered and inadequate Christian life, or die simply because he lacks nourishment for Life. And if I do not get these done to me by my local Church at the earliest possible moment, then my take-off into the Christian Life will be dodgy and dangerous, and I will struggle to get off the runway, much less remain airborne.

The divine provision for starting our Christian lives is free and perfectly clear. Just how silly are we to modify God's provision or not to use it at all?

SUMMARY

The entry gate to becoming a Christian is fourfold: to be born again by the Holy Spirit, baptised in water, baptised in the Holy Spirit and join a local church. Nothing less. And all done as soon as possible together.

Chapter 17
PREACHING, TEACHING AND PROPHECY.

There is a difference between preaching, teaching and prophecy, which I will try to analyse later. All three are biblical expressions, and are means whereby God speaks to us through other people. All three are very important. For instance, in 1 Corinthians 1:21, Paul says: "..God was pleased through the foolishness of what was preached to save those who believe." And in chapter 14 he writes: "But if an unbeliever or someone who does not understand comes in while everybody is prophesying, he will be convinced by all that he is a sinner ..."

But before I begin to analyse the differences, I need to ask this question: what is the fundamental purpose of all three? Very simply it is to enable God to bring *Revelation* to the listeners.

Revelation, as I have already emphasised, is the way God speaks to us. It is a living thing. It is *not* information. Revelation is life, understanding, faith, communion, fellowship with Jesus all rolled into one. It is how we become Christians, how we stay Christians, and is the essence of our relationship with God in Jesus.

We can get a Revelation through many channels, and we need to be open all the time to that. But, through people, preaching, teaching and prophecy are God's main anointed methods. That is, He speaks best through people through those media.

So let me be general to begin with. I used to be so unhappy as a speaker that all the work I put into a sermon would be mainly missed by the majority of a congregation. The theme was lost on them; the Revelation that was so precious to me was like a desert to them; the tangling with difficult and Biblical issues they saw as bordering on heresy, and they were not open to the vast mind-stretching promises of an Infinite God. After a while I gave up. I wanted to enter dialogue with them, but I used to get more interesting reactions from my teenagers than I did from the adults. So I decided to simplify my subjects and tried to lead them forwards, but some were offended because they already knew that stuff.

And then I got Revelation.

This was it: there were only *two* people in a congregation for whom a whole sermon was important. That would be the preacher and Jesus. It was as if the precious Revelation that God had given me was confined to me alone. Everyone else had different Revelations.

This Revelation came to me as I sat and listened to someone else preach. The things I took out of it were snippets from the talk, highlighted by the Holy Spirit, and applied directly to my own situation. The rest was irrelevant - to me. I suddenly cottoned on to the fact that if everyone who was there was listening to the Holy Spirit like I was, they too would get Revelation from the Holy Spirit which was completely relevant to their lives, but very different from the ones He gave me. Thus God was enabled by what was being preached to speak to everyone there in a very different and a totally relevant way. Indeed, the whole sermon was probably only for the personal benefit of the speaker - he would have loads of Revelation as he prepared and new insight as he spoke.

Taken this way, every sermon is a miracle. No one knows the thoughts or Revelations of any other, and no one can guess what God is saying to anyone else. In John 21:21, when Peter asked about John, Jesus said, "Mind your own business. That's his story, not yours, and I'm not going to tell you anything about him." The only person who is exposed is the speaker who bares his thoughts and heart. This miracle happens, of course, when everyone is receptive to the Holy Spirit. It is satan's task to divert our attention by any means possible. But if we overcome those barriers and focus in on Jesus, every sermon becomes a corker. No one who gives an hour to Jesus will come away disappointed. (I used to say something similar to our children and teenagers at Upcott - no one who gives a week of their lives to Jesus will come away empty). Those who take notes during a sermon are going to benefit from it later, and it then comes under the heading of teaching, more of which later. I suppose the greatest hindrance to hearing the Lord speak to us during a time of collective worship is criticism. The spirit of criticism kills the Holy Spirit dead in our hearts, and very often spreads throughout the congregation. The age old practice of continually assessing whether the preacher is "sound in his doctrine" is the greatest hindrance to having God speak to us through a sermon.

One of the stories of Smith Wigglesworth (which I hope I have got vaguely right) was when he was in a church service, at which he was the speaker. The atmosphere was dead. He got up to speak and immediately pointed to two ladies sitting on opposite sides of the congregation. He declared that he was not going to speak until they had got together, apologised for the animosity they had felt for each other over many years, and become reconciled. All the eyes of the congregation turned on them and, humbled and exposed, they got up, apologised with tears and embraced. Whereupon the Holy Spirit descended on the meeting and many people came into repentance and faith and many others were reconciled. The body of Christ affects the body of Christ. And a word of knowledge can be very powerful.

Beware the human trends. It is trendy for any one of us so to respect preachers that we idolise them. We pick up this trend from the sports and music arenas (sports idols and pop idols), but it spills over onto Christians with preachers too. Look at the (silly) Christians who "follow" a preacher. Some even venerate them. Sure, we must respect them. Certainly, we ought to thank them. Regularly. But the only human being we ought to follow is Jesus Christ. Don't, I beg you, don't ever rob Him of His glory. Don't substitute any other human being for Him. Ever.

The difference between a spoken sermon and a written one is that, initially, more people hear it than read it. But in the final analysis, more people read it than hear it. The blessing of reading Christian books is that the "congregation" is spread far and wide and each person can return many times to the places where they received blessings. A written sermon is potentially unlimited in its blessing, the greatest of which are in the Bible, more of which later.

So let's look at preaching, teaching and prophecy. What is the difference? Preaching tells us what the Bible *means*, and makes life applications from it. Teaching expands and exposes what the Bible *says*. Prophecy says directly what God is saying Now. Let's look at each in turn.

Preaching.

Preachers often preach on themes. They take their texts from all parts of scripture, clarifying the application both from the scriptures and to the people. Then they make life applications which, in the Holy Spirit they feel are relevant to today's people. Often they speak from a text. Every preacher has a different style, and if a regular preacher is open to the Holy Spirit, there will be no limit to the number of themes and applications he can make. The main problem a preacher has is that there is always too much information, and cutting it down is difficult. I have found that every sermon that I can recall preaching leaves, at the end, some important issue I have left out. I have learnt to live with that regret.

Every preach-in contains some teaching or other. And every teach-in contains some preaching or other. Also, both may contain a prophecy or a word of knowledge.

Every effective preacher must prepare in the Holy Spirit. Most need a long time alone with God and in their Bibles to draw from the Holy Spirit His message for the moment. Most weekly sermons are "top-ups"; that is, they are designed by God to keep the congregation active in Christ, remind them of some things they have forgotten (as in 2 Peter 1: 12-15), to encourage them in their commitment to Jesus against the flow of the world, and to take them further on and higher up. Occasionally a preacher will bring a mind-changing sermon, one that alters our perspective on Christian things radically. The Americans call it a paradigm shift. But all preachers in one church should start to repeat their themes every 10 or so years. In that time the congregation will have changed, a new generation will be attending that have never heard that stuff before, and the oldies will have forgotten you ever said anything like that. Besides, it will be dressed in new clothes. I maintain that every church leader should remain in his church for a minimum of 20 years. It's the only way to see a vision through and provide consistency in a church.

Evangelists are a special breed apart. They are nearly always preachers. But they have the specific purpose and skill of bringing outsiders into the knowledge of the Gospel and into a relationship with Jesus. Generally speaking, evangelists don't make the best shepherds or the best Bible teachers. They seldom know how to take converts forward into becoming disciples. Once a child is born it needs nourishment that would enable it to grow. That's when evangelists need the grace to hand over to other church leaders who can shepherd their sheep and take them into deeper discipleship. Teachers, on the other hand, often discover converts emerging through their teaching, for, certainly, the basic issues of the Gospel will appear at regular intervals through the texts.

Teaching.

Teaching is telling people what the Bible *says*. So, the teacher takes a passage and makes clear to the congregation what God is saying when He caused that passage to be written. Bible passages have consistency, and themes spring out of them like branches from a tree trunk.

Bible teaching is often far more potent than preaching. People have difficulty remembering preaching themes unless the preacher has a very good illustration round which to hang it. But that is less so with teaching. The passage itself remains intact and can be visited many times in the future, thus bringing back to remembrance the teacher's exposition. Besides that, the closer one keeps to the original, the more the Holy Spirit is able to work in the heart of the listeners. Bible teachers bring their listeners into more spiritual depth than preachers. They deal with the difficult themes dotted around the Bible texts, where preachers often skim across the top, or avoid the difficult bits altogether. A Consistent Bible teacher disciples more people by his teaching than a preacher does. And Jesus wants disciples, not converts.

In my opinion, proclaiming what the Bible *says* is far more effective all round than proclaiming what the Bible *means*. But then, I'm a Bible teacher (teaching is in my genes), and each to his own. Thank God there are not two like me in this world!

Prophesy.

Prophecy is hearing the voice of God and retransmitting it as accurately as we heard it. I have expanded on this elsewhere in this book. Prophecy as I have heard it during the latter years of my Christian life is formal, boundaried, and, I therefore believe, restricted. I think we limit the Lord by putting such boundaries around our prophecies. But I classify words of knowledge, words of wisdom and interpretation under the same canopy and heading as prophesy. I think it's all much the same sort of thing. And as such can often come into preaching or teaching. Embedded in a sermon, completely unprepared and largely forgotten by all except the person(s) for whom it was intended, God generates the odd revelation that the preacher never knew was there. Sometimes it's the casual remark. Sometimes it's the story that suddenly springs to mind. Sometimes it's an illustration from life - all these God uses to cut straight to the heart or to grant to someone a special encouragement.

But let me repeat - the one single purpose of preaching, teaching and prophecy is to allow the Holy Spirit to bring Revelation to the listeners. These three are God's work, not Man's. Pity the preacher who wants control over his listeners and leaves God out. His message is dead from the start.

Ian Andrews once said, "On a good day, 70% of prophecy is from God, and 30% is from man. On a bad day, 30% is from God and 70% is from man." We just have to be careful and wise.

I have asked the Lord for a prophecy for the couple involved in every wedding I have attended over the last 20 or so years. And He has given me one for each of them. It has often been written down on the back of the Order of Service, but it has been there. If you want a prophecy, or need a word of knowledge to inject into a tricky situation, just ask God – and be sensitive to His inputs. Many people put a lot of mystery or mystique on such things – as if the prophet is some way–out spiritual phenomenon. But it's not so with me. I am just an ordinary thick-headed dullard. If I need one of those prophecy things, I just ask and get it, and move on. It's good to be a child and know nothing; God loves children and fills His Heaven with such (Matt 18:3).

Every preacher, teacher and prophet is a limited human being. Therefore everything they do is going to be less than 100%. We should not strive after perfection - that's a sin. We should simply accept that we live with our limitations, and God is mega gracious to use us at all.

But let's go to the Bible. What is the New Testament? It is simply a series of preach-ins, teach-ins, and prophecies all rolled into one. The unique nature of it is that it is uncontaminated. It is not perfect - in that every translation has its limitations, but it is perfect in that the whole Bible contains everything that God wants every person in every generation to know. It is fixed, and cannot be added to. Nor can anyone take away anything from it. It is the clearest, most barrier-free channel for God to speak through, as I have already pointed out in the chapter of that name.

The whole Bible is a direct preach-in, teach-in and prophecy by God. That's why He speaks to us better through it than through anything else. And still He used men through whom to speak.

God is well able to give Revelation over and above the specific details contained in the Bible. But He will never contradict it in any way at any time. That is why I am bold enough to write the things I have in this book.

I pray that both my (written) preach-ins and my (written) teach-ins will bring comfort to you, encouragement to you, and Revelation from the God of love.

SUMMARY

Preaching tells us what the Bible means. Teaching tells what it says. Prophecy what God is saying Now. The Bible originally was all three rolled into one book.

Chapter 18
UNITY.

Ladies and gentlemen, we've forgotten "The us-ness of we." If we ever knew it. We may be learning the blessedness of Me. But we still have little handle on the blessedness of We.

I cannot believe the self-centredness of the Christian Church. My salvation. My sanctification. My ministry. My giftings. My destiny. My life. My place in the body. My contribution. My peace, joy, patience, income, prosperity. My future in heaven. Where will I fit in the Bride?

Need I go on? Songs, even some modern ones, are more about me than about Jesus or about us. A friend of mine says he prefers the old hymns to the modern jingles because, he says, they have "words". And those which are the best are those which exalt Jesus the most. But so few there are which express our destiny - to be one together as one Bride for the King.

But some will complain – "Surely the Bible gives many indications of a personal salvation." Well, no. Some certainly. But the majority are plural, not singular. I have pointed out elsewhere that we are very much deceived in English by the word "you". The majority of "you's" in the Bible are plural. But we don't distinguish singular and plural in modern English. So, in accordance with our self-centred perspective, we invariably interpret "you" as singular. The only thing I can do to help us get our perspective right is to point you to the KJV where "you" is almost always singular, and where the plural is rendered "ye". Better still, go for the Greek. Learn the difference and start to see salvation from a collective view point, rather than a personal one. By way of illustration, Ephesians chapters 1 and 2 are all plural. I bet you've always interpreted them as singular!

"But surely," you might continue to argue, "The "us" of the New Testament is made up of lots of "me's"." I would agree with you. There certainly is Biblical precedent for the salvation of the individual, and I will analyse that in a jiffy. But those who stay there just haven't yet got hold of the purpose of salvation. That purpose is collective, not individualistic. *We* are the body of Christ, not me. *We* have the mind of Christ, not me (1 Corinthians 2). *We* are the Bride of Christ, not me.

Everything that the Holy Spirit is trying to generate within us is collectiveness. He is trying to make us like the Trinity. Why does He exalt humility so much? Why servanthood? Why did Jesus choose to be a slave, not a king, when He already was a King? Why did He lay down his life for us (not just for me)? Because in all these things He is pushing us towards the Unity and Oneness of the One Bride.

There is indeed a necessity for personal salvation, and that is very clear in the Bible in a good number of places. So, if the final vision of God is a collective one, why the need for individual salvation and holiness? The only sensible reason I can muster is to bring you the picture of the human body.

We all have a body. But this body is made up of countless trillions of cells. Each cell is complete in itself. They are perfect, full of life, and functional. Each cell is a living organism in its own right. But its purpose is not to function for itself. It does not exist to self-perpetuate. Nor does it grow; it will not expand to take over other neighbouring cells. It functions to serve the body. Each cell is a transmitter of life to the cells surrounding it. And each cell is specific; it has a specific shape, a specific function, one place in the body where it functions best and for which it is designed.

Now there is no way that we ever think of ourselves and our bodies as a bunch of cells. We think of our bodies as One Body. My One Body walks around and does things. The purpose of the trillions of cells is to form together as a unity to be One Body doing one thing at a time. Each cell is crucially important, and we know the result of rogue cells. We call them cancer and they can kill the body. So each cell is crucially important, carrying out a specific function in a specific place so that the whole body can work together as One unit.

It is not for nothing that God gave Paul the illustration of the Christian Church being like a human body in 1 Corinthians 12. There the comparison is of larger units: "Can the eye say to the hand I have no need of you?" "If the whole body were an eye, where would be the sense of smell?" And, indeed, the illustration of larger units of the body is far more apt than cells. The picture of the Christian Church as a series of cells is too small an illustration for us to grasp and might imply that we are either unimportant or not valuable. Yet God made the human body in the way He did because that is the way it functions best - indeed, perfectly.

To think of ourselves as one cell in the Bride of Christ may be, perhaps, too difficult. It reduces each individual down to microscopic proportions, and because it's so small and therefore so invisible, none of us can cope with such insignificance. Yet I think that is exactly what we are and will be - one cell in the Bride of Christ. But by this we should not despair. I also think that the Bride of Christ is going to be so enormous and so overwhelming that we cannot cope either with its enormity. God says in a number of places that no one has ever conceived what He has in mind for each of us for the future. He only writes in superlatives, because He knows that our little minds could not possibly cope with the truth even if we were told it.

So what is God doing with us?

I think He is building the Bride of Christ cell by cell. Just like He builds a human body in the womb cell by cell from just two microscopic cells, so He is building the Bride of Jesus cell by cell, and taking 70 odd years to form and complete each cell with infinite patience and care.

You already know that you are unique. Each one of us is uniquely different. Therefore each one of us is infinitely valuable. No one is insignificant. We should already know that God has a special place for each one of us in His Bride, planned before the foundation of the Earth, but based on our travel through time because of God's foreknowledge. Therefore none of us Christians is lost. How God works it out is far beyond any one of us to ponder. And it's not our job either. We just have to trust that the consistent God of love has got it all sussed and is working out His plan as time travels forwards. I can believe Him for that, and can trust Him too. I pray you can as well.

Both the "too small" and the "too big" idea may be too much for us to cope with. But we can cope with our own identity, significance, importance and uniqueness. And that is probably why we think selfishly in most of our own Christian thinking. We do not like losing our individuality - and, for sure, we won't. But we cling on to it as if it's the thing of maximum importance. Why can't we trust God with His promises (and the scripture cannot be broken) and move towards the way He wants us to be?

So where does He want us to be?

God is building the Christian Church. The One Church. Jesus' Bride. The One Bride. In order to give that oneness, God has to change our "me-ness" into "us-ness". He has to change the whole of our naturally human way of life into God's natural way of life. To do that He has to generate in us humility. I've written about that elsewhere, but humility is basically voluntary death to all that is self-exalting within us. Before we can get to a place of delighting to honour others, we have to die to "me". The more I die to myself the more I like other people, and the more I appreciate them and long to bless them. So I cannot operate collectively as a member of the One Church until all those little selfish ways and self-indulgent desires are just there no more. It has to be a strong desire in my heart to be humble, but it's only Jesus who can generate God's beautiful version of it in my soul forever. Cry to God to give you humility.

From humility comes servanthood. Most of our lives we are called upon (often forced) to be servants to other people. So here is a test to see how far down the Christian pathway you have got: - how much do you delight in being a servant to others? *Every*one else.

Compare yourself to Jesus. He was delighted to serve everyone He met. You too. He is our servant and our humble friend. In it He finds no resentment. He delights to bless and help and serve.

That delight of His is also something He delights to generate within us. Did He not talk about laying down our lives for our friends? And, in a thousand little things we resist doing it and resent the intrusion it makes into our me-centred little lives.

Without humility and servanthood we cannot even begin to be "collective" in our thinking or act as One Thing in this world. Yet that is what God wants of us. We have to start learning here on earth what we are going to be forever in heaven.

Every cell in every body, and especially in the Body of Christ, must be perfect and whole. There is no way we can be perfect encased in these bodies, or "these bodies of death" as Paul puts it. But we have to aim there. Please don't get me wrong here - if we aim for perfection we plunge deeper into hell. Our concept of perfect is not that of God's. Perfection must come under God's definition, and be generated in us by the Holy Spirit and not by us. To be perfect is to be Christ-like. It's a soul thing, not a behaviour thing. That is, it is generated from inside out by the Holy Spirit and not from outside in by us. Do you know what my definition of Perfection is? Forget behaviour! It is walking in fellowship with and obedience to Jesus every waking moment of every day.

So what God is doing "through all the changes and chances of this mortal life" is to surgically remove demonic self-centredness and generate the Trinity's collectiveness. The sooner we realise and recognise that, and the sooner we develop a "collective" mentality, the sooner disasters and difficult discomforts get erased from our lives. Difficulties are the sand papers that God uses to move us out of self-centredness into Christ-likeness. People too. Most of us find that the most difficult and most emotional issues that cause us the greatest distress are people. Personality clashes, resentments, bitternesses, disagreements et al are all fired up by satan and used by the Lord to humble us. I wonder if it ever occurred to you that every single Christian is one day going to be your best friend, your closest companion and someone you delight in more than your best holiday? It's inevitable. So the sooner we can reach that place with all, the more Jesus will be pleased with us, will use us and will bless us. The Christian way is upside down - the more down we put ourselves, the more up God puts us. On the other hand, the more we exalt, justify or promote ourselves, the more ineffective, unhappy and clobbered we become. God and man hate arrogance.

This self diminution is particularly tricky when it comes to leadership. Surely, you might argue, leaders don't just have to be capable and competent - don't they also have to stand at the front and take authority? Well, kind of. Jesus' requisites for leadership are typical of both Him and His Father:

> "Jesus called them together and said, "You know that the rulers of the Gentiles lord it over them, and their high officials exercise authority over them. Not so with you. Instead, whoever wants to become great among you must be your servant, and whoever wants to be first must be your slave"." (Matt 20:24-27).

Now isn't that crazy? How can anyone lead by being a servant? It's difficult for me to give you a detailed rationale of "How". But I do recommend you watch what Jesus does in your own life, and follow in His footsteps. Copy His style. He does it and is it. In your own heart, don't you seriously appreciate the way He leads? It's non-threatening, non-proud, non-aggressive, non-heavy, and is helpful, humble and delightful. We love Him, not just because He has told us He does, but by the way He approaches us, addresses us, encourages us, supports us, helps us and empathises with us. It's the most effective form of leadership in the universe. And it works best. People will love and appreciate us as much as they love and appreciate Jesus if we follow His lifestyle in dealing with them.

Jesus' style of leadership works best among submitted people. If all of us are laying down our lives for each other and honouring each other, then we all recognise leaders, recognise their anointing, and are glad to follow them. Not to is rebellion.

There will certainly be times in every leader's Ministry when they have to exercise the authority God has given them, and deal with the demonic, with sickness, and with rebellious people. But still their lives should be spent as servants and "ministers". (A Minister is not a general name for a church leader: it is someone who ministers; that is, serves).

From that do you see the style of unity and collectiveness emerging? God's kind of leadership is collective, as is mere living. We *are* One. So we must aim to *be* One.

I wonder, too, if you have ever thought of who else may possibly be with us in the Bride of Christ in heaven? Let me make some suggestions:

- Perhaps those who have never had an opportunity to hear of Jesus on this earth but in their lives they have honoured God? When they meet Him at death, then perhaps He will fulfil all their unfulfilled dreams? ("Will not the Judge of all the earth do right?" Gen 18:25)
- Zealots of other religions? Those who have genuinely sought God and found the only god who was available in their lives?
- Aborted babies? Those who genuinely were but ended up might-have-beens; maybe God who formed them will bring them into His kingdom because He knows what chances they would have had if their mothers had not chosen to abort them? Methinks they are far more likely to belong to Jesus in heaven than their mothers!
- Miscarriages.
- Special needs people on this earth - those rejected by society through mental or physical disability will be perfect in heaven. Will Jesus' perfect them *for* heaven?
- In the days of Elijah, when he thought he was all alone, God had 7000 who had not bowed their knees to Baal. I believe the Grace of God and the zeal of God is seeking and saving many more insignificant people than we are aware of. They are His, and He is theirs - particularly those under persecution. I think Christians, particularly Bible instructed

evangelicals, make entrance to heaven an awful lot more exclusive and an awful lot narrower than God does. By that I am not modifying what Jesus has said in the scriptures. It's just that the specific requirements for entry into heaven come to completion slowly, and the system is a process. Many people die before that process is complete, and some just after the process has started - like the thief on the cross. Isn't this why we are called to love and appreciate *every* human on earth? We just don't know who we are talking to (especially children) and thereby "some people have entertained angels without knowing it."

- Christians in all denominations. Evangelical Christians (and Calvinists in particular) are very scathing about Christians who don't toe their own doctrinal lines. I really do not accept a philosophy current today that "All roads lead to God." But I do subscribe to the view that "Many roads lead to Jesus," where "Only Jesus leads to God." Indeed, because all humans are unique, it occurs to me that that is the number of roads that are possible that lead to Jesus. Everyone treads a different pathway to heaven and everyone at a different rate. I'm sure that not everyone takes the narrow path presented to them, but it is their own, and I have no right to say that it is a wrong road, or that Jesus is not there with them. Therefore my criticism that other Christians don't believe what I believe, or do not worship in the way I prefer is arrogant, unbiblical and judgmental in the extreme. May God deliver us from such criticism, and make our hearts inclusive and unconditional.
- All those millions of people who die daily in this world through starvation, genocide, and the oppression and greed of man. The story of the rich man and Lazarus springs to mind here. I am so glad I will never have to make the kind of decisions that accept or reject others into heaven. They still have to choose Jesus and He them. But how does He find them? When and where? People in extremity are far more likely to seek and find the Lord than the rich and comfortable – as in Jesus' story. So let's be magnanimous in our thinking,

shall we? Let's love *everyone.* Their salvation is God's responsibility, not ours. Ours is to love and accept them unconditionally.

So what about unity?

There are some mega promises in scripture for those who operate the "One Body" system on earth. God knows how self-centred we are and how long it takes to come out of it and come into a "One Body" mentality. Therefore He loves and exalts any "One Body" operations in our Christian lives.

For example, Psalm 133 stands out, and I have mentioned this elsewhere. Where brothers live together in unity, there the Lord *commands* the blessing. And it's true. It really does work. Great blessing enhances all the actions of a group that is one in heart, unity and purpose. We need to remember, too, that "The blessing of the Lord makes rich, and adds no sorrow with it."

We can see what God's blessing does by considering its two alternatives - a curse and a middle way. The middle way is neither of God nor of satan but of man. If what we do is of man, then it is not only neutral but extremely hard work. We slog away to achieve very little. That always characterises the work of man. Curses, on the other hand, produce negatives, so not only is our work ineffective, what we do actually destroys what we want to achieve. Moreover, curses generate negatives in other people - anger, resentment, rejection and lack of cooperation.

On the other hand, the blessing of the Lord enhances what we do, provides effectiveness with little effort on our part, and makes everyone associated with that work happy. The presence of the Lord is not necessarily seen. It is barely felt. It is more sensed. And it is delightful in every way. Those whose work has the blessing of the Lord accompanying it make giant strides in what they do, and what they do is accompanied by a beauty and a glory that brings joy and peace. Psalm 1 is the good illustration: those whose roots continue to be in the water live fruitful lives continually, and "whatever they do prospers."

Many Christians are not proactive in seeking God's blessing in their work. We often assume it, and assumption doesn't work. If we assume God is with us and He is not, then our work immediately reverts to man's, and we find difficulty, labour and fatigue kicking in, making everything hard graft. One minute of prayer and surrender at any point in a day restores our vertical submissiveness and releases the Lord's blessing. We should never be afraid of, ashamed or embarrassed about praying with our Christian companions at any time of a day or at any point in our work. The moment we recognise hassle, gather together and pray it away.

The key to receiving the Lord's blessing is unity. That's what Psalm 133 tells us. Surrender to Jesus and submission to our fellow Christians brings the unity that releases God's commanded blessing

So what do you make of Jesus' prayer from John 17: "That all of them may be **one**, Father, just as you are in me and I am in you. May they also be in us so that the world may believe that you have sent me."? Or "I have given them the glory that you gave me, that they may be **one** as we are **one**:"? Or "I will remain in the world no longer, but they are still in the world, and I am coming to you. Holy Father, protect them by the power of your name—the name you gave me—so that they may be **one** as we are **one**."?

Jesus' statements point us in the direction He wants us to go. Moreover, the consequences of being "One" please God enormously. Don't they point always away from the exaltation of Me and the promotion of Us?

Paul, too, points to this necessity. "Do nothing out of selfish ambition or vain conceit, but in humility consider others better than yourselves. Each of you should look not only to your own interests, but also to the interests of others." (Phil 2).

All these scriptures are not just for this earth, as if unity is a jolly good idea, chaps, and could be beneficial for your health and your pocket! It is the essence of heaven, the certainty of eternity, a lifestyle for ever. I've written about it in chapter 14 on the Church.

Throughout the whole history of this earth and cosmos, God is forming, building, creating One Body. He is doing it carefully and methodically, cell by cell, soul by soul. But we must never forget, brilliant though our individual salvation is, that we belong to One Body, the Church. God is looking for “A People” not “person's”. The extraordinary self-centredness of modern Christians is a throw-back to the Anarchy or Legalism of previous Epochs. In the total surrender that each individual has to the whole, none of our uniqueness will be lost. The Trinity themselves surrender totally to each other but never lose their individual uniqueness. I believe it will be the same for the Bride. *Together* we reign - I do not. Let's not skip over the major import of plurality that the Bible emphasises throughout its pages. That surrender and plurality are a major lesson for the Christian Church today. Let's start becoming what we have been destined to be.

A car or an aeroplane works because every component is useful, every component is designed to function fully, is in its designated place, and is contributing to the whole in exactly the way it was designed. Many components - One car.

A jigsaw puzzle, before it is started, is a mess. Lots of little pieces, all with barely identifiable patterns on them and looking nonsense, all spread haphazardly over the table. Individual pieces are all irrelevant and useless on their own. No piece serves a useful function unless it is in its right place and collaborating together with all its other pieces. Anyone who has put a jigsaw together will know how vital one piece is to the whole. One piece of a jigsaw has no function whatsoever unless it is united with its mates. Many pieces - one jigsaw. So it is with us.

A sheep in a lane is a pain. It gets in the way of other lane users. It tries to climb the hedges and can't. It panics, and more so when a car or a person passes by. On the other hand, a sheep in a field is beautiful. It's at peace; it has plenty of grass to eat; it's in its right environment doing what sheep do best. Moreover it is happiest when all its other friends are with it in the same field, contentedly chomping the same grass.

Our selfish human culture drives us into individuality – the exaltation of Me. We are encouraged to do all things through Jesus Christ – does that mean *self* driven and *self* exalting? Which of us is multi-functional? None. Which of us can live on our own with no reference to other people? Think again. But also think what an enormous and fantastic unit we turn out to be if we function fully in our designed way, in our designed place, and forming One Thing in God's kingdom! Unity is for ever, guys and gals.

Every human being is most contented when he or she is in their designated place, doing the thing they were best designed to do, and working alongside the other people they were best designed to complement. Didn't Jesus often compare us with sheep? On the other hand, a person trying to operate outside their gifting, or in the wrong place, or promoted beyond .their ability, is a pain in the neck. They are a sheep in a lane - out of place, out of sync, out of ideas, panicking, destroying rather than enhancing, and a proper nuisance to everyone and everything. Such are the ambitious. Such are self directing humans. Such are Christians, too, who are in the wrong place at the wrong time. They are square pegs in round holes. They damage the Body of Christ, regardless of what they claim to be doing.

But when we do the will of God, we will never be led wrong. We will never be in the wrong place. We will never be acting beyond our capability or our capacity. We will always be "together" with other Christians in an attitude of submission. What is more, our lives will be characterised by the Blessing of God. Shouldn't they be? We will be as beautiful and contented as a sheep in a field; and, like the sheep in the field, we will have plenty of pasture to feed and grow on alongside our friends.

SUMMARY

God's work on earth only comes through a united Body. Separation, individualism, isolation or division are wicked and destroy God's work.

Chapter 19
OUR BESETTING VULNERABILITY

If you got as far as reading my chapter on Sin, you will see there that I came to the Biblical conclusion that the degree of sin into which we are born is absolute. Body, soul and spirit are born absolutely sinful. There is no vestige of righteousness in us and we cannot please God. Sad but true.

This chapter is mainly about how we acquire sin and then how we get rid of it. I will deal with the title at the end.

That sinful inheritance actually made us available for every kind of contamination the moment we were born. That is, if we had, say, an abusive parent, he or she could cause us all sorts of physical or psychological damage when we were young. And the fact that we were sinful would mean that we would be open to receive, absorb and retain that damage. I can only assume that any such abuse given to Jesus in His early years (it's only a hypothesis) would roll away from Him like water off a duck's back. Whereas all of the rest of us would soak it into our souls like a sponge. Let me say now that satan is a dirty fighter. If he can get us at our most vulnerable, he will. We all know that as adults, when we are hungry or tired or frazzled, that's when he tempts us and we are most vulnerable to sinning. But what about our childhood? There we have by far the most vulnerable stage of our lives. If our parents do not protect us then, we soak up negativity by the gallon and it becomes incorporated into our personalities. I would maintain that the greatest negatives in our lives are given to us and received within us before the age of 7. The same applies to positives. Good, healthy, wholesome attitudes are brought to birth within us by good, healthy, wholesome inputs from adults before that age. Of course, more come in later. But the ones at greatest depth come in roughly before that age of 7.

From where do they come? I have two major ones for the negatives, and two for the positives. Let's look at the negatives first.

The first of the negatives comes through "Authorities". Every child is automatically under authority. The main two are parents and teachers. A child automatically believes what their parents and teachers tell them, and receive consequent attitudes into their souls. A mother can influence her baby even in her womb. If she wants it, she can sing to it and talk to it, and there certainly are instances of babies responding to that. On the other hand, if the baby is not wanted, an attitude of rejection can be transmitted to the unborn child, and there are some people who have never known what it is not to feel rejected. It is built into their psyche and personalities from before birth. Fear and anxiety are others. Women can be more vulnerable to these negatives than men are, and mothers with them hand them on to their children. What we sow, we reap. If mother takes little interest in her child while she/he is young, that child will have little time for mother from teenage onwards. Fathers too. An abusive or absentee father builds negatives into his children. It is nonsense to say that a mother can replace a father's authority and position. And fathers who abandon their responsibility in marriage and run after other women and/or things are building the same irresponsibility into their children. The place of Authority is very, very important in the life of a child, and good, honourable authority at that. The Bible says that sins are handed down to the 3rd and 4th generation. That comes through both Nature and Nurture. By Nature we inherit characteristics from our parents, as we all know. But we can also gain characteristics by Nurture – that is by example. All of us are aware of attitudes, ideas or opinions from other people that have moulded our lives.

Teachers. They come into the same category as parents. What a teacher thinks of a child can govern that child's whole life. For instance, if a teacher says, "Oh, you'll never be any good at Maths" (or Science, or English or whatever), then that becomes a belief in that child's life. And, unless counteracted by the word of God, can remain for ever with them. Jesus often said, "According to your faith it will be to you." He was referring to faith in Him, and it led to healing and deliverance etc. But the principle remains intact, and faith in negatives is just as strong as faith in positives or in Him.

If I believe that I will never be good at Maths because my teacher told me I wouldn't, according to my faith it will be to me. The place and words of Authority Figures in our childhood are supremely important. The odd frustrated word from a frazzled teacher or parent can be a life-time's tragedy to an individual. And it's not good enough to say that when they grow up they will get over it. It's not that rational. Negatives that are buried deep in our souls become part of our make-up and character, and are certainly not easily removed. Indeed, we adjust our whole life-style around them regarding them as an inevitable and immoveable part of our characters. "I have always been a "worry-bug" – or fearful, or rejected, or control-freak, etc."

As I said, satan is a dirty worker. If he can establish a human being in his kingdom, he will do so from their earliest age. Through whatever means he will put his negatives into our lives. What form do these negatives take? How can we recognise them?

They take the form of attitudes of heart: fear, anxiety, resentment, rebellion, rejection, bitterness, anger, selfishness, greed, independence and so on. I have said elsewhere that it is easy to distinguish human attitudes that come from satan: they break or divide people from people – they sever good relationships. Any attitude that causes separation between people is from hell. Any attitude that exalts me above others is also from hell – pride, superiority, dominance, control etc. And any attitude that refuses to change (the opposite of humility) is also from satan: - obstinacy, intransigence, etc. But you will see that all these divide and do not unite people. If satan can birth any of these attitudes within us, he's got us. And, from his perspective, the earlier the better. Let me give you some examples of how some of these attitudes come into us.

Rejection I have already mentioned. It can come in in the womb – transmitted directly through mother. It can come in through bullies at school, or through teachers at school who obviously don't like us. Or we can set our wills "to go it alone" with as little reference to others as possible, rejecting "people influence" in our lives as much as we can. All these I have witnessed as a Christian minister. Rejection is one of the hardest spirits to get free from.

Why? All humans have been built to love and be loved. It's an innate longing within each one of us. Rejection is the feeling that no one loves me and no one wants me. So it causes a battle inside. The desire to be loved makes the person seek more and more attention and seek more and more to be honoured, respected, appreciated and loved, and at the self-same time reject any love, respect and appreciation it receives. It gives a person an addiction for being appreciated, but it is never enough. It is an insatiable appetite that is never fulfilled. It can lead to power-hunger. I reckon that Hitler had a strong rejection spirit within him. No amount of power satisfied him. And it's the same for other dictators.

Rejection is also the key to control. People are identifying "control–freaks" more and more nowadays, but few have identified the cause. It's rejection. This is how it works. A person longing for appreciation and hating rejection starts to control all the inputs into his life as a form of protection against getting hurt. He therefore tries to control what others do and say around him. The last thing he can handle is someone rejecting his suggestions, inputs or decisions. So he either withdraws, gets angry and/or goes further into trying to control others. It leads him to select carefully those he has around him, so that all outspoken people are evicted from his company, or they are very tightly controlled. Do you see the separation it causes? Any Christian in this position will be unable to lead properly. He will either become a dictator, a bully or a control-freak, and he will certainly not like sharing leadership with anyone else. The only way out from any of these symptoms is deliverance – more of which later. Someone has said that 80% of the British people have a rejection problem. I was born into the generation of fathers whose philosophy was, "I don't praise my children: it only makes them big-headed." My own Dad used to say it, as did my father-in-law. It's a lie from hell. Praise never destroyed anyone – it always built them. And I guess most of the British people have been brought up never being praised, and never being appreciated, especially as children. How much better is the U.S.A. where they constantly affirm children.

Rejection is not by any means the only negative and I have already listed a few. But how do these negatives "enter" our souls? Here I have to go back to the Gospels, to an area of truth that has been long rejected or ignored by the Christian Church, and dismissed as irrelevant nonsense by the world. It is the presence and activity of demon spirits.

Jesus set people free from demonic bondage, and the gospels are full of it. Jesus knew that demons were real and "cast them out" of people. In addition, demons knew Jesus was real, and addressed Him personally. There was quite clearly a serious clash between them. I have discovered, over a long period of time, and trial and error, that demons really do exist, that they are real and that they "possess" people. Indeed, that every negative attitude inside a human being is the mark of the presence of a demon. It's not part of human nature – it's a barnacle stuck onto our souls. I really do not want to write pages on demonic bondage; there are others who have done that in greater depth and at greater length than I want to here. Enough to introduce you to the idea, confirm that it is real, and encourage you to get rid of all of them you unwittingly find within yourself. But let me give you the experience in my life that confirmed and high-lighted it. Then I will tell you how to get rid of them.

I had left the RAF and I was a Bible Teacher at Upcott, the Christian Conference Centre where I was working. Because I had not been to Bible College, I had to do all the research myself, and allowed myself to be led by the Holy Spirit as to what I should study and where. At one point I timed my preparation at 21 hours for every hour of teaching. So, one day I was in my study/office preparing for a talk. Not long into it, I started thinking about a local Christian leader who had done me a dirty – said something nasty to me or about me behind my back. At that time one of my major vulnerabilities was resentment, and I started to get my teeth into this guy. "That is what he said. That's how I would reply, etc." It must have been chewing round my mind for a good hour. The preparation was forgotten. Eventually I saw that what I was doing was no good, shook myself, and said, "It's really not right to get so resentful about that Christian brother." Immediately into my mind came the name of another person who had done me dirty. So I started chewing them up inside. Again, after a long time, I recognised this wasn't good either and shook it off. A third name came into my mind, and I was off again. This went on all day. People came into my mind from way back in my life – at least a dozen – one at a time. (I realised later that my pet demon had a whole library full of resented people that he could call on from my computer memory. As yours has with your particular weakness!). Round about 5 o'clock (having achieved nothing but resentment all day), I had Revelation from the Lord. I suddenly cottoned on to the fact that the one common factor with all these people was Resentment. "It must be a demon" I thought. So, instead of addressing *people* that I had been resentful over, I addressed the cause of the resentment. "Demon spirit of Resentment," I spoke loudly. "I bind you in Jesus' Name. I reject you in Jesus' Name and I command you to get out of my life for ever." I coughed. And then I thought about the people I had spent all day chewing up. Amazingly, I felt no animosity, no resentment for any of them. It was gone. Fully delivered. It was astonishing. And the brute has never returned. The vulnerability stayed for a couple of weeks, and then it went for ever and I was free.

I learned some very valuable lessons from that which I have never forgotten. The first is that I have a personal demon as well as a personal angel (Matt 18:10). How did that spirit know the names and details of those people and what they did to me? It was obvious I have been trailed through my life by a personal nasty. I had read CS Lewis' "Screwtape Letters," and had never really believed it; now I did. Secondly, I was alerted to the personal presence of demons, and I could identify them by the *attitude* they projected. What its name was, that was its nature. Thirdly, I stopped pussy-footing around trying "to get the victory over" such negative attitudes in my soul. A direct confrontation with the attitude worked all the wonders that were needed, and I had no need from then on to try to win a battle inside that had already been won for me. So then I asked the Lord for Revelation on such matters. This is what He came up with:

1. There are such things as demons. They are fallen angels, and have chosen to be on satan's side in the cosmic rebellion. Revelation 12 tells me that ⅓ of the angels fell. That leaves twice as many good ones as bad ones. Fantastic!
2. I have authority over every one of them. Luke 10:19 gives me that right. *("I have given you authority to trample on snakes and scorpions and to overcome all the power of the enemy; nothing will harm you.")*
3. No demon has the right to enter my soul without my permission. Rom 6:16. *("Don't you know that when you offer yourselves to someone to obey him as slaves, you are slaves to the one whom you obey..")*
4. A demon enters my soul (me) by my specific invitation. Clearly, demons all know that they cannot be truthful, open and honourable because they operate in deception by nature. For example, say you are walking home alone in a dark street and a cat jumps out with a loud meow. You leap out of the way, terrified. You then acknowledge you are terrified, and, whoops, in comes a spirit of fear. You have been deceived by the spirit of fear and have surrendered to it. Fear is a good illustration, because if we don't get rid of it, it gradually multiplies over the years –

extending its kingdom inside us. Then we find fear of spiders, heights, dark, dogs, being alone and a hundred other phobias (a posh name for fears) gradually infesting themselves within us. Once we have yielded to one, it's twice as easy to yield to more.

5. According to Matthew 12:43ff, demons inhabit dry places, and are hunting for people in whom to live. Presumably they feel comfortable and at home in a human soul?
6. I am a unique Son of the Living God, and neither demons nor satan have authority over me. Indeed, I am a greater species than they are. My choices are mine alone. If I choose to have one possess me through opening up my soul to a negative attitude, then that's my choice. And I can choose to reject it again – or any that I inherited from my parents or childhood.
7. I have no need to carry any negative attitude round with me any longer than I choose.
8. "Fear" is faith in satan's negatives. Satan can only work like God works – through faith alone. The pattern is the same. As we believe a negative thought, that's what we get. Job said: "What I feared has come upon me." Precisely. Faith in Jesus' inputs releases positive outcomes. Faith in satan's inputs releases negative outcomes.

Let me give an illustration of demonic work. I had been away on one of my expeditions, and when I returned I took my wife Eileen and daughter for a day out at Cricket St. Thomas wild life park. Joanna was about 7 years old and was cautious about a number of things. When we crossed a narrow bridge over the flamingo pool, Joanna kept right in the middle and walked at snail's pace. I thought she was just having fun, and I urged her forward as we were holding others up. But she ignored me and continued. It wasn't long before I said to Eileen, "She's crippled with fear. Where did she get that from?" We confirmed it as we continued around the park. That night, after Joanna had gone to bed, Eileen and I discussed it. Because we were the authority over Joanna, we took authority over the spirit of fear in her and commanded it out. We were not in the same room because we didn't want to wake her. The following morning she was shinning up trees in the front garden, as fearless as she always used to be. Delivered. She never knew and we didn't tell her until she was an adult.

I tell you, it has been freedom. I also tell you it really does work. If you are a Christian, try it.

I picked up a very useful tip from Rick Warren's book "The Purpose Driven Life" (p 210), concerning avoiding temptation:

> "**Refocus your attention on something else.** It may surprise you that *nowhere* in the Bible are we told to "resist temptation". We are told to *"resist the devil,"* but that is *very* different, as I'll explain later. Instead, we are advised to refocus our attention because resisting a thought doesn't work. It only intensifies our focus on the wrong thing and strengthens its allure. ... Since temptation always begins with a thought, the quickest way to neutralise its allure is to turn your attention to something else. Don't fight the thought, just change the channel of your mind and get interested in another idea. This is the first step in defeating temptation."

That's quite enough on demons. The Lord uncovers each negative or difficulty inside us in His own time. And when He does so, He provides the means of removing it. He has to be sovereign over all our cleansing, and only He can plumb the depths of wickedness in our souls, like Jesus said: *"Everyone who sins is a slave to sin."* (John 8:34). Until He exposes it, we remain ignorant of it, and should be happy in the state we are in. There is no condemnation to those who are in Christ Jesus, so we should all be happy people, regardless of any negatives still within us that Jesus has not yet revealed to us and removed from us. And, please, don't dredge up internal negatives by yourself – it is very unhealthy and will lead to greater bondage to them. Wait for Jesus to tell you what negatives *He* wants to get rid of next, because His healing is total freedom.

All right. So let's look at the four major sources of positive inputs into our lives.

The first is parents and teachers again. It's astonishing what a positive perspective we can gain on life if our immediate Authorities encourage and promote us. We can actually *make* good citizens by good inputs. Parents have to establish good relationships with their children from the very first. That means spending time with them. I have watched Mums in the street talking to their kids, ignoring other adults, giving priority to their children, and taking an interest in the things their kids delight in. In fact, it's a lovely thing for an adult to enter a child's life and see things from their delighted new perspective. The world for a child is a place of exploration, intrigue, interest and delight. So should it be for their parents. School teachers, too, can enjoy the delights children find in new discoveries. I have had a card printed for parents and adults, which says:

> "If you want to create wonderful people, give your child the 4A's treatment every day:
>
> 1. Acceptance
> 2. Appreciation
> 3. Affirmation
> 4. Affection"

What you sow you reap. Positive seeds generate positive attitudes.

The other major source? Jesus. Parents need to live a consistent *Christian* life in front of their children. Children catch life-style much quicker than words, although words are useful too. Children are instinctively smart at seeing hypocrisy, especially in their parents. "Live the life if you're going to talk the talk" wrote Pastor Cecil Radford.

In addition, parents need to be praying the life of Jesus into their children's lives. Prayer changes our lives, and changes other's lives too. Let me tell you how prayer works. God has deliberately restricted His inputs into the lives of people so that they only come through other people. (John 17:9 Jesus said: *"I am not praying for the world..."* Thus He leaves *us* to pray for the world). Through My words; My actions; My prayers. My inputs set God free to do the best for the other individual that's possible. So with prayer. My praying for people releases God to do good in their lives. No prayer, no input. People argue that if God knows what's best, why does He involve us? After all, He could run this whole earth without us. But He has chosen to run it *with* us. In the Body of Christians, the Church, Jesus is the Head and we are His arms and legs. No human head operates on its own without its body; it works *through* its body. So does Jesus. Prayer is part of that involvement. Therefore pray! Let's change things and people through prayer.

So, I have looked briefly at inputs into people's lives – bad and good. Nevertheless, there comes a time when Jesus challenges every individual with His gift of salvation and offer of an eternal relationship with His Father. Jesus is the "Light that lights everyone that comes into the world" (John 1:9), as I am continually pointing out. He is the perfect lover. He is perfectly attuned to each individual's uniqueness. His "drawing" is perfect in terms of content, time, and length of time it takes. He knows the perfect way. Sadly, not everyone responds and comes to Him when He calls. But they could never have a better opportunity. And Jesus often uses the tragedies, difficulties, demonic oppressions and all sorts of other negatives to bring people to Himself - "By all means saving some."

What happens when people yield to Jesus and become Christians? Their spirits are turned from darkness to light, and they "see God" (but not with physical eyes). Their spirits move from being 100% sin to 100% light; they are now locked in to God and have an open access to Him by Grace through faith.

God allows for a honeymoon period. And then the cleaning up process begins. All that darkness which has characterised their lives up till then has to be faced and dealt with. They have to come out of all their bondages, and be loosed from their chains of sin and wickedness. This takes a life-time. We should not be discouraged by that, for it means that the Lord is dealing with us gently, carefully, and one bit at a time.

Some of the freedoms come through deliverance from demonic bondage. Others by the power of the Lord. Many unconsciously. Some of our bad habits fall away in the first months of our new life like autumn leaves from trees. The nine fruit of the Spirit in Gal. 5:23-24 are a good place to start if we want to see what Jesus is up to in our lives: Love, joy, peace, patience, kindness, goodness, faithfulness and self-control. Those nine (and loads more) represent God's *character*. None of us had all nine by birth, and those we do have are contaminated by sin. But when God starts working these characteristics inside us, we recognise that we are reacting in ways that we never reacted before. We find ourselves being patient and calm astonishingly, knowing that we have always been an impatient person. The thing all Christians need to know is that all nine fruit of the Spirit are a blanket requirement for *all* Christians. We *all* have to grow in *all* nine, and the power of the Holy Spirit is available to enable that to be accomplished inside us.

The rate at which these things are dealt with is both up to the Lord and us. There will certainly be issues in our lives that we do not want to give up. It may be career, position (in Church or in the world), prospects, or habits. As I have said, the Lord deals with a bunch at the beginning, and then one at a time. The more we resist the Lord's prompting to get shot of them, the longer it takes. I have noticed and others have said that the Lord deals with the One Thing, and does not lead us further in our cleansing until that One Thing has been surrendered and has gone from our lives. Only the Lord knows which Thing must take priority next. What I am absolutely certain of is that when the Lord puts His finger on an issue in our lives and reveals it to us, the power to sever it from us, root, fruit and all, is immediately made available. There are some things that will never go until the Lord's time.

The second element is God Himself. There are certain issues within us that He will not get rid of within us until old age. He has His timing, and it is always perfect. So now is the moment to tell you an experience or two.

I left the RAF at age 38 and started at Upcott, a Christian Conference Centre in Seaton. It had already been going 6 years when I joined. Its major feature was people. During the summer there were 6 or 7 weeks for children and teenagers, and throughout the rest of the year groups of adults came for conferences. Sometimes I was the speaker, and sometimes they brought their own. I very soon realised that I really was not good with people. I think the words "defensive" and "aggressive" best described my heart attitude. I had been in the RAF for 20 years as a bachelor, and it told. I was quick to notice that these attitudes turned people away from both me and the Lord, and that was not good. I chanced upon a book by Dr. Ross Campbell called "How to Really Love your Child", and found it very helpful. He recommended 4 procedures:

- Give them Unconditional Love (see my chapter on The Four Loves).
- Give them your undivided listening when talking to them.
- Give them eye to eye contact (that is don't let your eyes wander onto other people or things), and get down to their level (especially with children).
- Use touch (appropriately) as a means of showing appreciation and affirmation

I tried these techniques, and then found they worked wonderfully well with all ages. I was, of course, acting. But it was a class act. I got to know and appreciate people and they got to know and love me. I made many friends, and was available to minister into their lives. It became my normal behaviour and I soon forgot the style and pattern and just loved and appreciated people. Some 15 or so years later I was doing something innocuous in the building when the Lord dropped a Revelation into my mind. He said, "You don't really love people do you?" I was floored. It was a bombshell. I protested "Of course I do", but then realised that if God says it, it must be true. Then I was stuck. I didn't know what to do or how to do it. I thought that issue had been dealt with a long time ago. So I simply said to the Lord, "Well, if you say so. But I have no way of changing it. You've made the statement, you deal with it. It's all yours," I deposited it there and then with the Lord, forgot about it, and got on with my work.

Six months later I was doing something else innocuous in the building when the Lord dropped another Revelation into my mind. "You really love people now, don't you?" I was floored again. It was another bombshell. I stood still and examined my heart. And, certainly I had changed in relation to loving people. But in what way I couldn't then tell. And how it had happened I could tell even less. So far as I had been concerned, I did absolutely nothing towards it, except to let God do what He suggested. Moreover, I have absolutely no knowledge of what He did inside nor how He did it. All I know was a before and after, with nothing in between, and both were Revelation into complete ignorance. Those are the facts.

So, that's enough background. Have you noticed that I have not even looked at the title of this chapter yet? So now I will.

Our besetting vulnerability.

Having said all I have, I must leave you all with one other factor: the Lord never removes *all* our negative attitudes. He leaves us with one or sometimes two that will be a weakness to us all the days of our lives. That weakness will be characterised by its ability to tempt us on a daily basis. Not weekly or monthly, but daily. We will be vulnerable in that area continually and regularly. It will remain as an open door into our souls through which our personal demon will find access, bring temptation and often cause us to sin.

Let's first of all get a Bible passage for it. 2 Cor. 12:7-9. *"To keep me from becoming conceited because of these surpassingly great revelations, there was given me a thorn in my flesh, a messenger of Satan, to torment me. Three times I pleaded with the Lord to take it away from me. But (God) said to me, My Grace is sufficient for you, for my power is made perfect in weakness."* (I suggest you read the context yourself if you are unfamiliar with it). I praise God that Paul described his limitation as "a thorn in the flesh" and never told us what his particular vulnerability was. There are those who have tried to analyse what it was, and that, in my view, is foolish. I think God deliberately made it vague so that the principle could apply to every Christian on earth. We all have a thorn in the flesh. Moreover, God will not take it away. I'm amazed at Paul – he only asked God three times to remove it. I've asked God 3000 times (approximately) to remove mine, and still He hasn't.

So why does God leave us with one that will nearly always defeat us? It's very simple – so that we will not get proud, think we are perfect and talk as if the Christian life is easy-peasy, and all you other people who still struggle are 2nd class Christians. We are forced to call on Jesus in our weakness and temptation and plead with Him to grant us victory in His name – at every distressing point in time. *His* strength must then continually be being made perfect in *our* weakness. Do you see how necessary it is that we are all kept vulnerable all the days of our lives?

God removes all those wickednesses that do not "belong" to me. But the one He leaves is the one we have to exercise our own self-control over. ***I*** have to say to that one vulnerability: "NO!" Without my "NO", God will not come in and help me defeat it on that or any occasion.

Every person's vulnerability is different and unique – so that's why we can help other people; I have victory over their weakness and they have victory over mine. And it brings us each into tremendous empathy with other struggling Christians for, in their distress, there but for the Grace of God, go I.

But do not get depressed with your one last besetting weakness. God does not condemn you for having it – it's a deliberate gift from Him. It keeps you humble, submissive and running to Jesus daily. What could be better? So let me end with Paul's conclusion to his own thorn in the flesh – *"Therefore I will boast all the more gladly about my weaknesses, so that Christ's power may rest on me. That is why, for Christ's sake, I delight in weaknesses, in insults, in hardships, in persecutions, in difficulties. For when I am weak, then I am strong."*

SUMMARY

God will remove all wickednesses within us except one or two. These He leaves as gifts to drive us closer to Him daily.

Chapter 20
THE COMPLETE GOD

God is One. Three persons, one God. They are indivisible because their individual humility is perfect, their love is perfect, their commitment to each other is perfect, and their communication with each other is instantaneous and perfect. Notice how Jesus on earth never came into His Ministry until He had been "completed" by the addition of the Holy Spirit (a practice all Christians need to heed)? Notice also how together, it only took Them three years to complete His perfect mission on earth? Old Aunt Cath said, "Never split the Trinity." She was right. Although we can try to analyse the roles of each member, we come across such scriptures as: "God was in Christ reconciling the world to Himself." In other words, They Themselves will never be split. God is One. But even so, each Person in the Trinity has roles. Thus it was the role of Jesus to create the earth, carry the Responsibility for that Creation, be the Rescuer and Redeemer, and to keep it ticking until all is complete and perfect, after which He will hand it all back to His Father (1 Cor 15:24, 25). It is the Holy Spirit's role at present to be "God in us". But never split the Trinity.

Some Christians are confused. They say: "Who am I talking to when I pray? Father, Son, Holy Spirit, angel? Who?" Frankly, who cares? It does not matter. What you say to One you say to All. Even the angels are perfect transmitters of God's will to us, and none of them express their own personality (and must not be worshipped). None of us will ever distinguish the difference between the voices of the Trinity. They are One. Never split the Trinity.

But it is none of these things that are the subject of this Revelation. It is the immensity and completeness of God. There is no doubt that I will be unable to do justice to this theme and you will be able to add many other excellences from your experience or knowledge. There is no aspect of goodness that God is not. And every aspect of goodness He has is 100% perfect.

So let us start with His Intelligence. The physical, chemical and mathematical laws that hold this universe together are complete and perfect. There are many more that man has yet to discover. But everything needed to hold all things together is complete, and was from the beginning – or nothing would have worked. Biological laws, how the bodies of man and animals hold together, their gene pools, their digestive and nervous systems, the control they have over them and their automatics operating out of every brain – all is perfectly designed and works. Even the brain itself, a majestic biological computer, is amazing and immense. In addition, life may be analysed but not created. No man can create life – animal or vegetable – except by reproduction, and that only of mankind. In addition, the physical laws that hang the planets in a stable condition round the sun, the sun in our galaxy, the galaxies in the universe, all are complete and perfect. God has thought of *everything*. From the microscopic, and how each cell and atom works perfectly, to the running of a galaxy, all is complete and "very good". The Intelligence that thought through every detail, the power that hangs it all together, the Law-making that ensured it works, is immense and so far beyond our own intelligence that we are (or ought to be) awe-struck by it.

God has boundaried all creatures and given each creature freedom inside those boundaries. Even mozzies have freedom to bite whom they like. Man, too, is boundaried in his intellect as well as his geography. There are still many things man has yet to learn. But God is not boundaried. The only kind of boundary that He has let us know He has is that "He cannot deny Himself". His nature is complete, and He cannot be other than complete and perfect.

Have you ever wondered what makes some people masculine and some feminine? Of course, it's not just their sex. There are characteristics that we consider to be feminine, and others to be masculine. Who decided those divisions? Clearly, God did, at the creation divide when He divided Eve from Adam. We recognise them, catalogue them, and basically agree with them. "That's a feminine woman," we say, or "That's a masculine man." Or, sometimes "That's a feminine man." The characteristics of the opposite gender are designed to be attractive to each sex. But where did they come from? My answer is that all characteristics of masculine and feminine are to be found in God. He is perfect in all things. Both women and men find a corresponding response in God; He is attractive to both genders, and He can relate exactly to all people perfectly, whatever their combination of characteristics. He is complete and perfect.

He is good; kind; full of joy; just; careful; courageous; merciful; fair; loving; powerful; wise; gracious; happy; patient; omniscient; perfect in planning and organisation; responsible; accountable; faithful; consistent; omnipresent; controlled; gentle; compassionate; empathetic; perfect in judgment; righteous; consistent; forgiving; sacrificial; humble; servant; caring; generous; spiritual; full of light; the fountain of life; encouraging; positive; full of grace; fully masculine; fully feminine; glorious.

And many more I have forgotten and that you will remember. All these good things God is *full* of. We humans divide things up as a fraction of a whole. So we would tend to analyse God as part this, part that, part the other. But He is not. He is all this, all that, and all the others. He is fully and perfectly humble, fully and perfectly just, fully and perfectly wise, fully and perfectly everything. Just like Jesus was fully God and fully man – not part God and part man.

So why am I bringing this up? Because when God deals with us, He deals with us as a Complete God. Everything He says to us and everything He does with us is fully and perfectly everything He is. He cannot deny Himself. He can't leave one bit of His character out because it's inconvenient to use it in this circumstance now. How we wish He would sometimes.

Healing, for instance. How often we wish He would heal. Wouldn't life be so much simpler if He healed every time we asked Him? Think what it would save the nation not to have a National Health Service (NHS)! But God does not always heal. When He doesn't, it's always because He has another agenda, the implementation of which is far, far better than a straight healing.

Prosperity is another one, and I have written more about these two under the chapter on Faith. But don't you sometimes wish that He who owns the cattle on a thousand hills would sell a few to get us out of the present financial hole we've just dug for ourselves? But He is the Complete and Perfect God. His response to all our praying is absolutely perfect. He sucks out of each prayer the scraps that line up with His will for the earth and for our lives, and answers those bits. Always, invariably, astonishingly God's answers to our prayers take us by surprise. The nature of those answers, their excellence, the depth of them and the timing of them – all are awesome. We are often left dumbfounded. Since this paragraph is on money, let me share something with you.

I have "Lived by faith" for some decades, and in my early days I tried to guess how He would provide income for our family. I almost heard Him say, "Wanna bet?" He fooled me every time. After a couple of months I gave up guessing how He would do it, and just worshipped when it came in. He has been generous, but wisely restrictive. It was complete and perfect, and it has kept me walking in faith day by day. There has been enough for today and/or this week; but never enough for this year or this life-time.

It's the completeness that is so awesome. How unlike us He is. We may not get angry very often – but when we do, everyone catches a whole eye-full and earful of it. God's anger is measured, controlled, tempered by grace, wisely administered, patiently withheld and perfectly timed.

Have you ever met any perfect people? Don't you find them insufferable? Their behaviour is precise, according to the Law. They are upright, honest, honourable and careful. But they are also so superior, so disdaining of failure, so intolerant of all who cannot match their standards. So unlikable. Have you heard the prayer of the Victorian child? "Lord, please make all bad people good; and all good people nice." No wonder Jesus had so much trouble with the Pharisees. How different is God's perfection! He is perfectly humble, perfectly gentle, perfectly kind, perfectly careful. When He meets us we can never be offended. His kindness and gentleness communicate and we feel so comfortable, so cared for and, yes, so loved in His presence. Human beings see perfection in terms of law-abiding. They therefore miss out on the essential qualities of God that would make them warm, friendly, approachable, happy people. Have you ever met a perfect human being who is happy? Come to think of it, have you ever met a perfect human being?

Communication, I have emphasized elsewhere, is the key to fellowship, companionship, togetherness. And togetherness is the name of the Christian game. God places great stress on unity, belonging and one-ness. That's because They are One, and They are training us all to be changed to become like Them. "People" are the only "things" we can carry across the divide of death. A friend of Tony Rogerson's, my Chairman of Trustees, was fond of saying, "There are only two things which are going to survive beyond the grave – people and the word of God. Give yourself to them." "Things people," (like I used to be) as opposed to "People people" are going to be very lonely in heaven (if loneliness is a possibility there). We carry friendships over death, and 2 Peter 1:11 says that we have a great welcome awaiting us in heaven when we get there. If we make few friends here – there will be little welcome there. And the key to friendship and unity this side of that divide is *communication.* Talk to people and you keep them. Stop talking or writing to people and you lose them. That's why God constantly communicates with us. He is into Relationships above all else. The *whole single purpose* for building an earth and a universe was that God might set up and keep loving Relationships with human beings. Indeed, this cosmos is going to be scrapped one day when all God's friends have at last found their home in Him.

So, have you ever analysed God's communication with you? He is speaking all the time – little nudges here and little suggestions there. Those are tricky to analyse because they run through so fast and so quietly. But the bigger, more obvious Revelations we can analyse – as well, of course, as taking notice of them.

The thing is this – *every* time God speaks to us His communication is perfect. It is precise – never one word too much and never one word too few. I've already told you that when I asked the Lord if I should up-sticks and go and live in Nicaragua, He just said, "Nehemiah." He did not need to say any more. He knew my Bible knowledge perfectly. He drew on what I knew, and knew that I would not misunderstand it, or misinterpret it, or under-understand it. It was perfect, and needed no further explanation from Him. Perfect. But when we then try to tell someone else what God said to us, it often takes a lot more words than His perfect few. Often it's because we have a background that God has drawn on, and we feel we have to unravel the concept just in case the rest of you don't have that knowledge. Take "Nehemiah" as an example.

I knew that what God meant was: "Nehemiah was a rich Jew living in a rich land. He brought the funds, equipment and encouragement to a poor nation, and got them to do all the work. That combination led to the rebuilding of the walls of Jerusalem in 52 days. Besides, it means that the style of missionary activity I want you to pursue is Biblical." That's what I collected from His communication. What He simply said was, "Nehemiah". Do you see the point?

This seriously applies to prophecy. God's words to a prophet are perfect. But that prophet often feels obliged to expand the prophecy God gave to "explain" it and/or make it more intelligible. But prophets need to beware of doing that – God has many interpretations He may want to use one prophecy for, and adding to it may weaken it, diminish it or destroy it altogether. The point I am trying to establish (vaguely so far) is that God is a complete God in all He does as well as all He says. He is fully everything, and all His "everythings" participate in full measure in everything He does and says. He told us (Is. 55) that His ways are not our ways, but as the Heavens are higher than the earth, so are His ways higher than our ways.

His dealings with us are *full* of wisdom, humility, kindness, grace, positiveness – all those things I have listed. By way of illustration, when I act, I act as a complete human being, in my Now state. When I was younger, I acted rashly, unwisely, resentfully, defensively, aggressively and overconfidently. I acted as the complete person I was then, and I spoke rashly and unthinkingly. Now when I act I am far more patient, kind, promotional, wise and generous. Jesus has changed me and I have a past and a present. All my actions and words at every moment of my life were the expression of the whole person I was at that point in time. I acted completely. All of us always do. Each action includes the full sum of all our personality and character.

Now take God. We are made in His image, so that same completeness of Personality and Character occurs every time He acts or speaks. Only He is perfect. That is, perfectly good and perfectly complete in all His goodness. I challenge you to find a flaw in anything He does or says. Didn't Jesus challenge the Pharisees (righteous prigs that they were): "Can any of you prove me guilty of sin?" (John 8:46).

God is full of reconciliation, forgiveness, salvation and rescue at *every* point of contact with *every* human being. His love is out to reconcile every human, and He does not take offence at being rejected (shades of Isaiah 53 – "He was despised and rejected by men – He was oppressed and afflicted, yet He did not open His mouth."). How does He not take offence when billions of people ignore and reject His suggestions daily? What an immense Character He is – amazing, stupendous, astonishing. Yet very loveable and totally reliable. How good it is for us limited and mainly wicked humans to have such a good God to fall back on, whether we are in difficulty or in delight. He is always open to us, always accessible. He meets every person's need whenever they ask in a wise and appropriate way, bearing in mind the long-distance transformation He has planned as well as the short-term situation. He is completely complete and completely whole. Nothing will faze Him and nothing will change His goodness and completeness – "whom to know is life eternal".

With great reluctance, and contrary to all my Christian instincts, I think this is the place to talk about God's judgments. I have barely mentioned it throughout this book, because God's judgment on those who have put their trust in Jesus is a prize-giving. As I have said elsewhere, the gold, silver and jewels of 1 Cor. 3 are, in my opinion, prizes for acts of faith, obedience and love.

Because Jesus is God's one solution to all sinfulness in man, God's judgment on all men is focused on their relationship with Jesus. God has made our choice as simple as He can: find Jesus and we have the whole of Heaven; dismiss Jesus and we have nothing, no God, no goodness, no heaven. Man cannot, on his own, find a solution to sin. We may strive after Righteousness today, but what can we do about all our failures of all our yesterdays? If God had not found a way of forgiving us and restoring His relationship with us, there would be no way back for any. And the solution God found in the Cross of Jesus was not only very costly; it was perfect in every way. God has nothing else to offer us but Jesus. And Jesus is everything good and wholesome and lovely. See, I cannot even bring myself to talk about judgment!

If God is everything Good, and is the Complete God, then what is there left if you take God out of every equation? Here on earth, we are left with man and satan. Man is desperately limited and satan is desperately evil. Here on earth there are shades of grey. No man is perfectly evil. Even Hitler and Stalin loved their nearest and dearest (I assume). So far as we know (and we don't), neither found Jesus before they died. If they had, the Redemption of Jesus could have transformed even them – there is no human being who has transgressed beyond the reaches of Jesus' Redemption. But it all comes down to choice. John 1:9 says that Jesus is the Light that lights every man that comes into the world. From that I gather that God gives every person the choice to choose Jesus or reject Him – and every person gets an individual Revelation that is perfectly tuned to his/her circumstance. CS Lewis once said that what we are right now a sum of all the choices we have so far made in our lives. What we end up as is a sum of all our life choices – whether good to Heaven or bad to Hell. The choice and choices are all ours and God cannot be blamed for any of them.

Which is where Jesus comes in. God has delegated all Judgment of human beings to a Human Being. THE Human Being – Jesus. And His Judgment on us is scrupulously fair. He will be in possession of *all* the facts, *every* circumstance that caused *every* choice we made, and He will judge impartially. There is no doubt that there are rewards for good behaviour and good choices – even in hell. In my gut, and knowing God the way I do, it seems to me that "punishment" is actually "the absence of good". Rather than a deliberate stoking of the fire to exact revenge, God seeks to *bless* sinners as much as He can. Where He can't bless and reward, what remains is not so much a deliberate infliction of pain, but an inevitable and automatic result of the removal of good. Much will be the same in Heaven. When God can reward, He will. Where He can't because we have chosen badly, He won't. Whether we end up in Heaven or Hell is pivoted entirely round our relationship with Jesus. For someone who, for reasons known only to themselves, has chosen to reject having a relationship with Jesus here on earth, then Heaven would be Hell for them. And it's obvious that God is not going to gather around Him in His perfect Heaven people who don't like Him or don't want to be there in His company.

So, what is it going to be like for a human being out from whom all goodness (as in God) has been extracted? Jesus described them simply as "worms" ("Where their worm does not die," He says). They will be still existing, but with no goodness and eternally no possibility of goodness. Here on earth we have choice between good and evil – God or self. After death there is no further choice down that line – either in Heaven or in Hell. There we will be either perfectly good, with no possibility of evil, or perfectly evil with no possibility of good. Hell was designed for the devil and his angels (Matt 25:41), and not for man. But for those humans who reject God's one perfect solution in Jesus, Hell is their eternal resting place. I picked up John 5:29 one day. There it tells me that *all* human beings get a resurrection body, whether they end up in Heaven or Hell. Demons don't ever get bodies. Therefore the agony of a human being in Hell will be more excruciating than that of demons; the torture and pain will be physical as well as psychological and spiritual. Terrifying thought really. And I still believe that, even in Hell, God will have done the very best He can (that is, the best possible) for each individual person. He is like that. So God is Complete in all His Being. Judgment, even of those who have rejected Jesus will always be filled with Mercy and Loving-kindness (Habakkuk 3:2).

Grace has daughters. Some of them are: love, kindness, empathy, peace, reconciliation, promotion, care, and an absolute refusal to believe anyone is worthless or useless. So, because God is full of Grace, He is full of all those lovely things too. So when He acts, even, say, in rebuke, He cannot help but include all those lovely attitudes at the same time. That's why you will never find Jesus being harsh with anyone. He cannot deny Himself.

That's why His instructions are so precise, so careful, so complete in every way, and bring crystal clear truth without being offensive. How does He do that? Why do people take offence when I say something straight, and they don't when Jesus does? I guess it's Grace, of which I obviously need more.

God is the Complete God, and cannot deny Himself. Of course, we learn of God's completeness bit by bit, which may be one of the reasons why I've been tasked to write this book.

It has been a real delight for me to get to know the Lord better. 50+ years of walking in faithfulness with Him have opened up doors in my understanding of Him that are so beautiful and so excellent in every way. Every aspect of His character and personality is delightful and addictive. He is intriguing and fascinating, and getting "stuff" out of Him is a challenging adventure. He is both shy and generous at the same time, inviting and restricting together. It's a bit like wooing a woman who longs to be wooed but runs away at the same time – just far enough away not to be lost but not too far to be fully caught right now. In God there is always more to be fascinated by, more to be found, more to be discovered, more to be enjoyed, more to be loved. I guess that discovery adventure is the whole reason for our being alive at all, and still being alive here on earth. He is the Complete God, who is everything good to everyone everywhere – if only they would gladly surrender to being loved.

SUMMARY

God's attributes are all good, are all 100% and are all perfect. When He acts, He acts using all His attributes together at once.

Chapter 21
INTIMACY

I remember sitting down one day and saying to the Lord, "There must be more than this. I have slaved for you for quite a few decades now, struggling to do what is right and good and honest and upright. But I'm tired of the struggle. It's all slog, and do I really have to wait for heaven to get some goodies in this Christian Life? Aren't there any compensations down here? Please don't get me wrong: I'm grateful for my salvation and sanctification, for the ministry you've given me and stuff like that. But it's just slog. Isn't there any more?"

Now I don't want you, my reader, to get it any more wrong than the Lord. I had been a faithful servant of God's for a long time. Many people had found strength and understanding though my teaching and encouragement. My wife Eileen and I had been given a prophecy by Selwyn Hughes before we got married, saying that we would be a rock to many. It has been true. And this negativity was not a sudden thing, like a sudden attack of gut-ache. It was a cry of an unspoken ache deep down inside that came to the surface that day, to be expressed.

And that's where I left it. I told the Lord and moved on with what I was doing. You must understand that there never had been, never was, and I pray never will be any thought of giving up the Christian walkway. That has never been an option for me. We just press on.

I have no sense of history. Ancient or personal. I am a person who exemplifies Phil. 3:13 fully ("Forgetting what is behind and straining towards what is ahead, I press on towards the goal to win the prize for which God has called me heavenwards in Christ Jesus"). I work today and plan tomorrow. I have forgotten the "when" of all my yesterdays. I never liked History at school – even though I took it (and failed dismally) at A level. So when this one-sided conversion took place I don't now know. Nor how long before the next incident. All I know is that it was before, and quite a while before.

I live in Devon, in the South West of England. I had been asked to give a talk to a Young People's Fellowship at Folkestone in the South East of England, and I needed to drive there. I remember it was May–time.

Just before setting off I chose which route I would take. I had the choice to go Motorway – M3, M25, M2. It was the easiest and least hassled. Or I could go the coast road past Southampton, Portsmouth, Chichester and Brighton. For reasons that escape me, I chose the southern route. I was not in a hurry, and it could have been "select the pretty route." Or it could have been the Holy Spirit nudging me. It doesn't matter.

I got into my car and set off. It was one of those beautiful May days, with wall to wall blue except for an odd fluffy cloud and a feather or two of high cirrus. The leaves were in Spring Green, light, verdant, vivacious and pretty. The Almond and Cherry trees were in bloom with their pink and white blossoms. It was gorgeous. I turned on my car radio, and soon turned it off again. I just felt like praising God for such a beautiful creation and such a beautiful day He had given me.

It was a time of sheer joy. The Lord was close and fun and we frolicked together through the journey. It was sheer heaven on earth. Everything was an item of praise and fun with the Lord, from the design of the cirrus through the beauty of the trees to the little girl pushing her dolly in a pram. All was deliriously happy, and words fail me to express the delight I encountered that glorious Spring day. And it went on almost to Folkestone, where I had to take out the map and navigate through unknown territory. As I navigated the last bit I needed to switch my mind back to driving. On motorways and dual carriageways one can switch off and just head forwards, reacting instinctively to vehicles and situations. But now I had to focus. As I meandered through the little lanes to Folkestone, I started to think. I was amazed and astonished, as I glanced at my watch, that I had been 4 hours in our happy frolicking. 4 hours! It had passed as if it had been a moment. There had been no sensation of the passage of time. All had been inexpressible joy and fun.

Then the Lord reminded me of an incident that had happened some 40 years earlier. I was a young Christian, certainly not more than a year old. It was a Saturday or Sunday evening in TCM Baptist Church in Lincoln. I was upstairs in the "upper horseshoe" that contained the seating. We were singing the hymn, the chorus of which went, "Draw me nearer, nearer, nearer, blessed Lord to the Cross where Thou hast died ..." And we had just finished singing the verse that went like this:-

> Oh the pure delight of a single hour
> That before Thy throne I spend
> When I kneel in prayer and with Thee, My God
> I commune as friend with friend.

Early in my Christian life I had learned to think about what I was singing; otherwise it is just empty words and hypocrisy. If something I was singing was not true for me, I made it a matter of prayer – "Please, Lord, make this true for me today." It was good then and it is still good to have the words in front of me, so that I could recapture the thoughts I had just sung or expressed, and pray them in again.

So it was, back in my youth, that I had thought about that verse. And I said to myself, "Wow! That guy must have been a saint. A whole hour! How could anyone manage a whole hour in prayer and find it non-boring? I can manage 5 minutes with effort, and then run out of steam. A whole hour! What a saint!"

And the Lord heard.

Now, 40 years further on He reminded me of that incident. "Well, son. Do you have to be such a saint to spend an hour with Me?" I laughed. Four hours! And I ain't no saint. What I might *know* about sainthood is one thing; how I *behave* is quite a different matter!

The new Revelation that came to me that day was that just being in the presence of Jesus is such fun. Not asking for anything. Not having a hidden agenda – like contacting God "for a purpose", which I suppose had been the greater part of my life-style up to then. Just being, and chatting to Him for no other purpose than just doing it. Of course, during that 4 hours I told Him I though He was marvellous. I admired Him for His clouds and trees and flowers and people and fun, and told Him so. I guess you could call it "worship". But it was different from what I classically had recognised as worship before. This was now just plain fun. I remembered a verse part of which flashed back to me and I later looked it up. I found it at Psalm 16:11 "In His presence is fullness of joy".

At last I had been given a taste of heaven while still resident on earth. Now I knew what to expect when I graduate from Earth School. I told the Lord that I wanted more of that for the rest of my days. I guess we all need encouragement. And it may surprise you that it took such a long time for me to come to the place of needing it. After 40 years of giving encouragement to others, this time the Lord repaid me in a way that was beautiful, satisfying, heavenly and, yes, addictive. The nearest summary of this experience I could find was the word Intimacy. I'm not sure how others define that word, but now you have my definition.

It has completely changed my Christian life-style.

I can't fully recall what life was like before-hand, but let me share with you what it's like now.

First, seeking the company of Jesus in this Intimate way has become my top priority. Just living in His presence and enjoying His friendship has become a place of joy every time. Just for its own sake. I volunteer to go down town often. And as I walk I look down and find Him in the pavements. Just telling Him how lovely and wonderful He is, is all I want or need to do. Instantly we are together and having happy moments again in each other's company. Whenever I can get the opportunity during a day, that's what I do. The "spare" time is taken up with a "love-in" with Jesus – an *agape* moment. That really sounds corny and soppy but I don't really know how to describe it better. It's far from either.

Secondly, it has ditched my prayer time. I used to have a regular time with the Lord on a routine daily basis. Now *most* of my time is a regular time, but not timed. It's a "whenever moment", and that has now become the routine. I run into His presence at any and every available gap in a working day. There are occasions when we have more than the odd few minutes together, but those are not planned, are haphazard in terms of when and for how long, and they are nearly always initiated by Him. Walking in His presence Intimately is a "whole-life policy".

Thirdly, the ditching of a specific prayer shopping list asking for things has mainly gone. I hardly bother any more. That's the style and stuff of prayer meetings. As we walk together He reads my mind and searches my heart, and, mainly, I don't need to ask Him. I said "hardly". There are of course occasions when specific issues need addressing and sharing with the Lord, and Jesus did say "Ask and it will be given to you." But by and large, they tend to be the exceptions. The rule is the time of Intimacy.

Fourthly, it has taken tremendous pressure off me. Obligations, particularly Christian ones, have mainly disappeared. Do I have to "witness"? Not at all. Witnessing has become a spontaneous overflow of love and appreciation with all people. I *am* a witness: I don't *have* to witness. I've picked up, as I mention elsewhere, "Random acts of kindness to strangers," and find tremendous fulfilment in keeping my eyes open and doing nice things for anyone and everyone just for the sheer thrill of blessing them. No hidden agendas. Jesus went about doing good, and so do I. It's such a fun life-style. Do I need to pray? Only when prompted to do so. Do I need to read my Bible? Here I regret that many might misunderstand me. I beg you not to. Bible Reading is no longer an obligation. The ancient Scripture Union Chorus and Life-style of "Read your Bible, pray every day…" is no longer applicable. It may have served its purpose for my early years. Now, the leading of the Lord out from His presence is the only priority. "Man shall not live on bread alone, but on every (spoken) word that comes out of the mouth of God" is a whole-life reality. He knows better than I do what the important necessity of this moment is, and I just like doing it His way. It has helped for me to have been a Bible Teacher for 30 years, collecting loads of information at the feet of Jesus; so I have a lot of background knowledge that the Lord can call on and reminds me of regularly. And every now and then He re-directs me back to His word. This is always a delight and full of new Revelations. I think the thing that has gone is Law. The *obligation* of "must, should and ought" has disappeared; I no longer *have* to read my Bible every day as the rules of the Saint Evangelicals demand that I should. To read it as part of my relationship with Jesus makes it a thing of delight, and there is always a flexibility in the "when". Coming under Jesus' Grace is a freedom for all of our time. Didn't Paul write; "We are not under law but under grace"? (Rom 6).

What about Church attendance? Well, for reasons I have written about elsewhere, the Lord urges me to continue to attend Church. There are some services which I don't attend, and those absences have no guilt attached to them. Often the Lord brings other needs to bear at Church times, so Eileen and I just walk with the Lord as to what we do and when. I know there are many Christians who do not go to Church any more. They feel they can live with the Head OK and not be a part of His Body. I don't think anyone can. "Beware the Christian who sits alone," said Aunt Cath. And she is right. There's something wrong either with their relationship with God, their relationship with other members of the body of Christ, with their Bible understanding or with their theology. Jesus entwines us tighter with people, just like Intimacy entwines us tighter with Him. Separation and division is from hell, whatever excuse we might have to justify it.

So let me tell you what Intimacy has accomplished in my life. It is quite extraordinary. It has enabled the Lord to have access to my inner soul (bits I have never known anything about) and transform them, and that completely without my knowledge. The "how" of transformation is entirely unknown to me. As is the "when". The "what" of transformation has only become apparent in retrospect as I find myself spontaneously reacting in an uncharacteristic and heavenly way. "Grace" is the operative word. I find that I am thinking graciously about people in a way I never did before, speaking graciously to them and about them, and acting graciously towards them. It's astonishing that such a self-centred, arrogant twit as me could ever act in the way I now do. I tell people how astonished I am at the unlikely, irrational and undeserved grace that has been imparted to me without asking. I am often astonished at myself. It all comes from walking Intimately with Jesus, and doing no work towards it. Just how astonishing is that aspect of Grace?

Now, please don't think I'm a sooper-dooper saint. I don't think nicely about *everyone*. There are still those whose life-style and behaviour patterns are an enigma to me. There are others with whom I disagree, and sometimes I get hot about it. I have a long way to go yet in terms of my behaviour and thinking. But just see how far I have come! I know that it has taken 50 or so years for the Lord to get me here. But then, I have always been a late-developer, and I'm certain all of you who are reading this can reduce my time frame in your own lives. God has taken me, a self-determining rebel, through the mill so that you don't have to follow any of my stupidities. "Experience" is trying something, getting it wrong, learning the lesson and not doing it again. "Wisdom" is learning from other people's Experience and avoiding what they got wrong.

It has also changed my understanding of the Bible. The Bible has always been for me a kind of text-book. Not a series of texts, but a compendium of truth. I have far more taught "what the Bible says", and far less "what the Bible means". I'm a teacher before being a preacher. So, I have analysed themes, evaluated passages and books, and directed others to what it says. It has been Truth for its own sake. But now, Intimacy with Jesus has caused me to identify with the writer and where they were at when they wrote. I understand now where they were coming from. It's almost as if I have intimate empathy with them as they wrote, and see far more the heart of the message rather than the truth of the message. These people wrote out from their own Intimate Relationship with Jesus, and not from their head knowledge of heavenly facts. David Pawson once said, "Truth is not a proposition: it's a Person." Truth is an unravelling of the character of Jesus, an expression of the heart and soul of God, rather than the mind of God. What before I had analysed as Doctrine I now experience as Fellowship. Thus sticky Doctrinal issues like Calvinism and Armenianism have become such unnecessary, miniscule, myopic irrelevances. Those kinds of debates belong to mind-centred people. For me, Doctrine has been replaced by Relationship. I no longer analyse God; I just love Him and want to be in His presence. And I hope that my preaching directs people far more in the same direction. Revelation is a series of heavenly experiences that transform our Christian world view from the Christian cultural world-view into which we were born again to a confident assurance of "This is who God is" and "this is the way God works". All His unnatural methods of Faith, Patience, Grace, Forgiveness, Encouragement, Promotion, Honouring, Humility, Servant-hood etc., etc. become not just the norm for a human life but a selected preference of ones' own life-style. I walk like Jesus and talk like Jesus because I have walked with Jesus and talked with Him. And I see that His way is perfect. Not only perfect but enjoyable and effective.

So, for example, how do we raise money for SIFT, so that we might transform the lives of the poor, marginalised and forgotten in Nicaragua? Bombard the fatigued public with more and more pictures and stories of emaciated women and children? Have raffles and coffee mornings? Invite ourselves to Churches to see if they will "take the hook?" Flood the world with relevant literature? Go for the Media? Advertise? Try the Lottery? Try the Government? Nope. None of these things. They are all ways tried by others, and therefore to me they are of man. They come into our minds as methods used by other charities, and therefore none of them are for us. So what is? One by one the Lord has killed every human idea that we have spent time and effort (and money) having a go at. All of them that we tried turned to worms. Most came out absolutely zero – not a penny.

So, what do we do? We take the simple route and ask Jesus for it. It's irrational and scary. But "Unless the Lord builds the house, they labour in vain that build it" (Ps 127). What happens is that new avenues open up spontaneously as we walk. Things we never thought of just "happen". And people we have never met before give – some £20, some £1000, some less, some more. God does for us what all our efforts have failed to accomplish for ourselves. And it is without sweat. Is the way of other charities wrong then? I don't know, and I am not entitled to know their stories (see John 21:20-22). But their ways must not be our ways – unless the Lord specifically says so. He is teaching us the ways of Intimacy. We do what we do His way only. This is His work, His plot, and it must run His way. I can see God establishing a charity style that we have to follow, so that all my/our successes in SIFT can continue down the pathway that we have dug and trampled into effectiveness. I know one or two of my successors will have a go at man's routes, especially as SIFT gets bigger. But I'm sure they will fail, just as we have when we tried them. I am the pioneer of this work, and God's track record is that every outfit follows the style of the pioneer if it is going to continue to flourish. My way is not hard, although it can be a source of anxiety. It is simply to ask God for what we need to fulfil the task He has laid before us, and let Him select both the provision and its timing. As I have said elsewhere, the gap between asking and receiving is either a gap of faith or a gap of anxiety. Intimacy kills anxiety, promotes assurance, restores our vertical relationship and gives us patience. No longer is there that nail-biting, hurried, frustrated worry, pleading with God until we are exhausted and fasting because we think it does God good. No longer do we try to twist His arm and squeeze our pathetic pennies from His hard-pressed reluctant hand. We just sit back in joy, get on with the work He has laid before us today, and leave all our tomorrows happily in His hand. That's what an Intimate Relationship with Jesus has accomplished for me.

For years I have taught Christian freedom. I now realise that I used to teach it out from a knowledge and belief in the truth that

God can give it to us through Jesus. Now I know it. The obligations of law have all gone. The inadequacies in my make-up, especially spiritually, have all gone, to be replaced by a new kind of character, woven into my own individual personality. Life is totally positive, and I find myself encouraging everyone regardless of who they are, that "All things are possible in Jesus." The work I do in Nicaragua, although hard, incorporates the Lord's multiplication, has a silver lining round it and smells like roses.

This is my story, my song. Your story and your song will take on a different shape, a different line, a different fragrance and a different time. And I hope now I have given you the key on how to make it as effective as mine has been.

SUMMARY

Intimacy is being in continual communication with Jesus and delighting in His company with joy.

Chapter 22
HUMILITY.

A couple of chapters ago I wrote some thoughts on the Complete God. The enormity of His character and attributes are such that any one characteristic diminishes in comparison with them all. But sometimes it is valuable to pluck out one of those characteristics and examine it on its own, uncluttered by the others.

The reason why that diminishing happens is that we humans see a thing as One, and therefore see parts of that thing as sub-parts of the whole. But we need to try to see God from His perspective (just how hard is that?). With God every thing is complete and every thing is whole and perfect. If you like, each part is as big as the whole and each as big as each other. It's not like putting 500 baked beans into one tin can (that's the way humans see it). It's more like putting one baked bean into the tin because the bean is so big it fills it. But every bean with God fills the same tin can, and they all fill it full. Don't ask me how it works, because it is not humanly logical. It just does. A better example is Jesus. He was both fully man and fully God; not half man and half God. That's the way it is with God. CS Lewis puts it: "The inside is bigger than the outside."

So let's consider Humility.

Of all the most unlikely characteristics that are to be found in the Trinity it is Humility. Why? Well, isn't He the most stupendous Intellect to put this creation together? Isn't He the most astonishingly powerful person to be "upholding the universe by His word of power"? Isn't He the law-maker, the law-giver and the law-upholder, and doesn't it all work perfectly in His hands? Isn't He the source of all Life, all energy, all good? Isn't He the sustainer, upholder, creator and redeemer? Omniscient, omnipotent, omnipresent? Indeed, He is all those things, and many more. So - shouldn't He be proud of it?

Certainly. But no, He is not. Pleased – yes; proud – no. He is a humble God. That characteristic is illogical in the light of His accomplishments. But we can't get away from the fact that He is perfectly humble and loves humility wherever He finds it.

How can I describe it? It's a bit like when I praise Him for painting a beautiful sunset. I stand in awe and worship Him at its beauty, innovation and perfection, and then tell Him how amazing He is to do something so gorgeous, so transient just for our enjoyment. And it's as if He turns shyly to one side and says, "Aw, shucks. Do you think so?"

I wonder where His humility comes from? Methinks the Trinity is involved here. How can three persons exist together and call themselves One, and act totally consistently in that vein? There has been no record or experience of God acting selfishly or proudly or independently. It's got to be humility (and love) that is the catalyst that draws Them together as One.

We could of course assume selfishness if we talked about "God" as one person. Then, certainly, we could accuse Him of being like satan – utterly self-centred. There would be only One. But He is not a He – He is a They (or a Them). The three persons act together, are one together, are in total agreement, act consistently and mirror one another's characters. They have differing roles, are different Beings, but are alike as three peas in a pod (so to speak). So let's see some of those characteristics.

They are infinitely powerful and all infinitely wise. All infinitely intelligent. Any one could break away and form a gang of His own. But No. THE characteristic that stops them doing that is their infinite humility. They submit fully to one another. The consequence is that the three act as One, fully submitted, fully in agreement with each other, fully honouring to each other, and the universe is upheld by goodness in gentle submission. That's why God is so pleased with mankind, and wants to promote us. In their humility they are constantly promoting each other, and consequently us. Of course, it has been made possible by Jesus being identified as a man, and redeeming us. God is therefore free to bless us. But He can now do that because His humility can operate to the full to promote us.

Look at Jesus. He claimed that none of His words (or works) were His own – they were given by His Father (John 14). Consequently we have no personal opinions of His – only that He agreed with His Father about everything all the time. He also did no supernatural thing for 30 years – until He had been anointed and filled with the Holy Spirit after His baptism (as I have said before - a good lesson for every Christian to learn). And see, didn't Jesus say how much better it was going to be that He departed, for unless He did the Holy Spirit would not be sent? And it will be *much* better when the Holy Spirit comes. That's humility. John the Baptist caught it too: "There comes someone after me the thongs of whose sandals I am not worthy to untie. He must increase and I must decrease." Humility. Throughout scripture, the New Testament particularly, we see the Father honouring and promoting the Son and the Holy Spirit ("This is my beloved Son with whom I am well pleased"). We see the Son honouring the Father and the Holy Spirit. We see the Holy Spirit honouring the Father and the Son. Humility in all three. So how come they are Three but operating as One? Humility – they mutually submit to each other perfectly and wholly.

I have lived through the charismatic movement that roughly started in the 1970's. The Holy Spirit was exalted because He had been forgotten. I remarked, at that time, that in the past some Christians worshipped Father, Son and Holy Church; and other Christians who worshipped Father, Son and Holy Scripture. What God did in those days was to cause *both* to change and start to worship Father, Son and Holy Spirit – together. But for those who travelled with me through those decades, did you notice that it didn't take very long for the Holy Spirit to stop being worshipped and His prompting referred us back (so very gently but persistently) to the Father and the Son? Humility. Self-effacing. Other promoting. That's humility.

So what is humility? It is me selecting the bottom place and promoting, honouring, encouraging, supporting everyone else. I put myself down to put you forward.

You might think that if we did that nothing would be accomplished. As if everyone is saying, "After you." "No, after *you*." "No, no no. I insist. After *you*." But the opposite occurs. When I stand back and encourage you forward, you get fulfilled, I give you greater confidence to step out in your giftings, and I make you feel good because I make you king (queen) at that moment. More things get accomplished because more people become actively involved.

Take the opposite to see the contrast. If I am the competent one, reckon I can do it all, have the energy and go for it, I leave all the rest of you standing around idly watching. So there's one person working his socks off and everyone else redundant. That's pride. That's man-centredness. That's being thick. John Smith, a guy in our church, put it this way: "The Christian Church is like a football match: - 22 people desperately in need of rest watched by 22,000 desperately in need of exercise."

Humility stops that. The dynamo of the universe, the Trinity, act together because their hearts' longing is to honour, promote and exalt the other Two. Perfectly. And it's what has caused God to initiate the Redemption. His finest creation, man, joined the great self-centred rebellion. But God wants to win them back without coercion, with gentleness and in love. How is He going to do that? By being consistent with His nature and bless us, promote us, exalt us, honour us. Is it not the *goodness* (or *kindness* in the NIV) of God that leads us to repentance? (Rom 2:4).

Throughout my Christian life I have had a most extraordinary experience: I cannot ever recall being rebuked by God. That is extraordinary for two reasons:

1. If the Bible is the word of God, which it is, then why isn't God being consistent with His word and regularly ripping me to pieces? After all, both testaments, but mainly the Old, are laden with rebukes, judgements, punishments and warnings. The Bible is certainly consistent with itself in that

you don't have to go far in the New Testament to find a similar load there as well. And to be truthful I expected to be regularly rebuked. My early Christian years were spent with a nasty conscience and I was consistently doing sinful stuff, rebuking myself and apologising to God. Moreover, I was pretty fierce with congregations I preached at in those days. I took these rebukes as Divine input. But they weren't. Every remembrance I have of the Lord's dealings with me is that He has only encouraged me, helped me, built me and supported me. And when I have sinned? No rebuke. No judgement, no condemnation. Only silence. And not a "silence with attitude" either. Just nothing. No comment. No suggestion. Just silence and not one that I could "feel". All that *is* in fact consistent with the New Testament Revelation of Grace. Does it not say that God has reserved judgement to the Great White Throne spoken of in Revelation 20:11-12? No judgement now. Only kindness, grace, help, support. All coming out of God's humility. I don't know how He does it. Although my nature has been transformed by the Holy Spirit from legalism and judgementalism to grace and forgiveness, I still find it difficult not to tell someone off every now and then when they deserve it. But not God. He is consistently reserving all rebuke and judgement to that last great event. And, to be fair, the Bible is also consistent with that side of God's nature. There *has* to be an accounting for every deed done by every human being in their lives. Even our beautifully constructed bodies are gifts that we are going to have to give up one day, and the Maker and Giver has got to enquire exactly what we've done with such beautiful artefacts for the 70+ years that we have been borrowing them. Methinks that God thinks that there is enough rebuke in the Bible for Him not to have to add any more to jeopardise His relationship with us. We *know* the "You shall not's" of both testaments. We hardly need God to remind us (although surreptitiously He might give us a nudge or two). And if we don't know the "You shall Not's" – say, in the early days before we've had a chance to read them – He steers us away from the things and places that are not good and towards the things and places that are good. It's very positive. But then, God is perfectly positive. Moreover, He does not change. Faithfully and consistently He directs us in a good path, in a good manner, and in a way that is consistent with His revealed New Testament gracious ways.

2. Secondly, I *need* rebuking. Lots of people know that because I think and say and do loads of silly, stupid and offensive things. So why doesn't God tell me off? After all, people do. It really is extraordinary that He doesn't. I am inconsistency and thickness personified into one being. If there has ever been anyone in this world that has needed the whip, it is me. (I got it a good few times at every school I can remember). That's the kind of character I am. If there was wrongful initiative that was needed, I would readily supply it. Indeed, I have needed curbing all my days. Looking back, I guess God did curb me. But never by wagging a finger at me. Always by kindness, gentleness, instant forgiveness, reprogramming my character with Divine attitudes and by being *nice* and appallingly *kind.* I can tell you, it has won me over. It has taken a long time, but then, God is never in a hurry, bother it! I am. He *should* be rebuking me. Why didn't He? That's why it has been an extraordinary experience for me.

I have one permanent memory of a bad atmosphere between God and me. I was in the RAF flying Shackletons at that time out of Malta. I did something I shouldn't have done (not in an aeroplane, you'll be glad to know). I then felt so ashamed of it that I refused to confess it to the Lord. It didn't take long for that shame to turn into stubbornness, and I just dug my toes in and said "Shaln't". The atmosphere was strained between me and the Lord. For 6 whole months (just how stubborn can one get?). I continued to do Christian things (I had a reputation to keep up), and the Lord continued to guide and direct me (He also had a reputation to keep up). But none of my work was blessed. Protected, yes; blessed, no. In the end I didn't care about the blessing – it was the atmosphere and the estrangement that I couldn't stand. So I sulkily backed down, acknowledged my sin and stupidity (and all the rest), confessed it and said sorry. Do you know what God did and said? Do you know how He reacted? You might never guess. He merely said, "That's OK. Let's move on."

Now folks, if ever I should have had the cane it was then. I thought of the many rebukes He should have given me, but there was not one. Astonishing? Very humbling. I learned four lessons that day that I have never forgotten:

- Always say sorry *immediately* after sinning. Don't let satan get what I have since called the Second Victory ("You don't think God can forgive you for *that*, do you?").
- God is astonishingly kind and instantly forgiving.
- God's friendship and company are better than anything else in the world.
- Say sorry more than you ever need to, so when you do genuinely need to, it comes very easily. Since then I have tried always to be the first to apologise – even if I was in the right. Some people are so right all the time they never or seldom apologise. That's not righteousness – that's pride. Stinking, obscene, horrible pride.

I need another of my little diversions here. It seems to me that no one moves forward in the Christian life without confrontation. Many people (possibly all) hate confrontations, but it seems to me that they are necessary. When people do it, it is often done in quite an offensive way – although we should certainly have got the message when it is. But confrontations do not need to be hostile. They can be done in kindness and gentleness, so long as they are straight. I have recently been told I am a dominating character by one of my close relatives. Quite sobering. What I thought was being positive and constructive has been taken as domination. So I feel bad about it, and have gone straight to the Lord. It is another of those things that I can do very little about changing, except to repent. So I have just had to ask Him to change my heart and change my attitude so that I can serve others and bless them better. He can change me inside in a way that I cannot – I have learned that through many many issues in my decades of wallowing in mud (often called the Christian Life).

But how about the Lord Himself? Does He confront? Oh yes indeed! But His confrontations are so different from those administered by people. He tells it straight, and *without rebuke.* There is no condemnation. He tells the facts and there's no emotion or feeling attached to it. He just says it simply and directly with no added flowery language to soften, harden or amplify it. There is no avoiding it. But there is also no offence given by it. Moreover, He always adds a "get-out" clause; - "This is what is wrong, and this is what you need to do about it if you are going to change." Shades of 1 Cor 10:13. My vast experience of being told off has changed the way in which I now tell others off. I have learned to pray about it first, and allow the Lord time to fix it before I put my hob-nailed boots in and cause mega offence. That gives the Lord the opportunity to sort it out without my interference. But to do that I need to acknowledge that if the Lord wants me to face the issues and do the confronting, I need to be ready and prepared to do it. None of us likes doing that, do we? But if we must, we must. In which case I pray about it and thereby give the Lord time and opportunity to work on the person's heart inside, so that when it comes to the confrontation, they introduce the subject, the battle is ¾ won, and all I have to do is to confirm what they are suggesting. It works a treat, there is never any offence caused, and we remain friends for ever.

So how do we get humility? Is it gifted from above by Revelation or what? The most helpful scriptures are in James and 1 Peter, where both authors parallel Proverbs 3:34 –

"God opposes the proud but gives grace to the humble." [Prov. 3:34] (James 4:6)

"Humble yourselves before the Lord, and he will lift you up." (James 4:10)

"Humble yourselves, therefore, under God's mighty hand, that he may lift you up in due time." (1 Pet 5:6)

Interesting. It says, "Humble yourselves ..." Not like Mr Micawber, who told everybody that he "was a very humble man". That's hypocrisy – thinking that you are competent but telling everyone how humble you are. Humility never says it is humble. Humility is an act of *will* – humble *yourself.* I *choose* to do it. Do what? Select a station and position that is lower than the person I am talking to. I deliberately choose to be a servant to the person I am with. I give him/her honour, deference, the benefit of the doubt and the right to their views and actions. I put myself at least one rung of the ladder below them. It's my deliberate choice. My confidence is in Jesus, not in my own abilities. And that confidence is measured by Jesus' humility. I stand in a position of strength, because Jesus has given me assurance that I am who I am and no one can duplicate me. So, from that position, I deliberately make myself a servant to the other person. I do not devalue myself in doing so. But I promote them. I honour them. I make them very important people in my sight. I tell the world how excellent they are. I hide myself behind and beneath them. This is specifically true when dealing with children – to promote and honour them and consider them very significant people.

Now where did I get that idea and attitude from? Simply by being with Jesus and analysing His style as we have walked together. He does or says something: I take heed, but then go back and look at His style. How did He handle me on that occasion? How can I learn from it? Then I try to pray it through into my own life.

He is my servant (but not my slave). Like Jeeves and Bertie Wooster, He is always the Boss, although still a servant. I still find it extraordinary that the Creator, Ruler and Sustainer of the universe chooses to serve. And He genuinely does. That's humility. He is, in all things, set to promote me. And I am set to promote Him. Shadows of John 17:1 – 10?

There have been a very few rare occasions in my life when He has given me a direct order. 99% of the time, God gives me choice. He puts before me a suggestion, but always gives me the choice to reject it. Because most of His suggestions don't come accompanied by a megaphone or a tag "This is God speaking", I miss most of them. And for most of those I do get, I reject His suggestions. He does not take offence. Indeed, it is impossible to offend Him. But for those promptings that I do recognise, I am always aware that I have been given a choice. Clearly this is to make me personally accountable for every thing I have thought, said or done. The heavenly assizes on that day are going to reveal what a spiritual pauper I really am – given the percentage of promptings by the Lord and the percentage of choosing the opposite. And still He does not take offence.

Another little aside. As a young Christian RAF officer, I was "driven" to read General Sir Arthur Smith's 100 days Bible Study. I did it reluctantly at first, but got gripped by it very quickly. One of those meditations included his view on the Christian's Judgement Day. I guess I haven't now got it 100% right, but this is what I have concluded – the Day of Judgement for a Christian will be a Day of Rewards. Why? Because for a Christian all their sins are forgiven and forgotten. Sins are below the line, and below the line is "under the blood of Jesus." What is above the line? Every thought, word and deed that has been a result of faith, love and obedience. For those few or many occasions throughout my life, the Lord is going to reward me. Of course, I don't know how brilliant I have been at any of them. I am certainly more aware of the disobediences than the obediences. But do you get what I am saying? There is no punishment for a Christian – his sins have already been dealt with and the consequences wiped away. What is left? Only the things that the Lord has prompted us to do and we have done in faith. From the above paragraph, if I really have been a spiritual pauper, then the amount of reward will be little. If, on the other hand, I have been better than I ever thought I have been, then the rewards will be greater. I think the question is this: am I travelling through earth with heavenly rewards in view? I sure hope not. I travel through earth in a close relationship with Jesus, enjoying His company. All the results of that are His problem not mine. One thing I am pretty certain of is this: we are all going to be absolutely astonished at the degree of mega reward that the Lord is going to give us. None of us will deserve any of them. We will be humbled into the ground by God's fantastic generosity. And there I am content to leave my heavenly future.

Sometimes I wonder how God accomplishes anything of significance in this world. Because He defers choice to every human being, and constantly gets His recommendations binned, how is it that He can still steer the world in the direction He has planned? I guess it gets harder every day as more and more sinful people are born and go round "doing their own thing". It occurs to me that His forecast for the world is that it will believe a lie (actually The Lie, whatever it is), increase in wickedness of every kind and eventually succumb to the one great world ruler, who will be satan in human flesh (an evil copy of God in human flesh). So wicked will the world become that it will require the Second Coming of Jesus in power and great glory to put it straight again. Presumably, since God has predicted all this, it is His will that it should be so. Even that reveals His humility. Is it not God allowing every person the privilege of deciding for themselves the pattern and purpose of their own lives? If you choose to reject God's clearly stated single pathway to glory, that's your choice. As are the consequences. He let's you decide. All of us. That's humility.

His humility leads to self-effacement. And I guess that is why so many people miss Him. He hides Himself, and waits for humble hearts to acknowledge their inadequacy and seek Him.

"If you seek Me, you will find Me, if you search for Me with all your heart," He said through Jeremiah (29:13). "Where meek souls will receive Him, still the dear Christ enters in." To them He opens a window into heaven. They have a secret that the world cannot see and cannot understand. Consequently, Christians get ignored, shunned, ridiculed, persecuted and killed – no one likes those who are "different", and because they don't understand them, they kill them. They did exactly the same with Jesus. They now do exactly the same with God. If you don't understand something that constantly bugs you, shoot it. At least that gets rid of it. Oh yes? You think so?

Sometimes I have a competition with Jesus. It's not a very serious one, of course. I tell Him that I bet I can get below Him to exalt Him more than He can exalt me. I fail. It's a very one-sided competition, but He enjoys it. The trouble is that I am fighting perfection. No one can get any better – or lower - than that. My trying to is not futile though. Every parent loves to see their kid trying to copy them, and Jesus loves to see me trying to humble myself beneath Him. God gives *grace* to the humble. God exalts the humble in His own time and way (1 Peter 5:6).

Over the years I have come to understand God better and better. One does if one walks with Him daily for decades. And the things I know about Him fill me with pleasure and delight. In His presence is fullness of joy. There is not one characteristic of His that is not wholesome, delightful, desirable, healthy and brilliant. But I have come to see that the one characteristic that I am more astonished at than any of His others is His Humility. It amazes me every time I think of it. And I am left dumbfounded by it constantly.

Dig this for an astonishing thing: in the Psalms, God asks us to Bless Him. What? Is He not the greatest in the universe? So do we not always want and need His Blessing? Absolutely. But our God steps so low as to ask *us* to Bless *Him*. "Bless the Lord, O my soul, and all that is within me Bless His holy Name." Isn't that just so extraordinary? And my greatest concern at the end of this Revelation on Humility is whether I have truly done justice to God's fantastic character.

SUMMARY

God's most extraordinary attribute after Grace is humility. It is our most becoming one.

Chapter 23
POVERTY.

Have you noticed in scripture that God prefers poverty to riches? Noticed how He puts the poor at the very top of His priority list?

Have you also noticed what an embarrassment the poor are to men? How we ignore them? Trample on them? Set them at the bottom of our priority list? Avoid them? Avoid dealing with them? Assume they are poor because they are ignorant, irresponsible or have squandered the good things they had? And have you noticed how diametrically opposite to God's perspective the view point of man is? So let's see what the scriptures say.

Firstly, and to dismiss it quickly, the Bible tells us that lazy people, stupid people and pleasure lovers will become poor. Like the prodigal Son, poverty gained that way is deserved. It's their own silly fault. Whatever a man sows, that he also reaps.

But it is not that kind of poverty that the Bible particularly addresses. It is to those who are poor through no fault of their own. Poverty of this kind is not just not having food for a day, a house to shelter in, clothes to wear, shoes on their feet, neither is it just being intellectually thick or untalented, nor is it just not having opportunity for education or work - it is not knowing what to do about it. It's a trap. People at the bottom of a pit are made exceedingly poor by not knowing how to get out of it. I have met many.

God sees these poor people. And He is concerned, in a world in which He has provided for everyone's need, that those who have give generously to those who do not have. In that way there will be equality all round. I remember reading a Moral Rearmament leaflet before I became a Christian. Among many other things, it said, "There is enough for everybody's need, but not for everybody's greed." 50 years on and it's still the same. In the Psalms it says that God provides for the poor, rescues the poor from those too strong for them, maintains the rights of the poor, scatters abroad gifts to the poor, raises the poor from the dust and secures justice for them. He hardly says much about the rich, except to rebuke them for using their riches wrongly. He hardly says anything specific about average people. But God singles out the poor and the needy as being especially precious to Him, and asks us to do the same. We need to single out the poor to bless them.

In the Law books, much provision is made for the poor, the alien and the stranger, and God required His people to seek out that section of society for special care, special provision and special protection. That law has not changed for us today. We Christians are similarly required to look for, look after and support the poor, the alien and the stranger in our midst. And what happens when we do? The Book of Ruth gives us the classic illustration. She, one of the hated and despised Moabites, became the Great Grandmother of King David and an ancestor of Jesus because a righteous man obeyed God's law to an alien.

Let us also see some particular scriptures from Proverbs, which expose and express God's heart in this matter.

> 14: 31. "He who oppresses the poor shows contempt for their maker, but whoever is kind to the needy honours God."
>
> 17: 5. "He who mocks the poor shows contempt for their maker."
>
> 19: 17. "He who is kind to the poor lends to the Lord, and he will reward him for what he has done."
>
> 31: 8 - 9. "Speak up for those who cannot speak for themselves, for the rights of all who are destitute. Speak up and judge fairly; defend the rights of the poor and needy."

God is a person of His word. He is consistently selecting the poor for special consideration. So, when He sent his Son to this earth, He deliberately selected poverty to be His lot. The wise men went to a palace to see the new King that had been born, and didn't find him in the palace. Instead, the star led them to a small village and to a room where the animals were stabled overnight. There was not even a bed for Him and his Mum to sleep on. There was "No room in the inn." But that was no accident. It was deliberately planned by God so that, of all sections of human society with whom Jesus could identify the best, it would be the poor and the destitute. Corruption, intrigue and usurped power live in the rich places - as we read with King Herod. Honesty and integrity of heart are more often found among the poor, so that's where Jesus preferred to live His life on Earth. "Foxes have holes, and birds of the air have nests, but the Son of man has nowhere to lay his head." (Matthew 8: 20).

The New Testament comments on Jesus poverty:

> "Who, being in very nature God, did not consider equality with God something to be grasped, but made himself nothing, taking the very nature of a servant (Greek - slave), being made in human likeness." (Philippines 2: 6 - 7).

Why should He do that? Because servanthood is His nature, humility its root. He who was (and is) rich beyond all measure does not find riches a draw in any way, but lived in faith that His father would provide everything He needed on earth in a perfectly appropriate measure. And so it proved.

> "For you know the grace of our Lord Jesus Christ, that though he was rich, yet for your sakes he became poor, so that you through his poverty might become rich." (2 Corinthians 8: 9).

So God's heart is one of poverty. He is completely empty of avarice, and full of faith. The Divine Exchange - God's riches for our poverty and our poverty for His riches - was and always will be His way with men. God loves the poor, and His heart's desire is to bring them into His riches of whatever kind.

By way of illustrating this, God says through James "Has not God chosen those who are poor in the eyes of the world to be rich in faith and to inherit the kingdom he promised to those who love him?" (2: 5). Note - *chosen.* And it is true. Stories from the persecuted Christians north of Nigeria would indicate that raising the dead back to life is almost commonplace out there. Divine healing is considered normal and is a daily occurrence. We are laden with medical services for our every ache and pain, and do not need faith in God to heal us. How poor we are in our riches! Or take South America. There are still reports coming from there of God growing replacement teeth overnight, with some made of silver and some gold. Whoever heard of such things before? Certainly not those who can pay a small fortune to have a new set of NHS dentures or crowns!

Need I emphasise that God requires us to do to same as He does? That we seek out the poor, with the specific aim of blessing them in whatever appropriate way, and just for the sheer fun of doing it? God knows the poor cannot reward Him. And that must also be our motive - none other than to bring joy and happiness to those who don't deserve it and cannot repay. When you hold a party, Jesus said, "do not invite your friends, your brothers or relatives, or your rich neighbours; if you do, they may invite you back and so you will be repaid. But when you give a banquet, invite the poor, the crippled, the lame and the blind, and you will be blessed." (Luke 14: 12 - 14). There is no need to comment further.

In the "Sermon on the Plain" from Luke 6, Jesus said: "Blessed are you who are poor, for yours is the Kingdom of God." They are blessed because the Kingdom of God is made available to them in abundance and the Kingdom of God is better than any earthly riches. He then makes it absolutely clear what God's heart and will is by saying a few sentences later: "Woe to you who are rich, for you have already received your comfort."

So what are we rich Christians to do? We may not consider ourselves to be rich, but we only need to compare ourselves with the poor of this world - defined by the UN as living below $1 US a day - then we are stinking rich. What are we to do? Do we do what CT Studd did and give away our family fortune so that we all walk by faith and live on fresh air? Well, for some that may well be God's leading. But only for a few. So what do the rest of us do?

God gave me revelation to both that and to another issue by giving me insight into a verse that had troubled me for ages - Matthew 5:3, the very first of the Beatitudes and the opener to the Sermon on the Mount. "Blessed are the poor in spirit, for theirs is the Kingdom of Heaven."

My trouble was that I could not see that, taken at its face value, that could possibly be true. Was Jesus recommending that we should be spiritually poor? Surely He wants us to be spiritually rich, doesn't He? It troubled me. I turned to Bible commentators. All I read tried to explain *away* the verse - so obviously they didn't understand it either. They said things like: what Jesus *meant* was those who *felt* they were poor in spirit and so on. I just didn't think they got to the root of it, and I rejected all their attempted logic. Neither could I get there, and it troubled me. I handed it over to the Lord and forgot about it.

One morning a few months later I was out for my morning jog down the road when Bingo! God gave me Revelation. God told me exactly what that verse means, and I will try to put it as clearly and lucidly as I can. What Jesus is saying is: "Blessed are those who have adopted poverty in their spirits as a lifestyle." "Blessed are the poor in spirit." That is, they have a heart that has selected "Poverty" as their total commitment, their chosen way of life and their permanent intention. "Blessed are the poor in their *spirits*."

When God brings a revelation, as I have pointed out already, He also grants the ability. So, at that moment I not only got understanding but also received the soul of poverty that is God's own heart. He gave me a Spirit of Poverty. Note, not misery. It meant that, from then on I would covet no one's riches or possessions, never hanker after money, never be jealous of those who had it, never seek wealth for myself or for my own ends -

ever again. It was a life changing moment - a paradigm shift for ever.

The consequences? I can live in other rich houses and enjoy other people's possessions without one ounce of coveting. I can enjoy other people's wealth, regardless of whether I am a participator in it or not. I can genuinely bless those who have nice things with no hidden agenda in my heart. Moreover, I can live an appropriate lifestyle in England, comfortable and provided for, and never worry if God took it all away from me. Hebrews 11:34 springs to mind. I tell you, it is beautiful freedom. Where the scripture says: "The love of money is a root of every kind of evil," and it is, it doesn't touch me. So I can live in England without being dependent on others, give generously from what I have got, make responsible provision for my wife and daughter, and be fully identified with the poor I love in Nicaragua.

It does not mean I am not tempted. Of course I am. But God's heart is God's heart, and He has given the poverty bit to me so that I can really enjoy being generous to all. It is such fun.

Have you ever thought seriously what Paul said in Philippians 4? There we have a verse often quoted out of context. That verse is: "I can do everything through him who gives me strength." The context? Money! Listen to the previous verse: "I know what it is to be in need, and I know what it is to have plenty. I have learnt the secret of being content in any and every situation, whether well fed or hungry, whether living in plenty or in want." (Philippians 4: 12). Paul also had God's heart of poverty. Look how it works. If he had abundance, he was not moved by it. No power manifestations, no oppressions, no "I can do all things because I now have money." He was content in Jesus. And if he had nothing, there was not an "I can do nothing and am miserable because I am penniless." He was content. God would provide all his needs and the needs of the ministry, and having or not having money did not divert that for one moment. Jesus was his strength and his provider. But without the heart of poverty Paul would have been in a sticky position, and would (could) never have evangelised the Mediterranean in his one lifetime.

Do you notice that word "contentment"? It's a key. If we are discontented with anything to do with money or possessions, then we've still a long way to go in our Christian lives, and need the inputs of Grace more than we ever recognise.

I need to point out that there is a very strong negativity, almost despair, about poverty. Physical poverty and deprivation can introduce a "Poverty Spirit" into people's hearts. Those who have been deprived for a long time lose the heart to fight for their survival any more. The flame goes out inside them. They sink into one of John of Bunyan's "sloughs of despond." It's a spiritual thing, and demonically initiated. The thief, said Jesus in John 10, comes to steal, kill and destroy. Satan comes to take away hope, kill expectation and destroy people's hearts. We can see this desperation and Poverty Spirit in the eyes of the hungry, the oppressed and the dispossessed. Once someone has succumbed to a Poverty Spirit, it's very difficult to bring them out of it into freedom. For ever they may be suspicious of help given to them, and unbelieving of others' generosity. The Christians behind the Iron Curtain in the 20th century never gave up, despite the genocide and the persecution from communism. It took them all but 100 years, but their faith and confidence in their God of justice enabled them to destroy communism from the inside. The human spirit is strong to resist oppression. But the heart that has yielded to a Poverty Spirit is sad indeed.

I have tried here to differentiate between "The Spirit of Poverty" from God, and a "Poverty Spirit" from satan. I have no biblical justification for defining either that way. But we all know that there is a heart of poverty that is triumphantly good and free and there is a heart of poverty that is miserable and crushed. I just want you to know the difference, embrace the good and seek to heal the bad. Someone else will be given revelation as to a better way to define each, and I would be glad for that contribution from the Body of Christ.

I have met very few poor people in Nicaragua who have a Poverty Spirit. Some have been desperately close, but we have been able to draw them out and bring a smile to their faces. For the vast majority of poor that I know in Nicaragua - the poorest Spanish-speaking nation on earth - I find contentment. They have little or no income. Sometimes they have little or no food in a day. Often they have no shelter - or the shelter they have is difficult to describe as such. Yet they have learnt "the secret of being content in any and every situation." They are marvellous company. They are delightful to be with. I find myself closer to heaven in their presence than I do in all the rich sophistications of the West.

I have found that the poor of this world are often the happiest people I have ever met, as well as the most generous. Heaven is going to be full of them.

My task and calling from God is to bring relief to their poverty. The fact that they are happy inside their poverty does not mean that either God or I want to leave them there. No sir! We all know the dangers of riches and materialism. But putting a whole new roof on a holey one is not introducing wealth. Nor is providing a mattress or a second set of clothes or a kick-start to a sustainable livelihood. To bring someone out of their poverty trap is God's calling on the lives of far more people than take it up.

Let me finish with a few lines from the end of a Christmas Carol:

> Therefore Christian men be sure,
> Wealth or rank possessing;
> You who now will bless the poor
> Shall yourselves find blessing.

SUMMARY

God's heart is a heart of poverty. To be gifted with that same heart is riches indeed.

Chapter 24
INSIDE OUT.

There will be many reasons that you can think of why God chose to reduce himself in Jesus down to a man. The hymn writer gave up: "Our God contracted to a span, incomprehensibly made man." Methinks it would be a profitable subject to meditate on - should you be lacking in ideas for a meditation and opportunities in which to have fellowship with the Lord.

Here are some suggested reasons: He loves us. He created the cosmos especially for us. He could not go back on His creation. He had to redeem us or lose us altogether. He wanted to demonstrate the riches and depths of grace. He loves us.

And many more, only one of which is the subject of this Revelation.

Because God is wholly Spirit and is therefore not limited or restricted by geography (only one place at one time), or by time (having to be here and now), or by power (limited in strength and initiative), He has freedom of a kind we can only dream of. Because he is so Big, it's difficult for our limited and restricted minds to think beyond our boundaries.

But because He is Spirit and we are Spirit, He is able to commune and communicate with us despite those limitations and restrictions of ours.

First of all, He has access to us from the inside. He can read us from inside out. Because He is a Gentleman, He does not interfere with us inside. He makes suggestions and observes dispassionately, but never *causes* us to do His will unless we choose to do so. So the Hitlers of this earth, of which there are many in every generation, from the little control freak in the home or Office to the violent dictators or revolutionaries, still have opportunity to decide their actions in the light of divine inputs, but without divine interference. I am of the opinion that every single human being, from their first few days on earth, is being gently nudged by God from the inside. John 1:9 says (and I again quote) that Jesus is the light that lights every man that comes into the world. And if that's what the scripture says, it must be absolutely (100%) true. God not only has access to all our souls, but is making suggestions all the time. I have already pointed out that few recognise those nudges. Certainly, before one became a Christian, there was no possibility of identifying those inner thoughts that always suggest righteousness and goodness as coming from God. We thought they came from ourselves. And when we became Christians it still took a very long time for our minds to be changed and for us to identify those thoughts as coming from God and not from me. That mind change has never restricted the Lord from carrying on His good work inside our hearts. And He knows just how hard it is for the habit of a lifetime (the habit of thinking I am talking to myself inside) to change to seeing and recognising the truth. That's one very good reason why He loves faith so much and rewards us for it. Recognition is three-quarters of the way to acts of obedience prompted by faith. "Without faith it is impossible to please God." (Hebrews 11). With faith God is mega pleased.

Quite clearly, God knows the best way to run a human life. He designed both us and our environment, and knows, from personal experience looking from inside out, what is the best thing for every human on earth to do at every moment in time. And prompts us accordingly. The fact that few human beings follow His prompts is exactly the reason why the world is in such a mess that it is. We prefer to follow our own ways, which is another way of saying we prefer to follow satan, and his remit is to steal, kill and destroy. It is amazing that God gets anything good done on this earth. It is also amazing that man has not destroyed his environment altogether. Someone has pointed out that man is one of the few creatures on this earth that fouls its own nest. And we are supposed be made in God's image! It is also amazing that God's love and ways get through the barriers to anyone, and that some people actually become Christians. It is even more amazing that there are those who stay Christians all their lives; the fall-off rate must be enormous. I'm glad I don't have to arbitrate at the end of time as to who qualifies for heaven and who doesn't. It's tricky enough getting there myself. Someone asked Billy Graham what his first thought would be when he arrived in heaven. He said, "Relief!" The point I am making is that God "is familiar with all my ways."

He is also familiar with temptation. He can read satan's inputs into my mind very clearly - otherwise He would not be able to council me so perfectly on how to combat it. (Remember, the sword of the Spirit in Ephesians 6 is the spoken (*rhēma*) word of God). It is the Lord's little nudges into good that, the moment I acknowledge them, accept them and use them, are mighty to the pulling down of strongholds (2 Corinthians 10) and defeating satan. So, from inside out, God knows every thought of every person on earth, every subtlety of satan, and always produces at exactly the right moment the perfect course of action that enables each individual to live a perfect lifestyle in the centre of God's will. The fact that no one does is not an indicator of God's failure, but of our inherent wickedness - as no doubt we will discover at the Day of Judgment when everything will be made abundantly clear.

God has been observing and nudging man from inside out from the dawn of time. That's one reason why no amount, degree or style of wickedness fazes Him - He has seen it all before.

But that observation point was not good enough for God.

He had to see it and know it personally for Himself. That's why He became a man. It was crucially important that He experienced personally, from the moment of conception, what it is to be a human being. From birth, through childhood, through teenage pressures and sexual development, through to adulthood, rejection, deprivation, pain and death, He needed to experience it Himself. He experienced poverty, was a refugee, lost His earthly father, and saw all His brothers and sisters reject His claims. (Those we know about only got converted after His death). He also lived under foreign occupation. He had already experienced every experience of man from outside in, if I could re-style it that way, from heaven from the beginning. Now He would experience mankind for Himself, with no internal interference from anyone else. All of us in our bodies are influenced from outside in. The only "inside out" bits are the suggestions of God and satan in our minds and hearts. All others are from the outside in. We are all isolated individuals, and God has made it that way so that it is impossible for anyone else to be blamed for any of our actions.

Neither satan nor God, as I have said before, are able to force their ways on us. (God won't and satan can't). All our decisions are our own.

And that is how Jesus was on earth. He was isolated just like we are. He was cut off from all other responsibilities - such as "holding all things together" (Col 1) - and lived under the same restrictions that we do. He also had the same divine and demonic internal suggestions that we do. I wonder what age He was when He recognised the difference between good and evil promptings inside? And at what age did He recognise that God was His Father, and not Joseph? What we do know is that He "was tempted in every way, just as we are - yet was without sin" (Hebrews 4). So from the earliest age He must have known the difference between what God said and what satan said. God would have been as kind to Him as He is to us, restricting satan's temptations to a developing appropriate level until Jesus had been fully equipped after baptism and was in the desert when God took His hands off the restraints and left Jesus alone to face satan neat, together with the Father and the Holy Spirit, and clearly, the remembered word of God. So the battle was joined from the start of His life, and, as a man, Jesus was isolated exactly like we are, with the only internal inputs coming from God and satan just like us. It is my opinion that Jesus never cheated. I believe He laid aside all the privileges and powers of Divinity, and lived 33 years on earth with exactly the same restraints as we have. I also find it quite astonishing that He always and only chose the Father's will. He was in the same place as Adam, knowing only God. But Adam had one rule, Jesus had thousands. Adam had one temptation (and failed); Jesus had 33 non-stop years of temptations (and never failed). The more I chew over what Jesus did, the more astonished I am with it. I bow in awe and worship. I used to think that He scraped through by the skin of His teeth. But now I see that He was never anywhere near sinning – the closest being in Gethsemane. He was so full of His Father and so locked into Him, that anything and everything else was miles away from even being considered.

I've gone off the point. He needed to live the life of man from inside an isolated human body. From that very same position that we are in here, He listened to both God's nudges and satan's temptations, and always chose God. "Because he himself suffered when he was tempted, he is able to help those who are being tempted." (Hebrews 2:18). In that way, no one can possibly accuse God of not understanding us. Or of ignorance. And that is why God has placed all judgment into the hands of Jesus. As a man who has been tempted and won, He is the only person who is qualified to make valid judgments on every human being's successes and failures.

So that's the point I want to make. God knows every thought of every human being from the beginning of time because He is Spirit and observes. He also knows what it is like to live as a man, under the same restrictions and isolation as the rest of us. That's the reason I'm emphasising why God became man.

But I have not finished yet.

Because Jesus lived a perfect human life, I believe His life now serves as a pattern for all human lives. That is, the things He did and the way He did them are the base from which *every* Christian life on Earth should be patterned and emanate. That's why every victory He won in the minutes of His life can be given to us by the Holy Spirit as we walk our own minutes. We are prompted to do it His way – and His way will always be successful..

Clearly, few of us live in Israel, and none of us lives in 4 BC to 29 AD. The culture and times in which Jesus lived only serve as a framework into which the principles of divine living are granted to all those who live in a different culture in a different century.

But it's not those things exactly I am getting at. Let me evaluate other issues.

1. Demons. Of all people on earth, Jesus' observation and analysis of the presence of demons is the most prolific. There seemed to be more demons in His day than there have been since. And that cannot be true. Certainly, they manifested stronger when He was around than when I'm around. (Perhaps I'm not causing them too much bother?). But we don't believe in demons any more. And why not? Is it us who are wrong or was it Jesus? (Some have actually written that He had a naïve and early medieval mindset and was clearly mistaken). But I maintain that it is we who are deceived. Demons are just as prevalent today as then; Jesus was not deceived, but we are. Moreover, His statement to His disciples that we have all authority over all the power of the enemy comes straight down to us. I believe that both His insight into the demonic realm and the way He dealt with them serve as a pattern for every Christian's life throughout time. We can do what He did, because we should think the way He thought.

2. Healing. I am of the opinion that God is the only Person in the Universe who heals. People talk of the body healing itself - but it can't. God can and does. Others talk about the medical profession or medicines healing. And certainly science has discovered marvellous chemical solutions to abnormal chemistry in the body. But it is God who is in everything and everyone bringing the "wholeness". Praise God for the medical profession. And praise God for the help and comfort they bring. In no way am I going to minimise the medics.

In Jesus' day, the medics were a long way behind the 21st century. Therefore the short circuiting of healing by Jesus through miracle was acceptable then, and still is in the modern mind. It's the same in the 21st century's Third World. There is just not enough medicine for doctors to keep the population healthy. So Jesus needs to short circuit the medics where there are no medics. They need New Testament miracles today, and many have them.

But Western Christians, with all their medical sophistications, have forgotten God altogether. We have substituted "Doctor" for "Jesus". So there is an ever-increasing area in our lives that is no longer open to faith nor open to God. So what am I suggesting? That we abandon medicine and run by faith alone? God forbid! That's letting the baby out with the bath water, and spiritual presumption. The advances in medicine are from God. But never as a substitute for Him. He has been a partner to the medics from the beginning. That is where He should firmly remain - always. And we 21st century Christians, First and Third World, should be expectant in Jesus' Healing Power, combined with any help we get from the medics. Partners, not substitutes.

3. Miracle. I have written elsewhere that the mathematics of the spirit realm are very different from the mathematics of the physical realm of which this creation is made. And, clearly, it is very much superior. If we could only tap into that spiritual mathematics, there are many things we could do on earth that bypass this Earth's physical, chemical and biological laws.

The great thing is that we can! And it is not by mathematical means: it is by faith in Jesus Christ. He is Lord over all.

"Providence" is God doing stuff using natural laws. "Miracle" is God doing stuff cutting across natural laws. A miracle is not something that can be explained in any natural way.

What is our expectation of God? Has it diminished down to practically zero? Whether God answers prayer providentially or miraculously is, in fact, immaterial. We do not put our faith in miracles, or in our ability to perform them; we put our faith only in Jesus (see Matt 7:22-23). It is God's proactive intervention in the things of earth and time that should be our expectation. We follow Jesus. And "we fill up that which is lacking in regard to Christ's afflictions." (Colossians 1: 24).

4. Authority. There are two aspects to authority: the authority we have and the authority others have.

First our authority. As living sons of the living God, we have authority over all things - but only at the prompting of Jesus. It can be expected, but it cannot be assumed. Jesus walked through the crowds unharmed, and they were powerless to stop Him. On the other hand, the soldiers were able to arrest Him, try Him and crucify Him. All was under God's authority, and, following a perfect agenda of which we are ignorant, God allows some of us to take authority over evil forces and others to be captured and tortured by them. Only eternity will uncover God's perfect rationale. In His humanity, Jesus shrank back from the Father's will in Gethsemane, but accepted it and went through to death. Before that, He was in authority over all things.

But, secondly, notice how He did not take authority over the authorities. He was courteous to the Romans and to Pilate, and never questioned their authority. Paul in Romans 13 says that every authority is appointed by God, and we need to honour and respect those authorities that are over us. If there is nothing good we can say about them, then we remain silent, as Jesus did before Herod. But Jesus reminded Pilate that he would not have authority over Him unless it had been given him from above. Jesus was not into changing the political scene. There are those He calls into such a work, but for the majority of us we follow Jesus and honour, respect and obey the authorities God has placed over us.

I have a true story of a young Christian friend of mine who applied to join the RAF. His interviewer asked: "If your Commanding Officer asks you to do something and God tells you to do something else, who would you obey?" The young man was stumped. When pressed, he said, "I would obey God," and he failed the interview. I have thought about it since. The thing is that, biblically, the question itself is nonsense. God always works *through* the authorities. Rebellion is always from hell. And if Christians live in wicked regimes, then they hand that authority to God's greater ability to bring justice, and still obey them. Just like

Jesus did. Christians in communist Russia defeated communism through prayer and not rebellion. From inside out. As did Christians in Uganda under Idi Amin. As we all should.

5. Prayer. I don't know if you've noticed that there are not many instances of Jesus praying? There are some classic ones, of course, and Arthur Wallis' little book "Jesus Prayed" gives a good meditation on those in Luke's Gospel. On certain occasions, Jesus "looked up" before a healing. On all occasions recorded (if I remember rightly), He "looked up" as He gave thanks for food. On certain occasions He prayed all night, or went out early in the morning. Or, when the crowd wanted to make Him king, He sent the disciples back across Galilee and took a half (three-quarter?) night of prayer alone on the hillside. But all those were special occasions. Are we therefore to glean that those are the only times we should pray? That is, only occasionally or when there's a crisis? Not at all! In Matthew 6 Jesus spoke about prayer. He said that when we pray we should go into our room or toilet and pray there. The point? Our praying should be in secret. And God, who sees in secret, will reward us openly.

So we can work backwards (if we want to). A Christian life that is happy, contented, effective and gets results comes out from a secret life of prayer. No doubt about it. Permanent and ongoing communication with Jesus leads to fruitfulness and effectiveness (2 Peter 1), or prosperity (Psalm 1) - which means success in all aspects of living, not just financially. It's obvious that the only way that every minute of Jesus' life could please His Father would be if He was in tune with His Father every minute. It's that kind of lifestyle of which He is the ace example. We follow His style. We do what He did. We copy Him. But it's more than that. His prayer life - the life of prayer that He lived in His 33 years on earth - breathes out from us as He breathes it in. Our prayer life is an overflow of His Now prayer life. We are not called to mimic Him; we are called to be an extension of His human soul on this earth. We blend together with Him in all things.

It's these things that we have forgotten how to do. We pray because we feel we must. We pray mechanically, and only on occasions. Or in special crises. What God wants is a life of prayer, and Jesus is both our example and our breath. He walked, talked, ate, drank, breathed and lived God. That's what we have to do also. And the more we do it, the happier and more joyful we will be, the more Christ-like we will become, the more effective will be our life and ministry, and the more our life will become a 21st century version of the first century model.

Mentioning that the crowd wanted to make Jesus King, this came to me: *Never, ever become famous!* It will be an appalling drain on your time, your resources, your work, your well-being, and it's a diversion to your devotion. Notice how demanding crowds are? And what about the obscene, wicked, biased and critical pressure of the media? Just see how Jesus handled it – if you ever have the misfortune to become famous. I have already mentioned Luke 12 – just keep listening to God and drive on to do His will, regardless of the pressures from people. Or, as in John 6:15 when the crowd wanted to crown Him King, He spent a half to three quarters of a night in prayer – just to re-establish and refresh the priorities in His life. Copy Him.

6. Wisdom. James says that if anyone lacks wisdom, he should ask God, who gives generously to all without finding fault. Wisdom is not gained by intelligence. It is only partially gained by experience. It is wholly gained by Revelation. We can have Jesus' wisdom if we ask for it and trust the promptings we get.

But it will not be our wisdom. It will be Jesus' wisdom recycled in a different shape for a different century, appropriately adjusted to our Now situation. When it happens to you, browse through the Gospels retrospectively. I'm certain you will find a parallel in the earthly life of Jesus.

Conclusion. Jesus is THE MAN. He is the second Adam. His earthly life was the template for all new creatures in Christ. Because we are His Body today, all Christian lives are patterned on Jesus' earthly body. We will not all undergo, for example, Crucifixion. But certain of our brothers and sisters in every generation will be persecuted and killed. Some will be refugees. Some alienated. All hated, marginalised or misunderstood because of our association with Jesus. All of us want to live a quiet life and get on with our work; but we will not be able to. And in our distress we will find in the Gospels (as well as in the Gospel) both a pattern and a benchmark for victory. Because Jesus pleased His Father in all things in His earthly body, He can repeat that accomplishment in all our earthly bodies.

Jesus is re-living His 33 years of earthly life through Christians in every century from Inside Out.

SUMMARY

Jesus is re-living His 33 years on earth through every Christian in every generation in every century.

Chapter 25

THE FOUR LOVES.

It's love that makes the world go round. Or so they say. It is love, flowing out of Grace, that causes God to do what He does, and in Him is a never ending supply of it. He is the love dynamo of the universe. It is love that draws people together, and causes them to do beautiful things for each other, to sacrifice their time, money and attention, and even to lay down their lives for each other. Love is a beautiful thing which does beautiful things for other people.

But what kind of love are we talking about? I would suggest that every person who reads that paragraph above, and thinks about what it said, has a different perception of what kind of love I was describing. And was it the same kind of love in each instance?

In this area of love, the English language is particularly inept. In many instances it is unhelpful, and in others deceitful. Someone can use the word "love" and mean one thing, and those listening can interpret it in a completely different way, and one that erroneously suggests something distinctly wrong. Not many other languages (so I have been told) have this restraint. But in English, the word love has many interpretations, few of which are clearly defined at the moment of use.

It is good to turn, therefore, to the Greek language. For a start, it forms part of the foundation of English. And then it uses four words for our one, and can help us redefine what we mean. There can hardly be a better book on the subject than CS Lewis' book of the same title. So here I will barely expand on the differences - only alert you to them.

In Greece, we presume, they never got confused about what love they were talking about. Moreover, the New Testament was written in Greek, so therefore we have no need to be confused by what God is saying. Two of the Greek words are never found in the Bible, so let us start with those.

Storgē. This word describes love in a family. It describes the proper love relationship between parents and children, children and parents, uncles, aunts, grand parents, cousins et al. When we say we love our Mum and Dad, there is affection in it, no sexuality and nothing illicit, illegal or untoward about it. It is a right relationship, a good and proper kind of love, one that most people experience, and it is nothing to be ashamed of.

Eros. This word is also never found in the New Testament. It is the word for sexual love. Eros was the Greek god of love, and we get the English word "erotic" and all its associates from it. Because our English culture and society is as it is at the moment, and sex is one of our predominant wickednesses, most people interpret the English word "love" sexually. If someone asks, "Do you love children?" they usually have in mind "sexually". Or, "Do you love people (girls, fellows or whoever)?" they are thinking sexually. Sexuality underlies much of what people do and say, and newspapers and magazines are rampant with it. Moreover, people are now conditioned to think sex for sex's sake. There is little relationship in it. God made sex beautiful and purposeful. It was designed round relationships that are honourable, stable, secure, permanent and life-giving. God has written good things about sex, and epitomised it in the Old Testament in the Song of Solomon. We are a long way from the wholeness of that perception. He made male and female to belong together, not just for reproduction, and certainly not for "a good night out." We are rational, accountable and spiritual creatures, and God requires us to be accountable with what we do with our bodies and minds. He loves sex with all its fascinations and wonders, but always only blesses it within the boundaries He set for it. Moreover, there are other kinds of lovely loves.

We need to consider another important point. In our teen years as puberty kicks in, all sorts of sexual feelings course through our veins, both girls and boys. In single-sex schools, a lot of hero worship occurs from juniors to seniors. Hero worship is not sexual. But because our hormones are jangling about in our bodies at that time and before they have settled down and been identified, a mixture of "loves" is very common. Nowadays this becomes apparent with worship of sports personalities or pop stars - both male and female. But during this pubescent development period, homosexuality can easily raise its head. It happens from seniors to juniors and juniors to seniors. It is important to recognise that this happens, and is OK provided it doesn't lead to sex in any way, and provided it settles at 18+ into legitimate heterosexuality. Many homosexuals and lesbians developed their orientation during puberty, felt society say it was OK then, and consequently took it on as a lifestyle. Which is error. Puberty is not a stable condition to decide on a life-style's orientation. Heterosexuality is the norm, and God made us male and female so that together we could operate as one human being. Romans 1 tells us that homosexuality comes directly out of an abandonment of God. There are some people who genuinely are homosexual, but very few – far fewer than claim it today. They may not be able to change that orientation, but they certainly can avoid homosexual acts. Who we are is not judged: what we do is judged. May I also say that heterosexual sexual acts outside marriage are just as sinful and wicked as homosexual acts? Just don't do either of them.

Philia. *Philia* means "affection". It is a warm, loving, companionable love. There is lots of *philia* in *storgē*, family love. And, not surprisingly, it can be found regularly in the New Testament. The American city Philadelphia is "*philia adelphos*" meaning "brotherly affection." Indeed, there are many words we still use that come directly from the Greek, and, apart from the little used word "filial" are compounds. For example, there is philosophy (love of wisdom) and philanthropy (love of mankind)

- and there are many others. Of course, common usage changes meanings, especially when transliterated into another language. But with *philia*, the fundamental concept of "affection for" remains.

We all experience *philia* in some way. It comes out among colleagues working hard together on a common project: the delight of the companionship, the going for a common goal, the achievement together in the face of adversity - all that produces the love that is affection and appreciation. Sports people often have *philia* in their teams. Families, of course, have great *philia* for each other that often springs up irrationally in their feelings.

But, particularly, *philia* is common with Christians and Jesus. Our appreciation of His inputs, His kindness and His companionship - these things give us a warm feeling of *philia* (affection) inside for Him. (Would that we had the same level of *philia* for our fellow Christians!). *Philia* is an emotional love, totally divorced from anything sexual. I remember someone saying that married couples should not only love one another (*eros*), but that they should also be friends (*philia*). That's worth taking note of, because *eros* dies, and if it's not replaced by *philia*, what is there left but loveless duty?

I have just mentioned, but need to stress that *philia* does not contain any sexual content. That is very important indeed. Because of the huge limitation in the English word "love", outsiders often put sexual implications into affections that are completely harmless. Indeed, are happy, legitimate and delightful feelings that people have for one another. Outsiders raise their eyebrows and give knowing looks as if to say, "There something sexually unhealthy in *that* relationship." The chances are that there is nothing of the kind. Let me give you an example. Schoolgirls often develop relationships with each other that are from *philia*. Moreover, girls are very good (much better than men) at retaining those close and loving relationships all down through their lives. They are often misinterpreted as lesbian. But the vast majority are not.

Agapē. The 4th Greek word for love is *agapē.* Now this is an interesting Greek word, and for this reason; it is very rarely found in ancient contemporary Greek literature. According to William Barclay, it is used only once. There its meaning is so obscure that no translators can translate it. The Holy Spirit has therefore dredged it out of obscurity in order to give it special significance in Christian terms. Really, the only ancient literature in which this word is found is the Bible. Also significantly, we can only get a definition of it from the Bible's use of it. All the other three forms of love have common use outside the Bible, and we get our distinctions between them from there. But not *agapē.* It means love, and can only be defined as God's love.

All the various kinds of love must come from God. He created all things, and therefore all kinds of love. But there needed to be a special description of the kind of love the Bible tells us of when it says: "God is love," or "God so loved .." (Of course, in case you wondered, the Bible uses it both as a noun and a verb). It has to be different from sexual love, *eros.* It has to be higher than the emotional affection of *philia.* It is also much more than the love connection between relatives as seen in *storgē.*

Here I am reliant on William Barclay. William Barclay says that *agapē* love is a love of the mind and of the will. If there is emotion in it, it is neither significant nor important. So let us look at both of these areas one at a time for I have found them very helpful.

First the mind. God's *agapē* love stems from His mind. Having thought something through, God needs neither to add to it nor to change it because He is eternally Now. So what did God need to think through?

He had to think through the whole of His creation before He created. Why should He create anyway? Why should there ever be an "other than Them"? And what would it involve to create - in terms of the cost in energy and maintenance? What kind of creatures would He have, and what responsibilities would they be given? What boundaries? What choices? What environment? What would it cost Him (Them) if He gave His creatures the same level of choice that He has? What would it cost Him if it went pear-shaped (wrong)? How was He going to end it? Develop it? What was His long-term view and purpose?

All these things God thought through before He put pen to paper (!) and drew up His plan. Because He knew and planned all things, and also knew everything that *might* happen, He had to think through every eventuality, determine every solution to every possible problem, and then decide mutually between the three of Them whether it was all worth it or not.

To our blessing and to my eternal amazement, He did.

His determination and motivation was and is and always will be love. He has decided that, regardless of what happened to His creation, whatever His creation did, He would always do them good. So *agapē* love is a *rational choice* to bless. No other and no less; God *is* love *(agapē)*. Because of this predetermined choice of His, God can do no other than good to His creatures, whatever it might cost Him.

One significance of this to us (me anyway) is that I am to do the same to my fellow creatures - human and other. I have to choose and decide that my mind set and my actions must be always to bless, encourage, help and support. You can see immediately that this is not an emotional issue. It is, firstly, a rational issue. It is something I see to do which is good. Also, I see that it is good to be good and do good to all people, regardless of age, or race, colour or creed. I must decide to believe in people, not ignore them, abandon them, or marginalise them. I wonder if you can see the necessity of the thinking through of this policy first and completely? Why should I do this? Because that is what God does, and I have been included in God's determination. "We love because He first loved us."

Secondly, *agapē* love is an act of the *will.* God not only decided to do good to all His creation, He makes sure He does it. All of God's carefully thought-through strategy to bless ends up in actions of blessings. He *does* what He has promised to do. That is why there is a Cross in human history.

In this respect, human beings are certainly made in the image of God (as in many other respects). In what respect? All our actions are the result of previous thought. We think first, decide, and then we do. Indeed, it is impossible to do otherwise. (I guess the only exceptions would be in the throes of illnesses or pain). We do because we have first thought about doing. This has to be the major reason why God judges us on our actions - our actions betray our motives and our hidden agendas. Didn't Jesus say that "out of the overflow of the heart the mouth speaks (and the body acts)"? What we are inside governs what we do and how we act. So, by judging actions, He assesses both the motive and the will. We often think to do things but don't do them. For those we are not judged – unless it is for disobedience. Our actions betray our hearts. It's no good saying things and not doing them. We assess other people, not by what they say they are, but by what they *do*. "By their fruits you will know them."

With God, all of His heart is goodness. He is love. That's why we can rely on all His actions being loving, kind, merciful and promotional. Negative things that happen on this earth (floods, earthquakes, natural disasters etc) do not come from God - He has an agent whose specialisation is evil. Fortunately God controls him. Satan can only think evil and do evil, but he is not a free agent to rush off and perpetuate the maximum wickedness he can. He is controlled, as is the degree of wickedness he can perpetrate (see Job 1 and 2). Then God turns it round to good (see Romans 8:28), because He is love. (I consequently coined this phrase that has rocked some people over my last few decades: "satan is God's agent for good on this earth." Think it through!)

As for us, once we get our hearts right, our actions will follow. But we must make sure that our motives and agendas are the same as God's - to do good to all people all the time, and not even wish evil or negativity on them. The pity is that it takes a lifetime to get there. We have no idea just how deep and extensive is the wickedness within us; but God will show us it all bit by bit. Meanwhile, guard those thoughts that pass through your minds moment by moment as they happen. At least we can *desire* to be like God, even if we have trouble accomplishing it.

"Grow in love" is the biblical recommendation. How? The only way I know is to learn it first hand from the Master moment by moment as we walk with Him. Where we find it impossible to follow His example or wishes, then prayer is the key: ask Him to "Create in me a clean heart, and renew a right spirit within me." That works. I can assure you with confidence - it works. I am today mostly made up inside by Grace alone. I now understand Paul when he wrote: "But by the grace of God I am what I am, and his grace to me was not without effect. No, I worked harder than all of them—yet not I, but the grace of God that was with me."

So, we need to grow in *agapē* love. We need to be thinking all the time; "How can I bless that person; how can I do them good? What do you want me to do to help them Lord?" So we need to *think* random acts of kindness to strangers, and *do* random acts of kindness to strangers. Thinking kindness enables us to speak kindness, rather than speaking the angers and frustrations with which we are so familiar. Thinking them is not *agapē*. Doing them is not necessarily *agapē*. Thinking them and doing them out from the heart of Jesus, or at His prompting, or in conscious collaboration with Him - that is *agapē* love. It comes from God, is initiated by God, brings glory to God and dispenses happiness and joy to all. I don't think *agapē* love is copyable; that is, we can't act it or pretend. It is a divine attribute which is imparted momentarily as the need and occasion arises. Constant use of it brings us into the habit of expecting it more and more. Thus we live the life of Jesus on earth in an ever increasing and effective way, and that's how we "grow in love and in the knowledge of Jesus Christ."

So, what about these four loves?

I hope this little chapter will enable you to distinguish between them from now on - both in your own heart and in the actions and words of others. From that, I pray and plead that you develop each love in your own heart in a good, honourable, helpful and kind way, so that love may continue to make the world go round in as beautiful and wholesome a way as God would like.

Won't heaven be wonderful?

SUMMARY

We need to differentiate between 4 kinds of love: Family, Sexual, Affection and God's Love, and use each appropriately.

Chapter 26

STUDY ON THE NATURE OF THE BRIDE OF CHRIST

Packets of cigarettes in the UK today come with a Government Health warning – SMOKING KILLS. This chapter comes with a spiritual health warning – it could break the Unity of the Spirit in the Bond of Peace. All unusual doctrines carry the same warning.

Why? We like all our doctrines to be conventional and safe. What does that mean? It means that we prefer everyone else to agree with us – so that we may feel secure and comfortable. I have already expressed the view that Doctrine causes more heat and division than anything else in the Christian Church – with the possible exception of personality clashes. (Les Ball said, "There is no such thing as a personality clash in the Christian Church – only carnality.") Far too many Christians listen to sermons on the lookout for "unsafe" doctrines to flow from a preacher's lips, and then to tut-tut about it – when they should have been listening to Jesus and dismissing those things that don't apply to them.

So in this chapter you might well find controversy. Relax - I'm a risk taker. If, at the end, you and I disagree, it will not make any difference to me – I am commanded to love every Christian regardless of what they think. But if you fall out with me because of this chapter, then the problem lies within you. But if you do disagree, can I ask that you do so from a Biblical basis only – not from a basis of negative emotional reactions, or logic, or Doctrine, or Theology or Tradition? My friend John Smith said that there is no such thing as new truth. True. But there is such a thing as new Revelation of old truth to a new generation. Hence the Reformation, Believer's Baptism, Congregationalism, Missionary evangelism, and, in my own life time, the recovery of the Baptism of the Holy Spirit and the Charismatic. All of those were old truths, but they came new to the generations to whom they were Revealed. In the end this Revelation will not affect any of our daily lives – so it is solely a matter of encouragement and discussion. Only Time and Jesus will prove me right or wrong.

I think the best way I can open this debate is to find scriptures and make comments on them.

Let me first make some common assumptions. Man is born spirit, soul and body, and is unique in the universe for that reason. Animals have no spirit (so far as we know), and angels have no bodies. God has made man unique. Because of Adam's choice, we have "sold" our spirits and souls to satan, and all are now born on satan's side. This God calls "dead". That does not mean that man's spirit no longer exists; it means that is has no life from God within it.

The nature of my thesis is that the Bride of Christ will be, in fact, as divine as Jesus. The illustration is the human body. If we could ask one cell if it was a human being, it would say No. *Together*, all the trillions of cells in our bodies make one human being. Individually, they are not a human being. They are human cells, but not a human being. So as individual cells in the Bride of Christ, we will be perfect and flawless by nature, but not God. It is only *together* that we make up the Bride of Christ, who will be the same nature as Jesus – human and divine. We certainly know that God considers every cell to be important in that future Bride, and He is taking considerable and personal pains to purify each one. So what enormous size will the whole be? And what dimension is Jesus – He who is greater than all of us?

Let us look at each scripture in turn, and I will make comments about each text below it. It is for debate and consideration.

So what is the nature of the new birth?

"Yet to all who received him, to those who believed in his name, he gave the right to become children of God—children born not of natural descent, nor of human decision or a husband's will, but born of God." John 1:12, 13

- Entrance into the new birth is by faith in Jesus Christ. All the necessary inputs to clear the pathway to that happening have been achieved by Jesus on the cross.
- The Bible talks often about it being a "birth". This verse makes it quite plain that the new birth is a direct parallel to all other types of birth that we know – and that we born of *God.* That which is created is created. That which is born is born. The two are very different. Man can create cars and houses, but cannot create a human being. Humans can only occur by being born. "Begetting" is the only way humans can happen. The process of begetting and birth is the only way a species can reproduce after its kind. This verse clearly states that in the new birth believers are "born of God". That is, they are begotten by God. God *created* human beings and other animals. But if God *begets* something, that "something" must have the nature of God. In the same way that begetting by animals reproduces after that animal kind, begetting by God reproduces God, after His Kind. That's why Jesus is called the "Only (or first) begotten Son of God". He was begotten, not made. So are Christians. It either means what is says or language becomes meaningless.
- That verse also stresses that our birth is definitely "Not of natural descent". God's new birth has no human inheritance. The backcloth to the new birth is totally Divine. We are "born of <u>God</u>". It is a divine conceiving.
- The word "children" here is the Greek word *teknon.* I will analyse other incidents of this and other similar words later.

> *"in reply Jesus declared, "I tell you the truth, no one can see the kingdom of God unless he is born again"".* John 3:3.
> The original Greek for "again" here is "from above". Jesus is stating very clearly that the new birth is from heaven and not from earth or man. The only two forms of "life" in heaven are God's or satan's. It is obvious that the "new" birth is from God since we are all already connected with satan.

"Jesus answered, "I tell you the truth, no one can enter the kingdom of God unless he is born of water and the Spirit. Flesh gives birth to flesh, but the Spirit gives birth to spirit. You should not be surprised at my saying, "You must be born again."" John 3:5-7.

- No person can enter heaven *unless* he is born of the Spirit. That is, the Holy Spirit. We all know that the Holy Spirit is Divine. He is God. So that which is born of the Holy Spirit is also divine by nature. It cannot be any other.
- Flesh gives birth to flesh, and we see that in every human and animal's reproductive systems. The very clear statement here is that birth by the Holy Spirit is a direct parallel to that of creatures. The Holy Spirit reproduces "after His Kind". That is, spiritual and divine.
- Once more, in verse 7, the word translated "again" is written as "from above" in the Greek.

> *"For God so loved the world that he gave his one and only Son, that whoever believes in him shall not perish but have eternal life."* John 3:16.
>
> - The word "Son" here is the Greek word *huios*, of which more later.
> - The word "Life" here is *zöe*, and is always used in the Bible to represent God's kind of Life. It is often prefixed by the word "eternal", as here. In John 1 we read that in Jesus was Life, and that Life was the light of men. The other Greek word for life is *bios,* from which we get the word Biology, and it means physical, vegetable or animal life. That is also found in the Bible, but when *zöe* is used, it always refers to God's kind of life, and is found 133 times in the New Testament. So John 3:16 is saying we possess Jesus' kind of Life within us – eternal Life. This is another indication of the nature of the new birth that Christians have received.

Birth. The extraordinary nature of Jesus' human birth is miraculous. He was "conceived by the Holy Spirit". It is beyond our concept that God should choose to be born as one of His own creatures. But the nature of Jesus' birth into humanity brought God down into the human race. The total effectiveness of the cross, coupled together with Jesus' complete obedience to His Father, meant that it was not possible for Jesus' humanity ever to be taken away from Him again. Instead, He took humanity into heaven and integrated humanity into the Godhead. Jesus was not human before his natural birth. But now and for always He is fully human as well as fully Divine. There is a man inside God.

Jesus didn't just carry a human body into heaven; He carried the whole of *humanity* (in principle) and human believers (in particular) into Heaven. In the same way that no creature in Eden could satisfy Adam until Eve was created, Jesus the *Man* will only find final satisfaction in His Bride. Eve was flesh and bone of Adam's flesh and bone. Jesus' Bride is the same Kind of Being as He is, just like Eve was to Adam. The Bride will be both human and divine – just like the Bridegroom. That's the enormity of the Redemption.

Jesus came down to rescue mankind. What kind of nature therefore would be satisfactory for God to redeem back into heaven with Him? Perfect? Certainly – nothing less would be good enough. Flawless? Certainly. The Cross and the promises of God confirm that we will all be such. Sons of God? Certainly. See these scriptures, with comments below:

a. *"because those who are led by the Spirit of God are sons of God."* Rom 8:14.
b. *"For those God foreknew he also predestined to be conformed to the likeness of his Son, that he might be the firstborn among many brothers,"* Rom 8:29.
c. *"to redeem those under law, that we might receive the full rights of sons. Because you are sons, God sent the Spirit of his Son into our hearts, the Spirit who calls out, "Abba, Father." So you are no longer a slave, but a son; and since you are a son, God has made you also an heir."* Gal 4: 5-7.

d. *"In bringing many sons to glory, it was fitting that God, for whom and through whom everything exists, should make the author of their salvation perfect through suffering. Both the one who makes men holy and those who are made holy are of the same family. So Jesus is not ashamed to call them brothers"* Heb 2:10-11.

e. *"For surely it is not angels he helps, but Abraham's descendants. For this reason he had to be made like his brothers in every way,"* Heb 2:16,17a.

a. The word "son" used here is the same that is used consistently for Jesus' sonship in heaven (*huios*). If language is to mean anything, then they must mean the same. Born again Christians are sons just like Jesus is a Son.

b. We are to be conformed to the likeness of Jesus. In 1 John 3:2 it also says, "*But we know that when he appears, we shall be **like** him.*" The idea given is of conformity in every way. He is the Head, and we are His Body. That can only mean we belong to the same Being, and will therefore share His divinity as well as His humanity.

c. We are no longer slaves, but sons. Sons belong to a family. Jesus is the Son of God. We are sons of God. Isn't it the same thing? He is the first-born among many brothers. Because we are sons, we are also heirs of His Kingdom.

d. In Heb 2:11, the NIV translates it: "*Both the one who makes men holy and those who are made holy are of the same family.*" The Greek for "of the same family" is "One Thing". He who makes us holy and we who are being made holy are "one thing". It is neuter. You can translate it just "one". We are One. Just as the Father, Son and Holy Spirit are One, so we are One with them. But it says that Jesus and Christians are "One Thing."

e. So Jesus is not ashamed to call us "Brothers". Is that a metaphor, or is it literal? He is our Elder Brother.

Surely that means that we are from the same family? We are not brothers from the same earthly family; but we are brothers from the same heavenly family – born of the same Father.

f. Jesus came to rescue mankind, not angels. His taking on humanity has brought humanity up to where He is. We are like Him. That is, both human and divine. Jesus is divine and human by spiritual birth before the dawn of time and by natural birth through Mary. We are human and divine by natural birth and new (spiritual) birth inside time. The cross was so effective that that was the least God could do with its consequences. So when Jesus marries His Bride, that Bride will be as divine as He is, and perfectly human like He is. But very diverse. God is bringing to birth something so radically new that the church on earth struggles to grasp it. We are adding a fourth dimension to the Trinity, and we will reign over God's new creation alongside our Husband. The redemption of mankind is complete, not partial. God has transformed humanity.

Sons and Children. There are a number of Greek words used in the New Testament for children and sons, and there is a useful study that can be made of each word. But the word used of Jesus' Sonship is always *huios*, and that is also mostly used for sons of God. The other main word is *teknon*, and that nearly always refers to human sons. Or Paul to "My son Timothy", clearly used metaphorically there. *Teknon* is an endearing word, rather than a technical word for someone generated by parents. *Huios* means "offspring" and is always used of a son reproduced by parents. So, Jesus is the "offspring" of God. We are also "offsprings" of God. That's what sons *(huios)* of God are.

> "*… and have put on the new self, which is being renewed in knowledge in the image of its Creator.*" Col 3:10.

So how does this theme of "Image" work? Genesis 1:27 says that we humans are made in the Image of God. Col 1:9 says that Jesus is the Image of the invisible God. Now we have Paul saying that the new human is being renewed in knowledge in the Image of God. It feels as if it is saying that both the new self and the knowledge are in the Image of God. If so, that would tie up with all the other verses that I have brought up here. And it says that Jesus and us (redeemed Christians) are both alike in being in God's Image.

"For you have been born again, not of perishable seed, but of imperishable, through the living and enduring word of God." 1 Peter 1:23
The Greek literally reads: "Having been regenerated ... by incorruptible seed." The word for "seed" here is *spora*, from which we get the English word "spore", the seed, for instance, of mushrooms. In the parable of the sower, the "seed" is the Word of God, which we know from John 1:1 is Jesus. The Greek word used there, and mostly in the New Testament, is *sperma*, from which, obviously, we get the English word "sperm". Both are the same. They indicate that divine seed has regenerated us. Divine *sperma* can only generate divinity, just like human *sperma* can only generate humans.

"No one who is born of God will continue to sin, because God's seed remains in him; he cannot go on sinning, because he has been born of God." 1 John 3:9.
Here the Greek word used for "seed" is *sperma.* This scripture makes it very clear that both the seed and the birth are God's. (For those interested in how we stop sinning, consider re-reading the chapter on Righteousness)

Adoption. We must not get confused or diverted by this word. Automatically we think of today's style of adoption, whereby a child from outside a family's DNA is brought into the family and given its new family's name. It is not of the same blood. But that is ***not*** New Testament adoption. New Testament adoption was Roman adoption. Roman children were confined to the nursery and put under a tutor (*paidagōgos*, who was a whipping slave / teacher). When a boy child came of age and was approved by his father, the family then "adopted" him into the adult family household, from the nursery. The adopted children were *from that same family* and parents. In the Adoption ceremony, the father would bring his own son before the Praetorium, dressing the son in a white toga and presenting him to the town council with the words "This is my beloved Son, with whom I am well pleased." From then on he was an adult and recognised by all as such. This style of adoption is spoken of often in the New Testament and very clearly given a spiritual evaluation as an illustration in Gal 3:23 – 4:9. Otherwise that passage loses its essential meaning. Our adoption as Christians is from childhood (the darkness of satan) into sonship (the light of Jesus) – but *we are from the same family*.

So what do we have revealed to us in scripture? Let me list the words that are used:

- Birth from God.
- By the Holy Spirit.
- From above.
- Through the Divine *sperma* and *spora.*
- Of the same Family.
- Conformed to the likeness of Jesus.
- "Brothers in every way".
- Sons after the same manner as Jesus.
- The new birth gives us the same divine life (*zöe*) as that of God Himself.
- In the Image of God.

So what is God trying to convey? There is clearly a truth that He wants us to know for certain, and the only way He has of letting us know is to use the only language that is available and that we can understand. God never minces His words; He always and only says exactly what He means. It is clear that the language is metaphorical. That is, it is a heavenly equivalent of a human truth. For example, God's sperm is not a literal one (except in the case of Jesus). But whatever God impregnated us with at our point of new birth is the spiritual equivalent of a human sperm. So, in the spiritual realm, we are literally children – sons – of God. We are inheritors of all God's Kingdom (heirs of God, and joint-heirs with Christ).

God, in all His excellence, is giving us an earthly picture of something heavenly, the details of which are beyond our grasp and deliberately hidden until the time is right for it to be revealed. These texts have been available for 2000 years, and seem to be very obvious. Why do we not believe them? Is it because it is too enormous for us to believe? Or to say so seems to be full of pride and self-exaltation?

What they seem to be saying is that the nature of the new birth is exactly the same as the nature of Jesus' birth. He was begotten of the Father before all worlds (the Nicene Creed). We are begotten of the Father by the *sperma* of God, through the Holy Spirit, enabled because of the death of Jesus. Jesus is the "first among many brothers."

So a friend of mine asked me, on a scale of 0 – 10 whether I believe it. I gave it a 10. He then asked on the same scale if I felt it was true of me. Will I be Divine? I gave him less than 1. But the truth is that *I* will never be the Bride of Christ. None of us as individuals ever will be. It is the *whole Bride* that will be Divine, not merely one of its constituent parts. Each "cell" will be perfect and flawless, but it will be *together* that we make up the Bride of Christ – both human and divine.

God uses the metaphor of the human body in many places. Rom 12 and 1 Cor 12 are the best examples. But also in Eph 1 God describes Jesus as the Head and the Church as His body. It is the spiritual equivalent of Adam and Eve – husband and wife – where the two become one unit; that is, two people, one human being. In the same way, God is three persons, one God. And, if I have it right, soon to be four persons, one God.

It is not surprising that the Christian church on earth finds difficulty believing that God has granted mankind divinity through the New Birth. After all, everyone in Israel at the time of Jesus had the same difficulty with Him. Even the disciples needed special Revelation to understand that He was God (Matt 16:17). Indeed, it was *exactly because* Jesus claimed divinity that they accused Him of blasphemy and crucified Him. If they had difficulty believing *Jesus'* divinity, how much more difficult is it to believe that divinity has been destined for grotty human beings like us? Nevertheless, the Bible seems to me to make it very clear that that is what God has initiated through the new birth. Even the disciples were harshly rebuked by Jesus for their continual unbelief (Mark 16), and it was Jesus' *resurrection* that convinced them and proved to them that He was in fact God. It is possible that the pattern is being reproduced among Christians today. Will anybody be convinced of the truth of the divine future of the Bride of Christ laid out so clearly in the Bible, or do we also have to sit in unbelief until our own resurrection?

Our own inadequacy and great imperfection is why I maintain that while we are here on earth we are only the foetus. The whole of the life of earth is the *embryo* of the future Bride. We are "being brought to birth". We are, while here on earth, nowhere near an adult human being, full of ability, promise and performance – either individually or collectively. One day "when the Sons of God are revealed", then we shall be for real what we are now only in potential. Notice, in this following scripture in Romans 8, that the whole creation is spoken about as "being in the pains of childbirth". That's exactly what I have been saying the Church is and will remain until the Second Coming of Jesus.

> *"I consider that our present sufferings are not worth comparing with the glory that will be revealed in us. The creation waits in eager expectation for the sons of God to be revealed. For the creation was subjected to frustration, not by its own choice, but by the will of the*

one who subjected it, in hope that the creation itself will be liberated from its bondage to decay and brought into the glorious freedom of the children of God.
We know that the whole creation has been groaning as in the pains of childbirth right up to the present time. Not only so, but we ourselves, who have the firstfruits of the Spirit, groan inwardly as we wait eagerly for our adoption as sons, the redemption of our bodies." Rom 8:18-23.

"What marvellous love the Father has extended to us! Just look at it – we're called the children of God! That's who we really are. But that's also why the world doesn't recognise us or take us seriously, because it has no idea who He is or what He's up to. But friends, that's exactly who we are: children of God. And that's only the beginning. Who knows how we will end up! What we know is that when Christ is openly revealed, we'll see Him – and in seeing Him, become like Him. All of us who look forward to His Coming stay ready, with the glistening purity of Jesus' life as a model for our own." 1 John 3:1-3 (The Message)

SUMMARY

The final Bride of Christ in glory will, as One Being, be both Human and Divine like Jesus. Not the individuals that make her up. And never on this earth.

Chapter 27
REINVENTING THE WHEEL

I wonder how that guy felt when he put his first wheel (or two) on his cart, and gave up lugging tree trunks from the back to the front? They say that the wheel was the most important invention known to man. I don't dispute it. And now, we have no need to reinvent it. What we do is use it, in a million varieties of ways.

"Reinventing the Wheel" has become an expression in common use. It says that what I am doing is using an awful lot of unnecessary effort because someone else has tried it before and got it sussed. Why don't I listen to him (or her) and copy their style? Bless God for pioneers in every sphere of life. I use their gadgets every day. And, frankly, they have made my life richer, happier, easier and more fruitful, living my life starting from those very foundations they laid. Who invented glasses, (reading and drinking)? Who invented clothes, towels, pillows, shoes, socks, computers, cars, trains, toilets, electronics, scissors, knives, central heating, air-conditioning, blocks, cement, tiles, roofs, windows, tools? All things? Thank you inventors one and all for your sparkle and initiative that has made my life on earth so good.

It's a little more serious but just as beneficial to recognise the Christian inheritance that I stand on. I am at the top of an ever-growing pyramid (along with you) standing on the Spiritual discoveries and behaviour patterns of previous generations of Christian men and women. It's a salutary lesson to read some of their life-stories, and see what struggles they went through to bring me where I am and give me what I've got. People were martyred to bring me my Bible in English. People died to give me a good safe home in England. They "worked out their own salvation" in the generations in which they lived, and I am benefiting from them all. But, I do not need to "invent" new Christian doctrines. That's actually called "heresy".

The 20th century has been overwhelmed with such heresies. They called it "Theology". It is nothing of the sort. It is human philosophy with a religious bent – what Francis Schaeffer graciously called "Upper Storey Christianity". It comes under the same heading of "novels" that I mentioned at the beginning of Chapter 1. Those were religious novels. These are philosophical novels. Both are fiction, new inventions by those who have no access to the Real God in Jesus Christ through the Holy Spirit. They used to burn heretics at the stake!

But there's no point in any of us wasting our time being vitriolic or condemnatory about all these man-made philosophies (unless it's our calling). The point is that if we travel those kind of roads (actually, *any* other roads) we miss out on the Blessing of the Lord. And what can replace that?

I also need to be careful about pursuing new sources from which I can glean methods of spreading the news about Jesus. "Bookaholics" could easily run fast after everyone else's ideas. As could "Meetingaholics". Books and meetings are fine – but to *pursue* them...? They think: Let's try this idea. Or that one. Will this one work? The Bible is a firm, stable and permanent enough foundation to give me the purpose I need, and the Holy Spirit is Divine enough and brilliant enough to give me my own new proclamation adventures all the days of my life.

Truth is one thing that never needs reinventing. But methods of disseminating that truth are permanently being reinvented. Let's not confuse the two.

Do we *need* scientific discoveries or facts to confirm or deny our faith? Surely not! They are nice to have – so long as they add to and do not subtract from our faith. To have extra ingredients in order to bolster our faith is nice; to *need* them could easily lead us down a slippery slope. It's because the rationale is rational, not spiritual. What is of man, not of God, is full of dangers, interesting and fascinating though they may be.

This principle governs so many of the things we try to do as Christians. Someone starts a Coffee Bar Outreach and we all start a Coffee Bar Outreach. We follow fads. We read in Christian magazines how someone has been successful doing something, and we try to reinvent the wheel by copying him. It's a substitute for simply following Jesus ourselves. If we followed Him personally, based our faith on the Bible, walked with the Holy Spirit, we would be doing the inventing. We are all unique, and no one can copy us. So why be silly and try to copy others? Invent your own unique methods.

Neither should we copy the styles of our ancestors. They did Christian stuff in ways that were unique to their characters and great for their generations. But not for ours. "So how do we do evangelism?" someone asks. You can bet that most of us would answer that question by giving examples of how others have done it. Silly us! The only right answer is "Do what Jesus tells you to do." There is no other answer that works. Let Jesus invent your own wheel; don't try to reinvent others' wheels.

However, there are those I have met who are so concerned that they pioneer a new work for God that they totally reject the foundations of the work in which they are involved. They are trying to reinvent the wheel. Why can't they add new life to their predecessor's work, instead of erasing it and trying something radically new? Their predecessors went through the "cutting a path through the jungle" stage. Why not walk the path they cut instead of trying to cut a new path through the same jungle? I've seen it happen with some missionary societies, and Churches are classical examples of it: New Pastor/Vicar/Priest - new broom. Silly really.

Some think it's their task first to dismantle and destroy the Christian work they have inherited before establishing their own unique work, in order that "I would not be building on some else's foundation." (Rom 15:20). Just how silly is that? Paul wrote that text 2000 years ago, in the specific context of preaching the Gospel to those who had never heard. That context cannot be extended to Christian *methods.* If we do, what proportion of 2000 years of Christian activities do we think we have to dismantle before getting going on our own? It's as silly as saying, "I refuse to speak English because all my predecessors did." Jesus Christ never calls *anyone* to dismantle another Christian's work. Won't Time and Entropy naturally do it anyway without any of us wasting our effort helping them?

Surely we have to start at the place we have inherited, draw from it the good things it had, and build our own unique work from there, don't we? To destroy the foundations we have inherited could leave us without premises, without colleagues, without friends, without work, without a congregation, without support from our local church, without finance, without a vision and without a ministry. It will kill us. It would be like a goldfish who feels he has to pull out the bung in his fish tank before he can really get going with what he wants to do. I would call it suicide. And I would suggest its motive is definitely unhealthy and certainly not from God.

What I am doing in Nicaragua is based on what Mike Cole pioneered in the Peace and Hope Trust. Why reinvent the wheel? I am building on his foundation, with joy and effectiveness, using his techniques, and then developing my own unique ministry in a different location and remit to Mike. Isn't that a style that we should all be copying?

Why reinvent the wheel?

But there is a sense I want to share with you where we really do need to reinvent the wheel. In what way? In the unique *methods* the Lord has for each of us. He has made us all different. And He has placed us uniquely into the century and nation that fits our uniqueness best. Every one of my ancestors worked and prospered in a different location in the world, did a different job, supported a different régime, and were children of their cultures. They each had to "work out their own salvation" in their way and their day. I stand on the foundation they laid, but I can never do the work they did. Their contribution to society (and to their Churches when they were Christians) was a unique work that was God's plan for their century. Now I have to find my own wheel.

I have to find the fulfilment of Eph. 2:10 for my own life. No one can duplicate me. No one can duplicate my ministry. No one can duplicate my calling nor the way I carry it out. I have to find my unique pathway and style in life, settle into the middle of it, and never leave it until I die. Starting from where I find myself, and trying not to be a clone of anyone else, I have to step out in faith with Jesus and find my own "wheel" to invent.

So do you.

SUMMARY

We each have to find our own individual and unique pathway on earth to fulfil our pre-planned destiny.

EPILOGUE.

Why did I start to write this book? Dunno really - the beginning just happened. But as I wrote I was picked up in the arms of Jesus and inspired. Maybe that's exactly how the writers of the Bible felt as they put their Revelations down on paper? What I felt I have done is to say that God's very very simple way of living the Christian life ***really works***. What is His simple way? Jesus only. It is so simple that it is almost puerile. How could something so simple be the means of living such a complicated life in such a complicated century? Yet it is. And Jesus does. He is the beginning, the middle and the end of all things, and it is time we came back to Him again, shed all our sophistications and complications and just listened and did.

Moreover, it seems to me that today's church has got cluttered. We have a thousand "systems", a thousand new schemes and ideas, and we expend tons of energy processing them all, and realise that most of them fail. They do not achieve what we had hoped, and at the end of all our efforts we sit back fagged out and dream of holidays on a tropical island somewhere else. We feel failures. That's probably because we are. We have to learn again that Jesus is the only successful human being that ever lived. His Today Way is still the only successful way, and Christians have the privilege of accessing it all the time.

In addition, we have got clogged with Theology. We try to cross "T's" and dot "I's" to purify our understanding, only to find that our understanding gets more cluttered instead of freer. When the emerging Christian Church in China opened its doors to Western Evangelical Theological books, it caused nothing but division. After a short while they burned them all and went back to their Bibles. That's why they are so strong today.

We are also contaminated by modern and liberal theology. It's a shame to call that stuff "Theology". It is no more the word of

God (the *logos* of *Theos – theo-logos*) than my little finger. Much of it is the ideas of men.

One thing has puzzled me for a long time: why do Christian leaders and teachers insist that those called into the Christian ministry are forced to learn all this theology nonsense? In the Old Testament there were schools for *Prophets*. Jesus learned at *His Father's* feet through His Old Testament for 30 years. The Disciples walked *with Jesus* for three years. Paul sat *under the feet of Jesus* alone in the desert for 3 years. In the New Testament potential ministers walked around with the *Apostles*. Where do we get the idea from that every Minister has to have a load of degrees after his name, and have his head cluttered and contaminated with *secular* philosophy and stuff that is not from God? (What good does it do them anyway? How does it enhance their ministry?) If we have to have schools at all, why don't we try doing what Jesus told us to do and have Schools for *Disciples*?

We run after men and men's ideas. Just where do we think that will get us? Why are there so few people becoming Christians in the West today? And why do so many people become Christians in other less sophisticated lands? Isn't the answer obvious?

What our modern generation needs is Revelation from God as to what to do and a single-mindedness to do it. Nothing else works. Nothing else succeeds. And nothing else is quite so much fun. King Jesus has a route for every one of us to take that is perfectly tuned to our characters, and individually adjusted to His plan on earth for our lives. If we all did His will, we would all complement each other's work, and revival would hit our nations.

Just what else are we playing at?

May King Jesus Himself enrich your hearts and lives for ever.

FULL SUMMARY

This summary is given so that you can see that *God's* way of running the Christian life is consistent, consecutive, carefully thought through and fully covered from every aspect of life. It is the only way for our lives to be successful in God's sight and effective on earth.

Chapter	Summary
1. Revelation.	It is impossible for mankind to know God. The *only* way is for God to initiate it by Revealing Himself to them.
2. Logos & Rhēma.	Rhēma is the *spoken* word of God. It alone has Life, power and creativity. God created and governs the universe through His *spoken* word. The Rhēma of God and Revelation are the same thing.
3. Hearing the Voice of God.	God directs Christians by His Rhēma word into our souls (minds) all the time. We need to identify them and receive them by faith.
4. Faith.	The only faith that works is that given and generated by God's Rhēma words.
5. The Bible.	The whole Bible was inspired by God's Rhēma words to the authors. God is hidden inside the written words, and can only be found individually when He reveals Himself by speaking Life through the Spirit.
6. Grace.	Grace is the attribute of God that caused Him to rescue mankind. It is the root attribute in God, brought to earth by Jesus.

	Salvation is by Grace alone through Faith alone. Grace is a very beautiful thing.
7. Sin.	The whole of mankind is totally sinful, inherited from Adam. That is, cut off from God eternally, and locked into satan. Sin was broken in principle for all mankind when God made Jesus to be sin for us. Appropriation is individually by God's initiative through Revelation and received by faith.
8. Righteousness.	Righteousness in God's sight is not now related to law. It is related to faith, is imputed and then imparted by Grace, and depends on our fulfilling our covenant relationship with Jesus. All Christians are already righteous, although still limited.
9. Genesis.	God's creation fiat as recorded in Genesis needs to be received as written if anyone is going to hear God's Rhēma words clearly.
10. The Four Epochs.	The whole history of earth is divided into 4 epochs. The single purpose of the earth's millennia is to be the womb in which God is conceiving and forming the Bride of Christ.
11. Death.	Death is separation, not annihilation. Life is fusion. Death separates man's spirit/soul from his body. It separates man from God and from other people. God used death in its various forms to be the channel for bringing Life to mankind through Jesus. Life is fusion with God.
12. Entropy.	The whole cosmos is decaying to death and chaos (entropy). It can only be slowed by the injection of energy. At the Second Coming of Jesus, entropy will be erased by God.

13. Time.	Time is an illusion. Eternity is the ever-present NOW, which is where we all live. NOW is the only place where we can access God.
14. Big C	God is creating something new as time goes by. The Church is His new creation, is excellent and wonderful in the extreme, is the Bride of Christ, and is the only purpose for the continuation of the earth.
15. Little c.	All God's work on earth pivots round local churches. People are saved and nourished through them. It is in them that we are discipled into Bride-likeness. We learn to belong together as One Body.
16. Christian Initiation.	The entry gate to becoming a Christian is fourfold: to be born again by the Holy Spirit, baptised in water, baptised in the Holy Spirit and join a local church. Nothing less. And all done as soon as possible together.
17. Preaching, Teaching and Prophesy.	Preaching tells us what the Bible means. Teaching tells what it says. Prophecy what God is saying now. The Bible originally was all three rolled into one book.
18. Unity.	God's work on earth only comes through a united Body. Separation, individualism, isolation or division are wicked and destroy God's work.
19. Our Besetting Vulnerability.	God will remove all wickednesses within us except one or two. These He leaves as gifts to drive us closer to Him daily.
20. The Complete God.	God's attributes are all good, are all 100% and are all perfect. When He acts, He acts using all His attributes together at once.
21. Intimacy.	Intimacy is being in continual communication with Jesus and delighting

	in His company with joy.
22. Humility.	God's most extraordinary attribute after Grace is humility. It is our most becoming one.
23. Poverty.	God's heart is a heart of poverty. To be gifted with that same heart is riches indeed.
24. Inside Out.	Jesus is re-living His 33 years on earth through every Christian in every generation in every century.
25. The Four Loves.	We need to differentiate between 4 kinds of love: Family, Sexual, Affection and God's Love, and use each appropriately.
26. The Nature of the Bride of Christ.	The final Bride of Christ in glory will, as One Being, be both human and Divine like Jesus. Not the individuals that make her up. And never on this earth.
27. Reinventing the Wheel.	We each have to find our own individual and unique pathway on earth to fulfil our pre-planned destiny.
28. Epilogue.	The Bible way of "Jesus only" really works.

NAMES OF PEOPLE QUOTED

Printed in the United Kingdom
by Lightning Source UK Ltd.
119523UK00002B/145-162